Industrialisation and Everyday Life

Industrialisierung und Volksleben by Rudolf Braun is widely regarded as a classic of modern social history, inspiring a whole series of profound debates about the transition from pre-industrial society to the modern world. Utilising evidence from an upland Swiss canton, *Industrialisation and Everyday Life* provides a comprehensive survey of the impact upon popular life styles of the development of widespread cottage industry, as land-hungry labourers added textile manufacture to their existing agricultural concerns. Professor Braun analyses the structure of such 'proto-industry', looking at the changes wrought upon family life, domestic housing and popular culture in general. A great variety of literary and artistic sources are drawn together in a vivid portrayal of the ways in which early industrial development and social modernisation became fused together.

Industrialisation and Everyday Life

RUDOLF BRAUN

Professor of Modern History at the University of Zurich

Translated by Sarah Hanbury Tenison

The right of the University of Cambridge to print and sell all manner of books was granted by Henry VIII in 1534. The University has printed and published continuously since 1584.

CAMBRIDGE UNIVERSITY PRESS

Cambridge
New York   Port Chester   Melbourne   Sydney

EDITIONS DE
LA MAISON DES SCIENCES DE L'HOMME

Paris

Published by the Press Syndicate of the University of Cambridge
The Pitt Building, Trumpington Street, Cambridge CB2 1RP
40 West 20th Street, New York, NY 10011, USA
10 Stamford Road, Oakleigh, Melbourne 3166, Australia
and Editions de la Maison des Sciences de l'Homme
54 Boulevard Raspail, 75270 Paris Cedex 06

Originally published in German as *Industrialiserung und Volksleben*
by Vandenhoeck and Ruprecht 1960; second edition 1979
and © Vandenhoeck and Ruprecht in Göttingen
First published in English by Editions de la Maison des Sciences de
l'Homme and Cambridge University Press 1990 as *Industrialisation and
Everyday Life*
English translation © Maison des Sciences de l'Homme and Cambridge
University Press 1990

Printed in Great Britain at the University Press, Cambridge

British Library cataloguing in publication data
Braun, Rudolf
  Industrialisation and everyday life.
  1. Switzerland. Rural regions. Industrialisation. Social aspects, history
  I. Title   II. Industrialiserung und Volksleben. *English*
  303.4'83'09494

Library of Congress cataloguing in publication data applied for

ISBN 0 521 353114
ISBN 2 7351 0376 5   (France only)

Contents

Prefaces   *page* vii

Acknowledgements   x

Note on measures and coinage   xi

Introduction   1

1 The preconditions for industrialisation   8

2 Changes to the structure of family and population in the industrial
   regions   37

3 Life and society of the population engaged in industry   61

4 The impact of industrialisation on the house and the rural economy   111

5 Work in the putting-out industry and its effect on the life of the
   common people   131

6 The outworkers' attitude to poverty and crises   154

7 Conclusion   184

Postscript, by Ulrich Pfister   188

Appendix: a note on the administrative structure and social
stratification in the countryside of Zurich during the Ancien Régime,
by Ulrich Pfister   193

Notes   195

Sources and bibliography   223

Index   227

Preface to the English-language edition

In the preface to the second edition I mentioned that since the publishing of this work in the year 1960 cottage industry – under the new terminology 'proto-industry' – has received increased attention in social and economic historical reasearch, a tendency that still continues today. Therefore, the publisher's wish to take this historiographic situation into account and to summarise in a longer postscript the more recent research history as well as the latest research results is quite legitimate. Two reasons prevent me, however, from writing such an outline myself. First of all, I feel more like the grandfather of the youngest research generation which is presently working on proto-industrial subjects and problems. Secondly, my teaching commitments as well as my own research interest have, for many years now, led me away from the subject of proto-industry so that I have not followed the most recent developments closely and intensively enough. I have, therefore, asked one of my assistants, Ulrich Pfister, to write the requested postscript. He is part of the younger research generation and works in the field of proto-industrialisation on his own projects. Thus, the pen is passed on to the grandson.

Rudolf Braun

Preface to the second (German) edition

Well brought up young ladies used to be taught 'not to put themselves forward', an essential part of the education provided in the better girls' boarding schools in the nineteenth century. It may well appear that I too have learnt not to put myself forward: for years I have been wondering whether to revise *Industrialisation and Everyday Life* but I could never decide to do it and even now I find it hard. Not that I am shy; my problem is more fundamental: this book was written as a thesis around twenty years ago. Although I have no wish to repudiate my first-born, the umbilical cord was cut many years ago and it has gone its own way ever since. So it is hard to identify with it, for I too have gone my own way, a way which my work on this thesis definitely helped me to find and pursue. It has led me away from folklore and towards social and economic history.

In spite of this, my little runaway has dogged my heels persistently; since the late sixties, cottage industry as a subject has aroused truly astonishing interest in very different fields of research, and, unless I am much deceived, will be cultivated even more intensively. My spinners and weavers from the Zurich Oberland have been caught up in this Renaissance and are regarded with respect, often to such a degree that I would tremble lest their frail shoulders should not be capable of supporting the weight of academic evidence which has been heaped on them in the texts or footnotes of relevant works.

One effect of this new evaluation of cottage industry has been to give it a new name: 'proto-industry', more suited to an object of fashionable research, subjected to new questions, methods and scientific analysis. In 1977, *Industrialisierung vor der Industrialisierung* (*Industrialisation before Industrialisation*) by Peter Kriedte, Hans Medick and Jürgen Schlumbohm was published and became a standard reference book in the shortest possible time; it provides what must be the most impressive presentation of the latest position in international research with its variety of methods, its wealth of views and its attempts at theoretical models. When compared with all this progress, *Industrialisation and Everyday Life* seems to belong more to the genre of *Heimatsromane* (tales of the countryside), with their titles printed in big letters so that pensioners can buy them too.

So much for my timid dithering over the question of a new edition. It is also the reason when the contents have been allowed to reappear unaltered, the text as well as the particularly problematical and antiquated Introduction. This little first-born simply cannot be dressed up in new clothes in an attempt to conceal his age and origin. Nor indeed could I do it.

This new edition provides me with an opportunity for remembrance: not long ago Herbert Kisch died unexpectedly and far too soon. He was a pioneer of research into cottage industry and shortly before his death he initiated, organised and conducted an international conference on proto-industrialisation. The new edition is dedicated to him; may his charm and personality not be forgotten!

Zurich, Spring 1979   Rudolf Braun

Preface to the first (German) edition

The present work is the first part of an investigation into the relationship between industrialisation and the life of the common people. It deals with the changes in their way of life under the influence of the putting-out industry in the seventeenth and eighteenth centuries. Part two will concentrate on the changes in their way of life under the influence of factory industry in the nineteenth and twentieth centuries. Both parts are to be considered as separate works, even though the first part leads on to the second and many threads run on from the first part into the second. The development is to be pursued up to the present.

In 1955 I worked for eight months as a temporary hand in a textile factory in the Zurich Oberland and lodged with a weaving family, so learning about a factory hand's sorrows and joys. I recall this period, which meant more to me than just a sociological experiment, with happiness and gratitude. The fate of the population of the Zurich Oberland has been spun in cotton yarn for generations. They have remained faithful to cotton through all the crises. In spite of frequent hardship the factory people have retained their cheerful enjoyment of life. Anyone who is able to get to know them will take much of their life as his example.

I take great pleasure in thanking my esteemed teacher, Professor Richard Weiss, for the help and sympathy which he has lavished on this work.

My thanks too to Dr Heinrich Krebser. He has been extremely kind in allowing me to look at the archives of the *Walder Ortschronik*, which he had built up, aware that even the most mundane expressions of life in his factory parish constitute valuable source material.

I owe very great thanks too to Dr H. Spoerry-Jaeggi for the understanding he has shown towards my research. He employed me for eight months as a temporary hand in his firm.

Thanks too to the gentlemen of the Zurich State Archive for their frequent friendly advice and information, proffered when I was working in the archives.

The publication of this work has been made possible by a generous grant from the Pro Helvetia foundation, for which I would like to express my wholehearted thanks.

My final thanks are to Frau M. Möckli and Fräulein E. Liebl for reading the proofs with me.

Acknowledgements

I must acknowledge the impressive achievement of Sarah Hanbury Tenison in translating this book, and also express my deep gratitude to Dr Ulrich Pfister, who undertook the difficult and tiresome task of finding equivalents for terms relating to constitutional and socio-political institutions of eighteenth-century Switzerland, and of translating contemporary Helvetisms. I wish to thank them both.

Note on measures and coinage

1 *Juchart* (of plough land)=32.7 metric ares=0.81 acres
1 *Mannwerk* or *Mannmaht* (of grass land)=29 metric ares=0.72 acres

1 *Gulden*=2 *Pfund*=40 *Schilling*=16 *Batzen*
1 *Schilling*=12 *Pfennig*=12 *Heller*

Introduction

The following enquiry is concerned with the social and cultural upheaval which took place during the seventeenth and eighteenth centuries in a rural environment under the influence of the putting-out, or cottage, industry. Given the folklorist nature of our enquiry, we need to recognise how the fundamental conditions of human life and society are changed when men depend wholly or partly on industry for their livelihood, and how these changes in the lives of the common people are revealed in popular culture. The countryside of Zurich has been chosen for our enquiry, especially the Zurich Oberland, a region which underwent very early and intensive industrialisation. Three hundred years later, this region is nowadays still faithful to the various branches of the textile industry.

A folklorist approach

Folklore is a branch of the arts, a definition which obliges us to understand the changeability of all the conditions of human existence in terms of people's changing mental attitudes. Without promoting a one-sided theory of the spiritual and causative interpretation of history and culture, it should simply be emphasised that the arts have the task of perceiving economic and technical changes – to wit industrialisation – against the background of a development in mental history which preceded and accompanied the changes.[1] It is from this vantage point that we will look for the driving forces of history and try to extrapolate them from their secondary effects. Deducing economic changes from particular constellations in mental history is essentially a matter for economic historians. The folklore analysis begins where economic history (and history generally) stops. The aim and object of folklore is to investigate the transposition of mental impulses within the sphere of popular thoughts and values and to pursue personal culture through its transformation into popular culture bound up with tradition and community. This purpose provides the basic questions of our enquiry: how is industrialisation received on the popular level and how is the life of the common people shaped by the process of industrialisation? Since their life can be perceived in the relationship

1

between people and objects, we can research into the links between the mentality of the industrial workers and the new material world and popular culture pertaining to this mentality.

The folklorist viewpoint is thus briefly outlined and distinguished from other disciplines in the arts. However, our choice of theme requires further justification. Folklorist research into those people whose work and basis for existence binds them to the process of industrialisation is still in its infancy. This is due on the one hand to the present state of historical knowledge and technical theory, which does not concern us. On the other hand, there are problems inherent to the object of our research: industrialisation seems by its very nature to be hostile to community and tradition. We stress 'seems' because we cannot share this attitude. Industrialisation and industrial labour has until now been perceived and judged almost exclusively from the point of view of 'uprooting, disruption and stereotyping'[2] and any discussion generally starts from hidebound assumptions and views: industrialisation and industrial work destroy old crafts, working patterns and associations; they displace ancient folklore, long-lived customs and practices and traditional forms of community; there is a dynamism inherent to the industrial system of production which disregards human and material ties, and so on. Industrialisation is only too eagerly made into a whipping boy and held responsible for our uncultured age, for our rootless lives and for our loss of centre. This is not the place to counter such views, judgements and preconceptions, or to discuss the cultural value (especially the popular cultural value) of industrialisation and industrial labour. Let us assume only that our investigation will show how the life of the common people and their culture are altered under the influence of industrialisation, not in the sense of disruption and destruction, but in the sense of being given a new shape, one adjusted to the altered conditions of existence. What is more, the investigation will demonstrate that it is only industrialisation which guarantees large sections of the population a homeland. Indeed, industrialisation provides people with a homeland, allowing them to stay put on their own soil among their own folk.

We are dealing here not with a factual but a methodological problem: if industrialisation appears by its very nature to be hostile to community and tradition, how then can we justify researching this subject from a folklorist point of view, which considers everything relating to tradition and community to be of central significance? Can substantive folklorist research be possible in this context?

Two fundamentally important preconditions allow us to place the folklorist approach alongside other disciplines in the arts: both the need for community and belief in tradition are deeply entwined in the human psyche.[3] Even the process of industrialisation is subordinate to the effect of these two fundamental forces, once it is rooted in the life of the common people and is accepted and supported by them. In any case, and this is of decisive significance, belief in tradition should not be confused with folklore, nor the need for community with traditional forms of community. Both folklore and traditional forms of community have to change along with the process of industrialisation, but belief in tradition and the need for community ensure that new forms of folklore and community emerge from the new industrial base. The changes in the life of the common people are revealed in a new popular culture adapted to the changed conditions. There can therefore be no danger that the folklorist approach is invalid. Let us start by referring these preliminary and general remarks to the problem in hand, in order to define our theme and to justify our monographical approach.

Defining the topic

Our field of research is the countryside of Zurich. The industrialisation of this area was an historical process and as such unique and unrepeatable. The nature and shape of the Zurich textile industry in the seventeenth and eighteenth centuries, with its putting-out (*Verlag*) system of production, were determined by the political and economic framework in which they developed. During this lengthy process the Zurich putting-out industry emerged with features peculiar to its locality and period. Man as the creator and upholder of cultural life shaped from his struggle with the prevailing environment the mental, social, economic and technical foundations of this early system of industrial production and manufacture, which attained its first peak in the eighteenth century.

The putting-out system was harnessed to the legal organisation and structure of the Zurich city-state with its territory. A feature of the putting-out system of production was that it extended beyond the city walls into the surrounding countryside and that its workforce included not only town burghers but also peasant subjects. The putting-out system thus involved representatives of both classes, distinguished politically and socially by their origins, i.e. their birth. The effect of this division was to give the members of each class different opportunities to participate in economic life. They were allotted, according to their origins, differentiated functions in the putting-out system.

The first social class was made up of privileged town burghers. As the originators of the State's political and economic system, they were keen to ensure that the new system of production and manufacture was under their control and management. They monopolised the putting-out system. Only town burghers were entitled to buy in raw materials and to distribute finished goods. Their monopolistic control was tightest in the eighteenth century, protected by a network of regulations. The peasant subjects formed the second social class involved in the putting-out process. They did not possess the trading and manufacturing prerogatives of the town burghers. They were allowed only specific functions in production and manufacture; processing the raw material with all the various associated functions. However, the range of these specific functions was so extensive that a hierarchical order was able to emerge among the peasant subjects involved in the putting-out system. Another feature of this system was that intermediate stages could be inserted into the production process with entrepreneurial opportunities of their own. Turning raw materials into yarn and cloth involved a complex process, and the distribution of the raw material and the allotment and coordination of the various tasks all allowed the peasant subjects latitude and opportunity to act as entrepreneurs (with all the associated risks) even when they could not infiltrate the upper echelons of the putting-out hierarchy – i.e. they remained excluded from the management. Within specific limits, then, the putting-out system provided the peasant subjects it employed with opportunities for social advancement and social differentiation. We will get to know these peasant entrepreneurs, the *Tüchler* (clothiers), who often described themselves proudly as *Fabrikanten* (manufacturers).[4] They formed an intellectual and social elite in the countryside and acted as a catalyst, which wrought the great upheaval at the end of the eighteenth century.

The two classes represented in the putting-out system are thus briefly introduced. As far as our folklorist enquiry is concerned, the second social class, the peasant subjects, forms its chief object, whereas a study in economic history would have aimed at putting the first class of town burghers in the forefront, they being the leaders and managers of the putting-out system. As the putting-out system developed, it drew great sections of the population of the Zurich territory within its catchment area. These peasant subjects' own social and economic structure gave the putting-out system both directly and indirectly its local and period character: the local environment and culture restrict or promote the process of industrialisation, and so participate in the process not only as passive receptors but by actively shaping it. We will pursue this aspect in Chapter 1. Our field of research is particularly suited to this; the Zurich territory comprises on the one hand regions which were predestined by their social, legal and economic structure to adopt the putting-out system. Consequently, these regions underwent intensive industrialisation. On the other hand, the territory also extends over regions where putting-out was not established at all until the nineteenth century because their social, legal and economic structures excluded or impeded such development. This provides us with a means of comparing and assessing the determining factors.

Putting-out was, as stated above, harnessed to the Zurich city-state system, which endowed the Zurich putting-out industry with its local character; its social structure as much as its forms of production, manufacture and trade. In the field of force between two magnetic poles the following configuration emerged; pulling from above were the privileged town burghers who represented the ruling class and shaped the putting-out system according to a tangle of laws and business regulations for town and countryside. Pulling from below were the peasant subjects who gave the putting-out system its character, according to the differing local byelaws and social and economic structures in different parts of the territory.

This brings us to the important matter of reciprocity; as the putting-out system developed, it changed the social and economic structure, altered the organisation and working of the State and prepared the ground for the great upheaval at the turn of the nineteenth century. This applies as much to the town and its burghers as to the countryside and its peasant subjects.

As we stressed at the beginning, the main object of this investigation is to pursue the changes to people's life styles under the influence of the putting-out system. People, with their traditional mental attitudes and life styles, bound themselves to an existence based on the putting-out industry, thereby necessarily producing more stable living conditions, which were ineluctably entwined with the process of industrialisation. People's behaviour towards their previous (chiefly rural) lives and community, to their intellectual and material world, changed. New life styles and forms of community developed, protected and supported by new compulsory norms of behaviour, which can be observed in human relationships. New forms of settlement, building and homes arose. Agriculture acquired a new face along with altered ground rights and land use. In short, the life and culture of the common people were altered under the influence of the putting-out system. The more deeply entrenched industrialisation became, the greater and more lasting was its impact, shaping both man and landscape. An established and settled workforce emerged, along with an environment and culture which can be described in the cultural morphological sense as an industrial landscape. While these brief observations represent at this stage no more than a working hypothesis, they do help to define the aims of our enquiry more clearly. Once again our field of research is shown to be particularly suitable, since the countryside of Zurich contains, alongside its highly industrialised regions, others which were not (or only slightly) industrialised until the nineteenth century. This provides a means of comparing the changes to life styles under the influence of the putting-out system: industrial landscapes, neighbouring and overlapping zones, as well as purely agricultural regions are all found within the same political and legal framework, providing material for examples and comparisons. The new creative powers aroused in the lives of the common people by the putting-out industry may thus be distinguished clearly.

The changes to the life styles, and the altered lives and values of the common people should, however, not be understood solely as a result of the putting-out industry. We stress this most emphatically and will often refer back to this during the course of our enquiry. Our task is rather to understand these changes as the product of a conflict between the process of industrialisation and the existing political, social and economic order. It is this which imbues the changes with their chronological, mental and local historical relevance; hence our monographical approach. It is only when comparable conditions are available, as is the case in the state of Zurich, that these changes can be analysed in the sense outlined above.

This brings us to a further delimitation: we are restricting our research to the countryside of Zurich and direct our gaze chiefly on the Oberland. We neither can nor wish to compare it with other Swiss or foreign industrial landscapes of the seventeenth and eighteenth centuries. This would fall outside the perimeter of this study. In the same way, we refer only seldom to parallel developments in the industrial landscapes of Switzerland or the rest of Europe. Although this may be considered a weakness, we must be bold and stand by our decision.

In the same way, our study is limited chronologically: we restrict ourselves to the Ancien Régime, although much of our source material extends beyond this period. The great changeover at the close of the eighteenth century is only briefly outlined towards the end of the book. As already mentioned in the Preface, we intend to investigate in a future study the transition from the putting-out industry to the factory industry, with its machine manufacture and the consequent effect on the life styles of the Oberland population up to the present day. The material for this sequel is in greater part already gathered. In order to understand the changes under the influence of the factory industry in the Zurich Oberland, we need to know more about the conditions of existence and how they gave rise to the early industrial putting-out system. The following investigation will provide more than sufficient documentation.

We must emphasise, in order to avoid misunderstandings, that this investigation cannot and does not intend to provide a history of the Zurich putting-out industry. In the same way the nature and shape of the putting-out system, in terms of its economic history and significance, is not presented.[5] Further, we have avoided describing the outworkers' spinning and weaving methods and the accompanying processes, in so far as this is not necessary to understanding this book. For all such information, we refer the reader to the comprehensive literature on the subject.[6]

The reader interested in economic matters will note the absence of a thorough presentation of the cost of living under the Ancien Régime. We have deliberately avoided providing a wage–price index because this requires specialised research. Wages and prices fluctuated so wildly in this period that only the most rigorous analysis could succeed and, so far as our folklorist approach is concerned, these questions are of secondary importance.

We have attempted briefly to outline the questions and aims of our investigation and to define our theme. We are aware that, in spite of the restricted range of our study, we cannot hope fully to grasp and present the transformation to the lives and culture of the common people. These are only snippets from the whole breadth of traditional life styles and cultural expressions. Nonetheless, we must attempt to project these painstakingly assembled pieces back into a living unity, to see them in their manifold relations to other spheres of life and culture and to consider them from different points of view. In attempting this projection, we cannot avoid blending past and future. Nor, indeed, have we avoided repeating ourselves in order to ensure that the connections and implications are grasped, or to emphasise mutual dependence. We scarcely need to emphasise that we are trying to understand how things were by studying the spirit and life of the age, and we have chosen to present this analysis in the form which allows the sources to speak for themselves as often as possible. Analysis and critique of these sources is to be found generally in the text or the notes at the end. At this point, we should mention that the greater part of the source material could not be used.

We hope that our study reaches conclusions of general significance to the theme 'Industrialisation and Everyday Life'. Although we have chosen a monographical approach, we emphasise yet again the chronological, local and mental historical relevance of the changes to the life of the common people and their culture under the influence of the putting-out system.

1 ♣ The preconditions for industrialisation

Those parts of the Zurich territory to be caught up soonest in the putting-out industry lay near to the city, in the regions around the Lake (the Zurichsee) and in the province of Knonau. In the seventeenth century the Zurich textile manufacture also drew the Oberland within the catchment area for cottage industry. Raw materials from foreign lands were brought to the forest valleys to be processed and with them came a system of production based on new social and economic foundations. The industrialisation of the Oberland had begun.

Before this process began, however, yarn was already being produced locally, as part of the peasants' agricultural output. Growing flax and especially hemp was an important item in the annual budget both for wealthy peasants and for poor day-labourers, and was as such highly regarded. Even the poorest families tried to get hold of a *Hanfländli* (little field of hemp) alongside their *Krautgärtli* (vegetable patch). Often enough such a *Hanffäckerli* (little acre of hemp) would be all the land they owned.[1] In numerous parishes the hemp pounds were part of the commonage enjoyed by those parishioners entitled to use it.[2]

In rainy or winter weather, no farmhouse was without its busily spinning wives and daughters, with their husbands and children, or an attentive lover, preparing the fibres for them. They also tried to produce more yarn than they needed, using the profit to offset their heavy debts. Yarn carders went from farmhouse to cottage, buying up their wares. In places with a weekly market (Wald 1621) the market regulations insisted on all spun fibres and yarn being sold there. Many poor families were dependent on spinning hemp and flax not grown and harvested by them, but taken on from neighbours and carders. The weekly market regulations of Wald acknowledged that many poor villagers had to earn their living by producing flax yarn; *flächsinen Garn der Orten vil arm volck ernehren muss*.[3]

Linen weaving, a characteristic peasant handicraft, emerged alongside this locally restricted trade in yarn. Both the trade and the handicraft, however, scarcely exceeded the demands of the peasant economy and the limited marketing opportunities open to them. Yarn was just one of a variety of agricultural market products. Preparing and spinning hemp and flax was just an additional harvest task and formed a usual and familiar part of the agricultural working year. Even when people had to earn their living by spinning flax, this source of income retained the character of a labouring task, not intrinsically different from other farmwork. The demand for such work was still determined by the local cultivation and field systems and depended to a great extent on the varying quality of the regional harvests.[4] The Oberland textile industry did not grow out of the peasant economy, although, seen from a purely technical point of view, this did prepare the ground for it. Instead, it was the product of bourgeois and urban conditions (albeit not the guilds), and not of agricultural and rural conditions.

We do not intend to pursue the post-Reformation history of the Zurich textile production and the development of the Zurich putting-out industry.[5] The emergence of a form of city-state mercantilism in Zurich caused many factors to intermingle, thereby influencing one another and becoming increasingly effective. Church and State, with their religious, political and economic powers, were involved both at the local Zurich level and on a European scale. One need only recall the Protestant refugees who brought a foreign economic philosophy to the city along with their new skills.[6] Forms of production and trade developed, whose social and economic structure was fundamentally different from the traditional guild trades. A system of production developed called *Verlag* or putting-out system, whose structure and organisation extended out beyond the town walls into the countryside.[7] The new forms of production and management were at permanent variance with the old order of guilds and trades,[8] which were to frame the political and economic life of the city-state for a long time to come. The new economic structure made only painful progress, bringing the old order into question and contributing considerably to the collapse of the Ancien Régime.

An early industrial entrepreneurial type emerged to represent the new orientation and organisation, who combined competence in business with his firm, almost puritanical, religious faith to achieve a more elevated aim in life. His business mentality and dealings were based on religious foundations and imbued with the moral and ethical values of the age. No accounts book is without its pious inscription, such as: L.D.S, (*Laus Deo Soli*) or L.D.M. (*Laus Deo Maximo*) or G.g.G. (*Gott geb Glück*).[9] The hand of God directed the course of manufacture and rich business profits were recognised and valued as the blessings of God. This religious base was still strong in the eighteenth century, although much of it had become mere form, and the *Zeitgeist*, together with the rich profits from business, was moving in the direction of secularisation, whereas the puritanical attitude to the world renounced luxury, ostentation and a worldly seigneurial life style. The degree to which the character of eighteenth-century Zurich was formed by her textile manufacturing families is well known.

An economic history of the nature and shape of the early Zurich textile industry would need to start by studying the putting-out system and the urban putting-out masters who controlled it. Such an account would trace local variants of forms of production and manufacture in the early industrial putting-out system. It would have to explain the technical processes and organisation, and set out the social arrangements and so on. But we are faced with a different problem: our focus is on the countryside of Zurich, particularly on the Oberland. It is here that we must pursue and understand industrialisation.

When an urban and bourgeois industry spreads out from the city into the surrounding countryside, it penetrates an unfamiliar environment and economy which receives industrialisation on its own terms. For those involved in the industrialisation process, it meant that the country inhabitants experienced industrialisation not merely as passive recipients, but also by actively shaping it. Although they were politically and economically dependent on the town, in whose order the putting-out system was anchored, they introduced preconditions which favoured or impeded, and sometimes prevented, reception of industrialisation. These preconditions can only be explained in relation to rural conditions in their regional variations. If we look for the primary conditions enabling the Oberland and other regions of the Zurich territory to become early industrial landscapes, we must attempt to trace the history of the deep-seated transformation of the economy and life style of the Oberland. Natural preconditions are muddled up with legal, social and historical preconditions, forcing us to look at nature and mankind in relation to one another and to understand the Oberland in the seventeenth century as a cultural landscape.

Given our interest in folklore, let us begin by studying man. In the 'Beschreybung der Armen uff der ganzen Landschaft Zürich' ('Description of the Poor in the Whole Countryside of Zurich') (1649, 1660, 1680, 1700) we meet that section of the Oberland population whose lives were linked earliest and most exclusively to the Zurich putting-out industry. The Poor Registers owe their creation and compilation to purely superficial motives. We know of the existence of the first people to fall into industrial dependence only through their common poverty, which forced them to place petitions for alms. An endless portrait gallery of poor people passes before us, 'humbly and piteously requesting' their weekly rations, shoes and clogs, Nordling cloth and warm winter clothes from the Alms Office. Spinning had become these poor people's most important, if not their only, source of income, a fact deduced from a few recurring phrases. People petitioning for alms were described in the records in the following terms: 'helps self by spinning cotton'; 'feeds self with spinning silk'; 'has to support self with spun work'; 'does her best by spinning cotton'; 'can support self miserably by spinning'; 'busies self with spun work'; 'supports self with spinning'; 'owns nothing apart from her spindle' etc.[10]

Putting-out work had become these alms recipients' usual and familiar occupation, as is illustrated very clearly in a report by the minister of Illnau (1680), in which he writes about two children of his parish, Lienhart Moos and Barbara Pfister, who 'were still quite young folk, but not fully versed in the usual work of spinning, because they served with farmers in their unmarried state'. Spinning silk, wool and cotton was so taken for granted that in the Poor Registers the word 'spinning' can be replaced quite unambiguously by 'manual work'. The minister of Bauma was able to write in 1680 that Heinrich Ruegger's unmarried daughter, a 'forty-year-old, sickly person, cannot support herself with manual work and consequently asks for shoes and stockings'. In the same way, the informant of Dürnten (1660) used the words *Gwünn* (earnings) to mean earnings from spinning. He described Elsbeth Grüningery as a forty-one-year-old widow, who had to stay at home, paid 12 *Pfund* in rent and 'owns nothing, beyond what she, with her children, earns (*gwünt*) each day'.

Greatly as poverty and hardship provide the dominant tones in the overall picture of the early industrial landscape, it would be a mistake to look only among the recipients of alms for those hands who reached out eagerly towards the new sources of income. The economically better-off sections of the population also made grateful use of the opportunity to employ their free time after working on their farms by spinning silk, wool and cotton. We must remember this, as we dally with the 'Description of the Poor' in the next pages.

We are looking at a phenomenon, whereby a source of employment, which penetrated the Oberland from outside and was directed from outside, had after a few years become indispensable to the majority of the inhabitants. It should be made clear first on which economic foundations these persons' existence was based. Let us start by asking a rather broad question: what sort of work opportunities did poor villagers have in the Oberland? This should clarify the position of the putting-out industry in relation to the work opportunities arising out of the land itself. Which jobs were supplemented or perhaps even replaced by spinning?

The following details about the fate of the day-labourers make us realise how terribly little the woodlands had to offer their poorest inhabitants. Jageli Wirth from Dürnten (1660), for instance, would go *uff den Tagwen, wo er Glegenheit findt* (out day-labouring, wherever he found the opportunity), although he had trouble walking. In wintertime he and his wife and children were reduced to spinning. He owned his own cottage, a vegetable patch and an orchard 'enough to winter a cow', as well as a *Handfländli* and 5 *Jucharten* of ploughland, but everything was burdened with heavy debts. His wife and children managed to earn 15 *Batzen* a week. She and twelve-year-old Anneli span. Fifteen-year-old Hans-Jakob span and chopped wood; while twenty-one-year-old Hans was 'this time away doing day-labouring work with his father'. The working year of able-bodied men would be summed up repeatedly by the formula *Geht uff den Tagwen, winterzeit muss er spinnen* (he goes day-labouring; in winter he has to spin). We do not meet many owning as much land and property as Jageli Wirth. Fifty-five-year-old Hans Jageli Weber and his family, from the same parish (Dürnten 1660), found shelter in his son-in-law's home; 'He goes looking for day-labouring work; in winter he has to spin'. Josef Caspar of Rüti (1660) was 'an impoverished day-labourer, with neither house nor homeland, a destitute man'; his *Völkli* (folks) tried to remedy their poverty by spinning. 'Day-labourer Jakob Frey of Tagenau and Magdale Vogler of Volketswil (1649) have a house, a meadow for one cow, one and a half *Jucharten* of ploughland, but owe interest on 300 *Gulden* for the main property', so that, despite their youth and strength, they were unable to feed themselves and their seven children without resorting to charity. One of the children, eighteen-year-old Jakob, 'herds the pigs and appears to look for a master to serve'. The others helped their mother with her silk spinning as far as they were able. In Fischenthal (1649) the day-labourer Heinrich Zuppinger had his own home for 6 *Gulden* interest a year; his wife and two remaining children span and could earn 16 to 20 *Batzen* weekly. Hans Lochmann of Egg (1660) was also a 'reduced, poor day-labourer'; Heinrich, one of the older children, served in the Black Forest area; twenty-one-year-old Anna and nineteen-year-old Barbara were also 'in foreign parts, but no one knows where'.

Meanly as farm-labouring work was paid, and obtained with the loss of so much personal and economic freedom, the poor day-labourer was none the less glad to get any at all. Felix Pfaffhuser, a pious and industrious person who 'works wherever he is employed' and owned nothing of his own, was unable to support himself without help and alms, on account of his many children and because 'nobody was giving him day-work'. When he did get work, he earned 'daily [except at harvest] only 4 *Batzen* and now [in wintertime] until Easter only 3 *Batzen*'. His wife span silk, which enabled her to contribute 10 *Batzen* a week to the family budget. The two oldest sons were in service (Wangen 1660). Hans Ehrsam of Mönchaltorf 'on account of no one providing day-work' and 'rising dearness of bread' was unable to feed his household. Such complaints about the lack of agricultural work were desperate and bitter. However ready people were to undertake any work, 'practically none, although ready to work just for his meals, of the poor people who go hungry in their poverty are given work' (Bubikon 1649).

Where the opportunity arose, 'people took to the woods'. Boys of ten and eleven were already chopping wood (Dübendorf 1660). Circumscribed by the local conditions of ownership and rights of usage, the forest was capable of providing even its poorest inhabitants with very little in the way of a livelihood. Those who knew how tried to make ends meet by doing wicker-work. Heini Vogel of Uster (1649) owned no property; he was forty, 'healthy in body and can make wicker baskets'. His wife span, and twelve-year-old Hans, ten-year-old Rudolf and eight-year-old Barbel were also kept at this work. Twenty-two-year-old Hans Jakob lived in Dürnten (1680) 'who chops wood and makes wicker lathes'. The son of Jageli Temperli of Dübendorf (1649), thirteen-year-old Jörg, could not only 'read and pray well', but could also 'make wicker baskets'. Nineteen-year-old Maater of Fischenthal (1649) 'makes platters and spoons' and manages to 'earn up to 20 or 23 *Batzen*, when the others carry the wood to him, which they must however buy'. His mother span, along with thirteen-year-old Anneli, ten-and-a-half-year-old Barbeli, nine-year-old Elsbethli and six-year-old Kly-Anneli. The whole lot of them were, however, unable to earn more than 16 to 20 *Batzen* a week. The children were not sent to the somewhat distant school, because the family 'is not able to provide them with dinner'. Many a poor family lived isolated lives deep in the forest and burnt charcoal. Jörg Müller of Fischenthal, for instance, 'this summer [1649] dwelt with the children in a hut in the Tösswald'; he was forty-four and 'burnt charcoal'. His wife was forty-six, 'strong, and has helped her husband. In rainy weather they all spin.' The four children still living with them were 'healthy, but stark naked'.

These few sources illustrating the fate of poor village families reveal that industrialisation did not begin by displacing any existing work opportunities. Spinning silk, wool and cotton brought in so little that it could not compete even with the badly paid farm-labouring jobs. We have already seen how Jörg Maater could earn 20 to 23 *Batzen* a week by whittling platters and spoons, while his mother's and four sisters' combined efforts at spinning could earn only 16 to 20 *Batzen*. The Poor Registers contain countless entries comparing spinning with other forms of employment; one person, for instance, was able 'on account of lame limbs to do no work but spinning', another was capable 'of no work apart from spinning' (Gossau 1660). Spinning was resorted to only by those who could not find or were no longer capable of other employment. In spite of this, spinning had become indispensable to the greater part of the Oberland population. Putting-out work not only contributed to the family income, but had become an important basis of these people's existence. Even with spinning, their standard of living remained at the lowest endurable level.

Among those receiving alms were herdsmen, school-masters, sextons and rural craftsmen. They too depended on spinning to get by. A sexton of Kyburg (1649) owned 'a poor cottage and a borrowed cow'. He fed himself and his four children 'besides his small sexton's wage and the day-labouring by spinning – but there is very little else'. Hans Baumberger of Fällanden (1680) 'keeps himself at this time by butchering' and lives with his brother in half a house. His wife had to help them along by spinning. The tailor Dännyler of Weisslingen (1649) had 'his own little house and a little orchard nearby and otherwise a *Mannmad* of meadow, that he may summer and winter a cow'. He owned four *Jucharten* of *Ruchfeld* (a field of rough, i.e. bad, soil). The whole property was burdened with debt. He had seventeen children, one of whom,

Jakob, helped his father with his tailoring, while the others were being taught to spin.

Our survey of the work and earnings opportunities available to the poor villagers leaves us in no doubt that demand for work far exceeded supply in the Oberland at the onset of industrialisation. The Oberland was not capable of feeding her poorest inhabitants. Able-bodied men and their families were unable to make ends meet by working all year round, and part of the population was unable to acquire even the most essential and basic necessaries of life.[11] While fluctuations in the demand for labour are an integral feature of an agrarian economy, in normal circumstances, however, a period of full employment should generate enough earnings to cover at least part of the subsequent period of unemployment. There was no question of this in the Oberland. Day-labouring and servants' work was clearly in short supply and it was difficult for the grown-up sons and daughters of smallholders, day-labourers and villeins to find a master in their homeland. Those who were employed for the whole summer were dismissed after the harvest in the autumn, like sixteen-year-old Samuel of Wald (1649), who complained that he had had a master in the summer but that now he could not find one. Hans, the fourteen-year-old son of Barbel Müller (1649), who earned her living in Uster by begging and spinning, was looking for a master. Earlier in the year, he had 'driven the team before the plough' for captain Meyer. The significance of these sorts of complaints can only really be understood when one knows that a few decades later, farmers in the Zurich countryside had great difficulty in finding local farmhands and maids. They were obliged to import them from Catholic districts and from the neighbouring areas of Swabia and Württemberg. In the second half of the seventeenth century, however, migration was still in the opposite direction and the inhabitants of the Oberland were obliged to move away for a while to seek their livelihoods 'in the land below'. Individuals and groups moved to the towns, to the ploughlands of the Mittelland, to Swabia, to Württemberg and the Pfalz. 'Going to Swabia' was an especially popular practice, as can be deduced from the expression 'has recourse meantime to the land of Swabia', as applied to Jageli Werndly (Mönchaltorf 1660). His wife stayed at home and did 'her best by spinning cotton'. The coupled owned 'in great poverty a derelict hut, full of holes, and a cow'. Jagli Trüb from the same village (Mönchaltorf 1660) also spent 'most of his time away in Swabia, to seek his living' and his wife Maria 'busies herself' in their home village with the *Gspunst* (spinning work). Conradt Zappert of Hinwil (1660) was 'a poor day-labourer, works in the land of Württemberg. He has half a cottage and half a village right, but he may not keep a cow.' His wife Dorothea 'subsists wretchedly by spinning silk'.

Children were also sent abroad. Jörg Müller of Mönchaltorf (1660) had sent 'his oldest boy to Swabia, to seek his living'. The widow Elsbeth Trüb of Mönchaltorf (1660) owned 'her own cottage and the right of the village, as well as two little fields of hemp'. She had two children; 'The little girl is with her mother, but the boy is staying meanwhile in Swabia.' Felix Müller of Gossau (1660) wanted 'on account of great poverty to send two small children into Swabia' but was prevented from so doing by his minister.

These people were driven into foreign lands by the most bitter poverty, the extent of which is clear to all who know how much Oberland people love their homeland. Many moved away never to return, leaving their families behind in poverty and anxiety. Jakob Steinmann of Wangen had spent 'several years now [1660] in Swabia serving in Pfüren', during which time he had been able to buy a 'half cottage'. But 'last harvest time, he took up with a woman of Niderhasli, who was working there too, and ran away with her. On account of this, his wife had to give up the cottage, but can stay there for a year yet. She, the abandoned and distressed Regula, is forty-two years old, spins silk.' Her seventeen-year-old son Caspar 'serves in Ehringen in Swabia'. Barbara (fifteen) 'spins silk'. Felix was only two years and Hans six months old. Barbara Schänkel of Mönchaltorf (1660) was 'a desperately poor woman, who knows not whether her husband, who went to Swabia a few years ago, is alive or dead. She has part of a tiny, derelict cottage, but owns nothing besides. She works hard at her spinning, but her earnings are poor.' Margret Erisman, Jakob Kindemann's wife, of Grüningen (1660) had also been abandoned by her husband. He, 'a worthless fellow, had run away from her and left her with three children round her neck, towards whose upkeep he had not sent even one *Heller*'s worth home'. Of the boys, one was in service; 'the other must also find a master at Candlemass'. Regula, Ruedeli Boller's wife, of Grüningen (1660) span silk. 'Her husband went away from her more than a year ago and promised cheerfully to send something back home in the meantime.'

Those who sought their living in foreign parts could also serve in foreign wars; single men and irresponsible fathers could take the bounty. Magdalena Burg was the widow of Hans Meyer, a carpenter who died in Dalmatia. Her property included 'her own cottage, cabbage patch and orchard'. She was a diligent and good worker, but was 'heavily burdened with many children, her *Gwünn* [earnings from spinning] consequently poor'. Her three eldest sons, Hans-Jacob, Hans-Heinrich and Heinrich, were in Dalmatia; twelve-year-old Vreneli span; ten-year-old Rüdeli 'goes to school and chops wood'; Anneli, nine, also span; Elsbethli and Urschy could not as yet earn anything. Jakob Oetelin (Russikon 1649) had twelve children; two sons were serving in the war, and a son and daughter 'with masters'. There were many such pitiable records of wives and widows whose husbands had 'moved to the war' (Illnau 1680); the late Jageli Winkler died in Dalmatia, leaving behind his widow, Barbely Meyer of Russikon (1649), who owned 'a dwelling, a cow, but nothing to slice'. Without alms she and her four children could not have survived.

When the pressure caused by the wretched living conditions in the Oberland was relieved by emigration, it was the strongest and most energetic family members who moved away to seek their fortunes in foreign parts. The population they left behind was made up of poor villagers obliged by physical weakness or family ties to endure lives of abject poverty. Truly distressing fates are recorded in the 'Description of the Poor', with 'destitute' people vegetating in hopeless dependence. Their very survival hung literally by a thread, those thin threads twisted from the imported plant fibres. Had there been no Zurich putting-out industry, their lives would have been completely unthinkable. Bosshart of Bauma (1680), for instance, had apart from his four small uneducated children 'nothing at all, except what he earns by spinning'. Jörg Spörri (Bauma 1680) was along with his five uneducated children 'diligent at the spinning work and has otherwise nothing at all, beyond what he earns every day'. Heinrich Hess (Bauma 1680) and his seven children also had nothing 'except what he can earn by spinning'. Hans Sänn and Anna Bodmer 'have a cottage and a hemp field, but are burdened with debts and keep themselves and their four children by spinning' (Pfäffikon 1680). Fifty-year-old Brüngger of Wysslingen (1660), 'a broken man, owns besides his cottage and hay meadow, where he keeps a cow, also a small field of hemp, for which he is however still much in debt'. He had four children, who 'feed themselves by weaving and spinning, by begging too, which the wife and children engage in a fair amount'.

Even skilled and diligent hands were at that time scarcely able to keep themselves with spinning alone. Those whose work was impaired by sickness or age were, however much they tried, completely incapable of surviving without assistance from the Alms Office. Eighty-four-year-old Hans Weber of Bauma (1680), for instance, could 'no longer support himself by spinning'. Martha Scheller of Dübendorf (1649) was sixty-one, 'ill unto dying and destitute. She spins cotton, but can do but little with it on account of the aforementioned reason.' Jakob Wettstein of Fällanden (1660) was twenty-one and 'not of healthy body, and so can earn only little by spinning cotton on the wheel'. Anna Straub (Fällanden 1660) could also earn only a little by spinning. Maria Russegger of Wangen (1649), 'a single person, fifty-one years old, lives in Bailiff Wäber's house, is destitute and has nothing, except what she earns. But as she is unhealthy, short-sighted and ill, she can not earn more than 6 *Batzen* a week, and without assistance would surely die of hunger.' Barbel Stucki, 'a poor spinster' of Fischenthal (1649) was 'blind, owns nothing apart from her spindle and what My Gracious Lords and other good people accord her. Her illegitimate child, Elsbethli Bosshart, has been to school and is now [at fifteen years] to be her mother's eyes: she helps with the spinning.' Elsbeth Rügger (Dürnten 1680) lived with her daughter 'in a house for 8 *Pfund* [rent], so the church pays it'. She was 'very poor and can scarcely breathe, but she spins most of the time'.

Instances of these abandoned wives' and widows' sad lot occur frequently in the records: 'Anna Wunderli, the departed Jörg Jader's widow, is forty-one years old, with six children still at home; three educated, three uneducated; attempting with difficulty to keep them by spinning; having to stay at home' – they too petitioned the Alms Office for assistance (Russikon 1968). The mothers complained endlessly that 'on account of child care they were constantly kept from the work [spinning]' (Gossau 1660). One patently obvious reason for applying to the Alms Office for assistance was when the children, in spite of being able to 'pray and spin well', were so small that 'they still could not earn anything with their handiwork' (viz., Bubikon 1649). We have seen plenty of examples of the tender ages at which these children were obliged to contribute to the family earnings.

Let us not dwell too long on these dismal portraits; these people barely managed to survive on what their spindles and spinning wheels earned them. For many of them, spinning did little more than legitimise their entitlement to Poor Relief. It is worth noting as a general principle that when wages are determined by market forces, they tend to sink to the lowest level required for survival, so long as the workers and the labour involved cannot resist this tendency. Because spinning did not require any specialised skills, it could not command a set wage. The putting-out industry did not depend on a qualified workforce; children as well as old and infirm persons were good enough for the work. The imbalance between demand and supply of labour in the Oberland (mentioned above) created a work vacuum which dragged wages down. On top of this, the peasant farmers began taking on putting-out work in their free time, thus competing with economically unviable persons, who had to spin to survive. These people's labour was undervalued, but when one considers their economic and political dependence,[12] their pitiable situation can no longer surprise us.

The life-saving role of the putting-out industry in the lives of people on the margins of an agricultural community is now clear, since it was the lack of employment possibilities among an economically dependent population which directed the industry towards the Oberland. As soon as the Zurich putting-out industry had acquired a certain structure and dimension, it was able to tap this demand for work opportunities.[13]

We have limited ourselves until now to observations of a very general nature about the work and wages available to the poorest inhabitants of the Oberland at the beginning of industrialisation. As it is, we have inspected only one side of the foundations supporting the lives of the poor villagers, ignoring the conditions of ownership, which we will now consider.

It may have been apparent that most of the alms recipients still owned a share of a cottage, although the numbers of those who 'have no abode of their own' (Wetzikon 1660) and had to be taken in increased steadily between 1649 and 1700. The house was the last possession to be alienated. Although one might not otherwise own anything greater than a 'hand's breadth' (Maur 1649), one tried to become and remain a shareholder in a house. However poor the accommodation, however many 'accumulated debts' had to be paid, people set their 'backs and stomachs to it' (Dübendorf 1700) and tried to retain their share of a house for themselves and their descendants. The houses of the poor were without exception hopelessly indebted. Widow Anna Sigg, 'a worthy old woman of Kyburg [1649], owns half a house, which is tending to collapse, is burdened with accumulated rents and debts, more than it is worth'; the other half of the house belonged to Anna Schmidli, also a 'sickly widow'. Her part was also burdened with debts. Wilpot Keller's half cottage was '*ful*' (rotten); it was all he owned (Dübendorf 1660). The day-labourer Wanner's house was 'very small, hardly a half, derelict' (Wangen 1649).

We can only understand the pre-eminence of even the poorest people's efforts to own a house, when we know that a house provided not just accommodation and shelter but also political and economic rights. People's political and social status in the village was directly linked to possession of a house. We will see later on how the peasant economic mentality, backed up by the urban economic order, could use the legal function of house ownership as a weapon against the economically weaker elements who had no political rights. This had important consequences for the industrialisation of the Oberland.

Even when a poor villager did own something, apart from his own dwelling and the share in the commonage pertaining to it, it was very little and even in the best cases could only provide him with part of his livelihood. Most often there would be a 'cabbage patch and orchard' and perhaps a 'little field of hemp' as well. As in the case of Hans Bertschinger and Anna Hübscher, who has 'a tiny cottage with a cabbage patch alongside'; he did field-work; she span with eleven-year-old Urseli and even nine-year-old Elsbethli, who could spin a little, to help (Dübendorf 1649). Jakob Wohlgemut has a further 'three small arable fields', but the whole family had to spin to make ends meet (Volketswil 1649). Not many of the alms recipients could keep a cow; Hans Halbherr, the cobbler (Hinwil 1660) 'has half a cottage and half a commoner's right, along with a hay meadow for one cow'. At his home, too, everyone was employed at spinning. Anna Hofmann 'has her own cottage, cabbage patch, hemp field and fodder for one cow'. But she had to pay interest on 25 *Pfund* yearly, as well as her ground rent. Her ten-year-old Jacobli went to school, while seven-year-old Jörgli span. Jagli Furrer of Wald had 'a cottage, summer feed for a cow and half winter feed', but everything was burdened with debts. His wife and five children, aged between seven and seventeen, span. Klein-Jagli Wyss and his family owned 'a house with a little orchard and another piece of meadow growing enough hay to feed a cow summer and winter, and 2 *Jucharten* of ploughland'. But everything was so heavily burdened with debts 'that they [the parents] and consequently their children [Anna, sixteen; Ursel, thirteen] cannot extract enough from spinning and other work to pay the interest on this property every year' (Weisslingen 1649). Other 'little properties' supported 'not even a cow' (Wald 1660). Even if there was enough fodder for the summer, it generally ran out in the winter. Hans Brunner of Wald (1660), for instance, 'has a house and a little meadow for one cow, but no fodder for winter'. Of his children, the older son (twenty) could 'work a little at chopping wood'. Two children were in service, including nineteen-year-old Bethli in the Pfalz. Clephe (ten) and Elisabethli (eight) span. The lack of sufficient fodder for the winter was also a reason why so many were unable to make full use of their village rights. Their more prosperous fellow villagers were keen to prevent 'anyone from summering more cattle than he can winter'.[14] Many alms recipients had 'half a commoner's right, but could keep no cow' (Hinwil 1660). Wherever the Poor Register contains details of property in land, they are always accompanied by the disconsolate remark 'but he is in debt over it'.

Among the villeins, day-labourers and smallholders whom we have already met were often families who owned neither land nor house, but had to seek shelter under other people's roofs. Hans Egli (Bauma 1680), for instance, had 'nothing of his own, but is accommodated, has nine children, several of whom are still young and uneducated, and can earn nothing'. Hans Lähner (Rütisalt-dorff 1649) and his family also rented a home. He has 'nothing of his own and little too in movable goods'. Many poor and abandoned people appear in the records as owning 'no more than the corner' of a relative's house (Wald 1649).

As we know, the numbers of those who were accommodated with a farmer in return for a yearly rent rose steadily between 1649 and 1700. This was a direct consequence of the new earnings provided by the Zurich textile industry, which alone enabled a large number of people without homes of their own to build up a means of existence, however inadequate, and to put down roots in their homeland. They could never have achieved this with the limited farm and forestry work available and the small demand for unskilled labour. Nor was there any hope that the local cultivation and field system would allow any rise in the demand for labour, so long as the traditional use of land remained unchanged. This did not, however, mean at all that the possibility of industrial earnings could 'cut [people] off from their own land and soil'.[15] These people were landless before the process of industrialisation began, as we see from a petition of 4 May 1584, by the village commune of Oberdürnten for an *Einzugsbrief* (entry charter) which stated 'that only two in Sulzbach are endowed with some land and property, whereas all the others are day-labourers and poor folk, who support themselves on alms'.[16] We have seen how it was only putting-out work which allowed many families to acquire the means to pay the interest on the crippling debts on their land. Earnings from industry did not therefore cut people off from the land, but, on the contrary, helped them to retain even hopelessly indebted homes and properties. A glance at the conditions of ownership of the poor shows that scarcely a family owned a viable amount of productive land. They all had to earn their livings in other ways. But the fact is that, even before the onset of industrialisation, all these people depended on inadequate pockets of land. Industrialisation only uncovered a degree of hardship and misery not previously evident, by tying growing numbers of economically dependent and completely propertyless people to the Oberland. How much industrialisation was responsible for the fate of the growing numbers of landless inhabitants is another question.

Introducing these poor families in this way, one after the other, is, I fear, monotonous, but this primitive method of exposition, based as much as possible on the sources, was chosen to ensure that poverty and hardship do not remain anonymous but are linked to the lives of real individuals. The few examples selected can provide only a faint overall impression of the dark and dreadful background against which the beginnings of the Oberland textile industry emerged. It should further be noted that the pressure of poverty at the onset of industrialisation was not due to failed harvests. Hunger and hardship were not limited to certain periods, but were permanent features of the Oberland.[17] We will investigate the problems of poverty, almsgiving and industrialisation more thoroughly from other angles further on.

With the help of the Poor Registers we have learnt about the conditions of work and ownership of those people who were condemned to slip into industrial dependence. We have established that the pressure of poverty was already present in the Oberland before industrialisation began. The alms recipient was isolated not only socially but also politically; as soon as he accepted alms, he lost his rights as an active member of the commune.[18] When property as such was a factor determining a person's status in the rural community, it was inevitable that the propertyless should develop a hostile attitude towards property, towards the existing order and towards the ideas behind it – ideas shared by the urban authorities and the villagers. A reduced property, even just part of a house, allowed many poor people to maintain an outward link with their homeland. But their land could not give them inner security, since even in the best cases it could provide only part of their subsistence. In order to keep their tiny property, perhaps only a fraction of a dwelling, these people were forced to look for work wherever they could find it, even when it took them 'out of the country'[19] for shorter or longer periods. These small remnants of peasant holdings led less to permanent settlement and much more to a desperate search for work and wages. Indeed, farm-labouring work within the homeland had a more stable and binding effect. Although the day-labourer did not draw a direct share in the produce of his labour, and he did not live on or from the land which he worked, his relationship with his peasant employer was at that time still shot through with many personal ties. This endowed the social structure of the rural economic unit with its organic involvement, radiating conservative and traditional strength. But poor villagers could no longer be considered peasants, so how could they be included in the medieval 'estate' of the producers, when not one of them was able to support himself and his dependants without outside help. They were marginals in a rural environment, which did not allow them sufficient living space, thus determining their mental and spiritual attitude towards that environment. These human conditions in the Oberland greatly influenced the expanding putting-out industry, which sought out people with no economic and social supports.

The preconditions for the industrialisation of the Oberland so far discussed were only symptoms of the social and economic conditions. Our enquiry should not stop here, but should seek to shed light on the forces which produced these effects.

Various authors[20] have pointed to the barren soil to explain the lack of living space in the Oberland. They talk about over-population, which industrialisation is supposed to have encouraged. We must treat this thesis with the utmost distrust, because the relationship between cause and effect is perceived far too simply and one-sidedly. The fact that in the seventeenth century a large number of the inhabitants of the Oberland could not earn a living in their homeland does not allow us to deduce that the Oberland was over-populated. It must be stated once and for all that the living space in a region is not a constant, but the product of constantly changing factors. The number of factors also varies, as the example of the exogenous Zurich putting-out industry shows, which affects any calculation of the living space in the Oberland as a new and initially unmeasured factor.

The same applies to the concept of over-population, which is always only relative. It is based on a numerical proportion, which cannot stand up on its own, but must be related to the type of local economy and economic system. Human society has many ways of dealing with nature's rigid laws; historical ground rights and ways of using the soil do not only determine the extent and fertility of the cultivable land, but they also direct the distribution of labour along well-established paths, according to the traditional system of agriculture. People's capacity for work has a neutral feather-gauge built into it, which can be stretched to over-capacity. For this reason demand for work can never be equated with supply.

The starting position is thus briefly outlined: poverty and hardship should not be considered in isolation. The living conditions of a population which (without enough land and with insufficient employment opportunities) is unable to subsist and is thrown back on public and private assistance, must be studied in relation to the type of the economy, the economic order and the social structure of the Oberland. In the following pages we will attempt to gain an insight into the legal and economic bases of a peasant culture and community, whose organic unity presents such a closely woven texture that it is difficult to unravel the threads important to us. Analysing this diverse world, the product of its locality and history, inevitably involves stylising it to some extent. We will restrict ourselves to a few vital features, and we have limited our source material to the late sixteenth, seventeenth and eighteenth centuries, conscious that they represent only the last phase of a long-drawn-out development.

In the seventeenth century a process, which had already begun at the time of the Reformation, reached its culmination. It was spurred on by the endeavours of the villagers, helped by the urban authorities, to protect their common property in money and unmovables against newcomers and small-holders. No less than the preservation of a major part of their livelihood and survival base was at stake. This process was a consequence of the collapse of the old village order, under which possession of a dwelling and hearth within the village boundary had sufficed to maintain a share in the commonalty.[21] Everyone had owned the same right, although in fact the extent of an individual's share was determined by the size of his property. 'So long as the old village order, under which new homesteads could only be established subject to particular restrictive conditions and to agreement between lord and villagers, was still in force, this principle did little harm to the interests of the inhabitants. But the village order gradually disintegrated. New settlers became common and the villages expanded.'[22] In order to counteract the dissipation of the commons, the community tried to make it difficult and even impossible to move in.

Exclusivity could not be achieved by means of a single legal document, because the legal basis of the commune did not allow this; it could only be achieved by indirect means and over a long time. This particular slice of rural economic history is overshadowed by future developments at the end of the eighteenth and beginning of the nineteenth centuries.[23] In our case, the driving forces were not enlightened, articulate and literate physiocrats with new ideas about the use of the soil and field systems, as in the second half of the eighteenth century, but they were villagers with the whole leaden weight of their conservative and traditional peasant mentality behind them. Conse-quently, the new barriers they erected to protect their property and their political and economic status were constructed from materials which seem to belong in a history of the agrarian Middle Ages. The village communities' petitions (and the reasons laid out in their preambles) to the city rulers for new entry charters[24] are instructive manifestations of ancient peasant economic thinking. When one compares these petitions and suggestions with the legal statutes respectively ratified and drawn up by the urban authorities, one has to acknowledge the extent to which the authorities defended and sanctioned the villagers' intentions.[25]

The earliest entry charters date from the first half of the sixteenth century, rising to a flood only at the end of the sixteenth century and slowly ebbing away at the beginning of the eighteenth century. In these entry charters[26] the Zurich Mayors and councils acknowledged the right of the village communi-ties concerned to demand a fixed entry fee from those who wanted to settle in their community and become members with voting and commonage rights. This was the first, purely financial, restriction which the community members hoped would prevent them from being 'inflicted with a mighty and very burdensome invasion and settlement of new inhabitants, each one with little and inadequate money, having moved here from other places'.[27] Only well-endowed new members were welcome to the communities. The reasons for maintaining or raising an entry fee vary only slightly in the sources: the petitions to the rulers by the village communities were mostly based on the grounds that 'meantime they are being overwhelmed by ever-increasing numbers of those moving in on them and dissipating their community right, and greatly burdening them in other ways, thereby causing great loss and depreciation to the common lands'.[28]

The size of the entry fee granted by the authorities depended on the extent of communal property: the greater the commonalty, the more the community could and would demand from new members.

How this admission policy (which amounted to an exclusion policy) affected the industrialisation of the Oberland becomes clear when we compare the common lands of the Oberland communities with those in other parts of the canton. The village communities of the mountainous Oberland possessed very little, if any, common land. They owned much less property than did the more level areas of the canton.[29] This last circumstance was crucial, since in these cases it was not the absolute size of the common land, but its relative size, which mattered. It is clear that this equation (the smaller the commonalty, the smaller the entry fee) must have had a profound effect on the unpropertied communities, which lay mostly in the Oberland. They were consequently much less (indeed not at all) able than the better-off villages to protect themselves from encroachment by poor people by charging an entry fee. The mountain communities either never or only late and in a roundabout way achieved a 'soft' entry charter, with the inevitable result that the quality of the population (in economic terms) was reduced, and that the Oberland was impoverished. Poor people were prevented from settling in the wealthy communities, with their higher entry fees and other opportunities for limiting immigration, and so the Oberland was necessarily colonised by the indigent. These terms of settlement, which had such dire implications for the Oberland, were able to wreak havoc when the putting-out industry spread into the uplands. As we have seen, it was only when industrial earnings supplemented public charity and the insufficient farm-labouring jobs that the poor achieved a subsistence minimum. Nevertheless, industrialisation also had the effect of encouraging the efforts and constant attempts by the propertied village communities to strengthen their entry charters; the new situation created by the industrial work opportunities strengthened these communities' tendency towards exclusivity. The relationship between industrialisation and admission policy was an important factor for change in the life of the common people.

When we refer to the colonisation of the Oberland, we do not mean, either at this stage or later on, that it was swamped by a flood of poor people (although, according to various sources, this was to some extent indeed the case). What happened was rather that a growing number of people without sufficient land were finding a steady livelihood in the Oberland. The legal preconditions for a natural population increase were already present and industrial earnings introduced the material conditions for settlement and population growth; questions which will be tackled in the next chapters.[30] At this point we will discuss only the admission policy as a factor inhibiting the reception of the putting-out system.

Having just outlined a theory connecting the village commonalty with the human and material preconditions for the industrialisation of the Oberland in a causal relationship, let us now fill in the picture with a few illustrations from the sources.[31]

In February 1638 the parish of Bäretswil received an entry charter from the Zurich government. The parish was able to acquire this, although it had no common land and was consequently 'devastatingly and increasingly invaded by too many new inhabitants'. They hoped to be able to free themselves of this 'excessive burden' by charging an entry fee. The parish members would then be able better to 'dwell and live alongside one another'.[32]

The driving force behind this Bäretswil entry charter was not the village community (because there was no commonalty) but, and this is noteworthy, the church parish.[33] The governor of Grüningen wrote to Zurich on 23 January 1638 that representatives of the parish of Bäretswil had appeared and informed him that their parish 'at that time was greatly overrun with poor people, who move here daily, not merely from Your Worships' jurisdiction and territory, but also from the Thurgau and other places'.[34]

The *Kilch und Gmeindtsgnossen* (parishioners and commoners) of Bubikon drew up a petition for an entry charter in 1653, addressed to the government, 'concerning the far too numerous foreign poor moving in'. They were granted it by the council on 23 November 1659 with this explanation: 'Since you have until now been accorded no entry charter, although for years now, on account of your albeit scanty commonage and church property, you have been increasingly overwhelmed by and burdened with many poor people.'[35] Pfäffikon announced on 30 July 1630 that 'the many new inhabitants have been no small reason for our having to call on Closter Rüti for charitable contributions to the Poor Relief'.[36] The Hinwil and Rüti sources are the most telling; on 2 December 1642 the governor of Grünigen sent the following letter to the town authorities:

For some time past all kinds of unrighteous people have moved into the church parish of Hinwil from abroad and home, and have settled down, on account of which many expenses and burdens have been slung round the necks of the parish and upright folk of our Worshipful Lords and masters; a whole church parish has been occasioned to limit the inhabitants here and where possible to set up barriers; and thereby is advised (because the villages and communities of Hinwil, Ringwil, Wernetshausen have secured their own entry rights, but apart from these same three communes, there are all sorts of little villages, farms and dwellings situated in the church parish, which, on account of having no commons, have no entry fee, so the above-mentioned people go there and move in).[37]

As a result, they were asking to be granted an entry charter, which would apply to all who settled in the church parish of Hinwil, and not only to the three village communities endowed with common lands. As a consequence, on 31 December 1642, the church parish of Hinwil received an albeit very mild entry charter, allowing it to demand 12 *Pfund* from those moving there from the Zurich counryside, and 24 *Pfund* from other members of the Confederation. Only six months later the minister of Hinwil had to apply once again to the Mayor and town council, because the little village and commune of Hadlikon, a little member of the aforesaid parish, refused to acknowledge these conditions. Hadlikon, the minister reported, 'is an open door into our parish for anyone'. The church parish was not concerned about the money, but wanted only 'to dig a ditch against ungodly dissolute people'.[38] These entry charters for church parishes apparently owed their existence to the circumstance that the effects of this admission policy had gone far beyond what was originally aimed at. The Rüti records speak out even more clearly; the governor of Grüningen wrote to Zurich on 18 Febuary 1711 that

Some time ago the delegates of the church parish of Rüti duly notified me what had taken place in the past time and year at great expense to their parish funds and at no small cost to state property and burdening other honourable people and damaging the woods, gardens and orchards, with all kinds of foreign tramps, unrighteous and homeless persons who are no longer tolerated in other parishes and who have used all kinds of false pretexts to crowd in, to such an extent that, so long as it shall continue, the inhabitants and parishioners with their ancient rights, who are being driven out of their homes on account of these foreigners, live in the hope that your Worships will graciously grant them an entry charter, like other parishes, so that in future they will be less burdened and overrun by these foreign people, so much more numerous than them.[39]

His letter remained unanswered and the governor of Rüti addressed the town council again on 1 March 1711, stressing that, among other things, great damage had been done by the 'unrighteous folk' to 'state property and the surrounding copyholdings' since nothing in wood or field was safe from them.[40]

The sources provide clear evidence of the deteriorating quality of the Oberland population. We know from our foregoing reflections that the destitute people under discussion formed and were to form an army of industrial wage labour. The causal relationship between the Oberland parishes' entry fees and the pressure of poverty in the Oberland is obvious.

Entry fees could only be demanded from those who wanted to acquire the voting and commonage rights of the church and village community. Let us glance briefly at the villeins, people who enjoyed the protection of the village community, without themselves being members of the commune.[41] The attitude of the parishioners towards this lowliest grade in the peasant social hierarchy emerges clearly from their letters of petition for an entry charter. The parishioners demanded of the council the right to decide themselves whether villeins should be allowed to settle among them. The village community of Hinteregg demanded in a letter of 28 October 1654 that the following motion be endorsed: 'First, no one without the prior knowledge and consent of the community be allowed to accommodate foreigners in their village community.'[42] Villeins were only tolerated reluctantly, and were considered as burdens. At times people tried to rid themselves of this class of inhabitant; the assembly of church elders in Wetzikon decided, for instance, in 1716, that all foreign persons should be sent out of the parish by the bailiffs and church elders and returned straightaway to their homeland.[43] By the beginning of the seventeenth century the custom of demanding a villein fee from these people was already becoming established, not so much to protect the parish but rather to limit the expenses incurred by the parishioners on the villeins' behalf.[44] In 1621, for instance, Fägswil–Rüti demanded from those who 'stay accommodated here and have chosen to live as villeins; each one of them is to pay 5 *Pfund* on entry'.[45]

A draft of legal articles, which the governor of Rüti enclosed with his letter of 1 March 1711 to the Zurich town council, helps to improve our picture of the villeins. Article two of this draft runs:

In as much as neither foreigners nor parish members should be permitted to take on villeins, whether whole households, or a few individuals, as spinners, weavers and the like, neither in their house nor otherwise at their table and meals, for a certain yearly, monthly or weekly wage, unless he has first duly reported this to an honourable assembly of church elders and requested permission and is able to show it a satisfactory form certifying that when these people run out of money, the parish will incur no expenses on their behalf, but their keep and care will be obtained from the place where they are members of the parish and community: and so when he receives permission, the father of the family is to pay for the villeins he takes on the usual villeins' fee, namely 2 *Pfund* yearly for a whole household and for one person 1 *Pfund*.[46]

In our attempt to identify the form of the economy, the economic order and the social structure of the Oberland as the preconditions and foundations of industrialisation, we started out from the villagers' tendency towards exclusivity, a powerful factor for change in the rural economic order in the seventeenth century. The first barrier we learnt about was the entry fee, but we have still to inspect the inner workings of the village communities. Following up the other ways and means by which the select groups entitled to the commonage tried to protect their property gives us an insight into the inner structure of the community and also into the different social grades in the Oberland. As with the entry fee, the restrictions interest us only in so far as they became important for the industrialisation of the Oberland. The restrictions necessarily also involved changing the structure of the village community. Many factors were involved, with lasting consequences for the whole life of the common people. Looking back, it is very difficult to link up all the processes historically, because two essentially different processes were caught up together: on the one hand, a change in the community's legal structure, which resulted in individuals acquiring rights, and, on the other hand, changes which affected the material possessions on which rights were based.

If payment of the entry fee was originally intended as the only precondition to acquiring the voting and commonalty rights of the community and was only to be tied to the individuals (the newcomers),[47] then it equated to a personal village right, which could be acquired through birth or by purchase. Since the middle of the sixteenth century the village right and commonage had been increasingly loosed from personal ties and made to depend on material conditions. The village right was tied directly to possession of a house: 'He who sells his house to a member of the village community shall have alienated his village right and commonage, until he buys in somewhere else.' If he sold it to a stranger, he had to buy himself back in again or move elsewhere.[48] Even those who lost their homes through blameless bad luck lost their political rights and their share of the commonage:

Since notwithstanding whether one or more has to sell his house and home either on account of outrageous fortune, it could be a failed harvest, hail, cattle dying, fire and suchlike (God preserve us from the like), or otherwise on account of wretched housekeeping, a community should then suffer them gladly wherever they find a place and refuge in the village community. And should not expel them from the village. But such persons should forfeit their right. And they should have no say in communal matters and business until they buy themselves back into the community property and inheritance, overcoming the past and paying the entry fee anew.[49]

It became the rule in the rural village communities pertaining to Zurich to link the right to vote with ownership of a house. When a member of the community lost or sold his house, he sank to the level of a villein obliged to pay the entry fee again on acquiring a new house. In this period the policy of the rural communities was above all economic. Losing the right to speak at a communal meeting signified the loss of economic potency. According to peasant economic thinking what was involved was not primarily limiting the right to vote (this was simply a secondary effect) but much rather safeguarding their common property, limiting the commonage. They attempted to give commonage material form by tying it to a house. We have seen that when a house was lost so too were the 'village usage' and the 'right in wood and field, river and meadow'.[50] It is clear from the following conditions of entry relative to the division of a house that the house had come to represent the right of commonage:

If in one house two or more families have their household or from one house two dwellings are made, nevertheless the right will belong only to the house, in spite of it being split up, and no more is to be sought after and demanded. That is, as if it were only one household and the dwelling were still undivided and in one person's hands.[51]

In short, these apparently simple legal relationships were confused by the developments which had overtaken the village community as a public legal entity since the Reformation: the right of the village and the commonalty were given material form at a time when the commune was acquiring new functions over and above its communal property and purpose. It is clear that the nature of the village community was fundamentally changed by this, affecting the attitude of the executive organs, the members of the village community, towards the other inhabitants. Using the private legal side of the community as a basis, this could end in complete exclusivity, with the people in possession of rights forming a real village aristocracy.[52]

Among the details concerning poor villagers' property it was mentioned that in the seventeenth century many village communities had ended by splitting up their houses, and the rights pertaining to them.[53] The subdivision of houses and rights widened the circle of people with voting and commonage rights. This was accompanied by a social and political differentiation of the inhabitants according to their share of entitlement to vote and to the commonage, a development which they tried to impede by prohibiting the subdivision of houses. An article drawn up by the communes of Hinteregg and Vorderegg runs: 'and that they shall be less overrun by people and that they shall be better assured their grass, fruit, wood and other things at home and in the wood, so shall their houses remain undivided in one person's hands as much as possible'.[54]

In some village communities they went so far as to freeze the shares of commonage or rights,[55] as with the common lands described by the commune of Niederdürnten in a letter of 2 December 1661. It owned 188 *Jucharten* of fields and 167 *Jucharten* of woods 'on the upper, lower and outer *Zelg* (boundaries) of the pasturage. There are twenty-one rights to this, with the price of one right in wood and field calculated at the present time at 220 *Gulden*, irrespective of whether it is sold for a higher price.'[56] Here the right was loosened from the house and had become an independent object of sale and inheritance. This course of development, too, provided for a division of rights.[57]

The question now arises as to how far these material reasons for restricting entry were responsible for the pressure of poverty in the Oberland and how they contributed to the industrialisation of the Oberland.

In general it can be said that common land as a form of land right resulted in bad use of the land as soon as it was divided up into quantum shares. Use of the land was no longer determined by personal need but by the predetermined share. The Neftenbach minister reported in 1692, for instance, that

Hardship and poverty are widespread, there are alms recipients in thirty households; the hardship and the number of the poor will increase week by week until harvest time. Little or nothing can be hoped from communal property, since Hünikon and Esch have almost none. Neftenbach, however, has got a considerable [property], namely ground produce of more than 30 *mütt* of grain, enough wood, enough meadow and also as much rough ploughland or pasture as will allow 20 to 30 *Jucharten* to be sown every year, but strangely enough nothing of this kind takes place for the good of the poor. The loss side [in the Neftenbach Communal property] accrues much more strongly than the profit side; during the period of my ten years' service in the parish alone, the tavern has accumulated debts of 300 to 400 *Pfund*, the interest on which now has to be paid by the commune, in spite of the fact that in this short period of only ten years, 2,000 *Pfund* of admission money has been taken from new burghers. And such fine communal lands could truly be cultivated much better; to wit, many *Jucharten* of pasture could be ploughed and sown yearly, as well as many such grasslands be turned into good water-meadows, which could also serve to solace the poor in times of hardship. But the will and dispositions for this are lacking, and so nothing is done.[58]

A variety of regulations concerning the use of the common lands heightened these effects still further. We have seen that many poor villagers could not use their whole or half right to the full, because they were not able to fodder a cow over the winter. Such people were not allowed to lease 'his right to another, who can make better use of it',[59] and their shares remained unused. The economic order thus had a direct effect on the level of food production and was also responsible in part for the pressure of poverty. It is in this context that the countryside prior to industrialisation must be viewed.

We have already mentioned the degree to which the propertied element, with its farming mentality, had a vested interest in the economic order. The oligarchical peasant and village aristocrat knew how to safeguard his economic viability and his political clout against the unpropertied. The fact that property also carried rights put a strong weapon against them in his hand. His dominant position was further bolstered by granting credit and other means.[60] All this prepared the social background for industrialisation. It was the people without any economic resources, without voting or commonalty rights, who were predestined, along with their descendants, to fall into complete industrial dependence.

We have said that the Oberland was colonised by the poor. The lack of commonage made settlement easier. The introduction of material grounds for admission, as outlined above, meant that the absence of commonage had a far greater impact in the sense of facilitating settlement in the Oberland. Far fewer impediments could be placed in the way of building new houses in villages without any commonage. This gave rise to a truly paradoxical situation: the obviously inhospitable mountainous parts of the Zurich territory became the preferred areas for new settlements. While this was indeed a 'settlement against nature', it was just as much a settlement against the laws of men. It seemed easier to subdue nature than to break the power of the legislature. Anyway – and this is significant – the Oberland could only become an area of new settlement when the putting-out industry with its work opportunities spread into the high valleys. It was only when the textile industry provided a means of existence independent of the land that the consequences of the Zurich economic order could fully unfold in the Oberland. Industrialisation meant dwellings being built in lateral valleys, wooded gorges and ravines, in places where there was ofen 'scarcely enough room to install one house and garden'. The soil could not even begin to feed its inhabitants. H. Bernhard writes about the high settlements of the upper Töss valley founded in the seventeenth and particularly the eighteenth centuries: 'They are mostly dwellings which have been established by the settlers with an almost complete disregard for the natural conditions on the precipices, on the highest terraces and even in the peaks region of the mountainous country.'[61] New settlements of this type, which owed their existence to the textile industry, can be described only in the smallest degree as agricultural settlements. We will deal with them later on. Our present enquiry is into the conditions presented by the Oberland which determined reception of the putting-out system there. Opportunities to settle, as derived from the legal conditions of the Zurich economic order, were factors restricting or favouring industrialisation.

The absence of common property in the mountain parishes was not the only reason why opportunities for settling were better in the Oberland. The problem must be looked at in a far wider context. The form of settlement in the Oberland, even before industrialisation, was that of hamlets and farmsteads. At that time the Oberland economy was still geared exclusively to primary production, which meant that the influence of the local climate and topography on the forms of settlement was all the more compelling. A peasant farm and dwelling had to be sited where the soil could also feed its inhabitants. H. Bernhard's comments on the natural conditions of the upper Töss valley also apply to much of the Oberland:

The upper Töss valley is absolutely unsuited for intensive agricultural production not only due to its relatively harsh climate, but also in respect of its peculiar topography and its in part inferior soil [with a *Nagelfluh* subsoil]. The natural conditions enable unbroken forests to spread relatively extensively . . . consequently the naural requirements for dense settlement by a native farming population are lacking.[62]

At the end of the eighteenth century J.C. Hirzel described the Oberland in the following words

The sixth section of our province contains the mountainous part of the Grüningen district close to the mountainous part of the yonder district of the county of Kyburg, which borders on the lands of Uznach, Toggenburg and Thurgau. It consists of two mountain chains, the inner one leading from Rüti through Hinwil, Bäretswil and Wildberg, the outer one from the Scheidegg, Hörnli, Sternenberg, Breitenlandenberg, as far as the Schauberg on Eigg. Between these two mountain chains are to be found the parishes of Wald, Fischenthal, Bauman and Turbenthal, and the wild Töss flows through much of it, since its source lies in the highest part on the Scheidegg side on the borders of the Uznach mounains. All this is real Alpine country. The biggest parishes consist mostly of scattered farms, and the houses only cluster closer together around the churches, forming small villages. Here and there the strong population increase has caused single farms to grow into small hamlets; Sternenberg, for instance, comprises 38 localities with different names; Fischenthal comprises 111; Bauman comprises 47, and so on. From Wald to Fischenthal the valley winds higher and higher up between both mountain chains, and then drops further and further down to Turbenthal. It is mostly very narrow, so that the farms lie scattered along the sides of the mountains, as in Toggenburg and Appenzell. The mountains consist mostly of firm or brittle *Nagelfluh* peaks, interspersed by gullies of friable sandstone and occasional veins of limestone. The country is essentially sterile, as its meadows demonstrate, since they are rated in quality far below those of the mountains of the county of Wädenswil, where the grass is richer.[63]

When the natural conditions of the Oberland, its pre-industrial settlements and cultivation systems are set in the context of our enquiry, it is clear that they would heighten even further the consequences of the legal conditions imposed by the Zurich economic order. As is obvious when one compares the farming methods of the mountains with those of the flat lands.

In places where the natural conditions allowed closed village settlements using a three-field system to develop, the peasant settlers' community and economy were trapped in a network of legal and customary obligations. No one was allowed to use or occupy the land as he liked. Every individual's working methods and timetable, as well as his share of the land, were laid down to the last detail. The exogenous putting-out industry had great difficulty in penetrating such firmly established economic entities, so long as they were still vital. The industry, being based on individual achievement, obtained scant leaway in the collective organism of these economic groupings. True three-field rotation with its open-field system relies as an economic entity on the comprehensive and obligatory participation of the entire village community. Since industrialisation was to destroy not only the material but also the human basis for such an economic community, they had to defend themselves by every means available against an uncontrolled expansion of the industry. The open-field system and the overall legal and traditional order provided valuable assistance in the shape of firm agricultural regulations; until the collapse of three-field agriculture, it was forbidden to build outside the precincts of the village (*hinausbauen*); where possible, it was forbidden to build any more houses at all. Such regulations gave rise to endless disputes.[64]

Natural conditions and the forms of cultivation and settlement were quite different in the Oberland. A countryside inhabited by isolated farms lacked the economic discipline of a village. These farmers could dispose more freely of their land, they could use it and arrange it as and when they wished. If, for instance, the ground of the lower parts of the valleys was still being cultivated according to the three-field system, it would be modified so as to fit in with the natural conditions. Hamlets and farmsteads had their own field systems. The higher settlements were given over to a system of individual land ownership and land use (*Egartenwirtschaft*), described in the report by minister Schmid of Uster report to the Naturforschende Gesellschaft (Natural Science Association) in 1762 as follows:

Concerning the meadows of the mountain folk in Fischenthal and Sternenberg, experience teaches that they could not remove the fences from their meadows without incurring great damage, since they have no pasturage in common, nor do they have any ploughland (which, when manured, can be sown with wheat in the third year) but only meadows, and indeed a proper mountain farmer generally owns six or nine of these; one of which he ploughs every year and in the first year he sows wheat and in the next oats and then he lets it rest again and takes another and does likewise until each one has had its turn. His cattle find abundant grazing throughout the whole summer on the fields which have not been sown. However, in order to prevent the cattle from running all over his fields, which are all close together, and trampling the grass into the ground, he has to divide them up with fences.[65]

In the Oberland region of hamlets and farmsteads the peasants' use of the soil and their farming associations were so arranged that industrialisation did not disrupt the basis of their life, materially or humanly. Many features of the industry fitted in with the homesteaders' way of farming. Whereas the village farmer had to act within his farming collective and derived his security from it, the homesteader's working group had a far freer approach to production. To a certain extent he was an entrepreneur, with the entrepreneur's whole spiritual attitude to economic matters. The specific and practical feature of homestead farming – its greater independence, its ability to change and adapt – was attuned to the emphatically individual character of the homesteader.

Although the Oberland was described by J.C. Hirzel as 'real Alpine country', the sort of corporate Alpine farming of the central and western pre-Alpine region of Switzerland was foreign to them. There were no collective farming associations in the farmstead country of the Oberland, with their rigid organisation and their manifold opportunities for limiting entry and building. There was no effective regulation of building and letting houses, and so agriculture and traditional ways of using the soil were able to enter into a fruitful symbiosis with the Zurich putting-out industry. Industrialisation did not happen at the expense of agriculture; on the contrary, large tracts of the Oberland were urbanised by the putting-out industry in the eighteenth century. Fallow ground was cultivated and settled. Established land was more intensively exploited. The cattle stock was improved and so on. We will discuss how agriculture and industrialisation in the Oberland affected one another later on.

In this chapter we have attempted to explain the early and intensive industrialisation of the Oberland. We have learnt about the area's natural conditions, its social, legal and economic circumstances, and how they affected one another, and we mentioned the driving and shaping mentality underlying them. Only those factors immanent to the Oberland have been considered. We do not claim to have been comprehensive and we are aware that important points have been left untouched.[66] When applying an analytical method, it is necessary to separate matters which in reality form a whole. Our selection does not reveal a series of causal connections, but simply a few main threads in a tangled net of causal relations.

Our analysis, which has been carried out using the Oberland as our example, applies only to a very limited extent to the other early industrial regions of the Zurich territory (the industrial regions around the Lake, the Knonau and Keller districts and the intermediate zones between upland and lowland). In these regions the legal, economic and social conditions were different to those of the Oberland. As well as this, the geographical and climatic conditions were different. Each of these regions contributed its own preconditions to the reception of the putting-out system. Similar factors do, however, emerge albeit in sizes and shapes different again to those of the Oberland. Similar forces obstructed or encouraged the process of industrialis-ation. All the industrial regions were distinguished by the absence of firmly established collective farming associations in the sense of the arable three-field system. Their legal, economic and social order no longer formed an organic unit, with the vitality and power to prevent industry gaining a foothold. While the agriculture and land rights belonging to the three-field system (viz., real restrictions on communal rights, open-field system and prohibition of build-ing) did indeed survive in many places, these forms no longer represented fact. They had become obsolete for a part of the population. When the existing order was no longer secured by the economic and social conditions, the door stood open for the putting-out industry. It was able to push its way in and become established. This was, for instance, the case in the Knonau district and in the intermediate zone between Oberland and Unterland.

Conditions in the industrial regions around the Lake were different again. Their proximity to major routes, their vineyards, forms of land rights and land use and other factors as well-established conditions here which were favour-able to industrialisation. As in the Oberland, these regions also achieved a fruitful symbiosis of agriculture and putting-out industry, which we cannot go into in detail, but merely mention here. Later on, we will show how the traditional, pre-industrial legal, economic and social order asserted itself in its local variations. It can be seen in the different industrial regions of the Zurich countryside, with their characteristic forms of building, settlement and farming, and it determined directly and indirectly the lives and culture of the industrial working population.

The upshot was that the industrial regions of the Zurich lordship were certainly not limited just to zones of individual land use and farmstead settlement, but also included zones with three-field systems and villages. We stress this yet again so as to avoid misunderstandings, but with the firm proviso that the regions in question no longer possessed true three-field rotation systems. They were places where the collective organism of a well-established peasant farming community had either never existed or had been weakened.[67]

Let us close this chapter with a look at a map showing the distribution of the Zurich cotton putting-out industry in the period of its first flowering at the end of the eighteenth century. In 1787 a census was taken of all the cotton spinners and looms in the whole of the Zurich territory. This census provides the data for the map, compiled by Paul Kläui for the *Atlas zur Geschichte des Kantons Zürich (Atlas of the History of the Canton of Zurich)*.[68]

The highly industrialised regions show up clearly on the map, but, contrary to what one might expect, they do not form a circle around Zurich, the centre of the putting-out industry. Some of the most intensively industrialised regions lie far away from Zurich, in the lower Alpine zones of the territory, although these peripheral regions were only drawn within the putting-out circle later on, and presented terrible problems of transport. By studying the map we become aware of the strength of the legal, economic and social forces which we have analysed and presented as the preconditions to the industrialisation of the Oberland. These forces were strong enough to overcome the natural obstacles and the problems of transport. The Oberland formed a hinterland of scattered settlement areas, gulleys 'which afforded a dreadful aspect',[69] unimaginably bad roads and a harsh climate. Bringing in and distributing the raw materials and carrying away the finished goods was extremely difficult. This was also the reason why the Oberland was only slightly involved in the first flowering of the Zurich cottage weaving industry. The transport of the warps and bales of cloth must have been too much trouble, since, until the collapse of hand spinning, the mountainous parts of the Zurich territory remained committed to this branch of the industry – spinning, that is, not weaving.

We could illustrate our argument further by comparing two maps showing emigration patterns, also to be found in the *Atlas zur Geschichte des Kantons Zürich*.[70] A reference to them must suffice. They show how in the time of the greatest population growth (which applied especially to the Oberland) the Oberland was able to feed its inhabitants and keep them in the country through the putting-out industry. Very little emigration took place, whereas in the arable regions (with very small population growth) many people were forced to emigrate. The map of emigration between 1734 and 1744 clearly shows that the bulk of movement was away from the arable zones. The emigration map for 1660 shows the movement distributed fairly equally over the whole Zurich territory. Without making too much of our interpretation of these maps, it may be said that they illustrate the difference in the legal, economic and social conditions between the flat and mountainous parts of the canton. The inhabitants of the arable regions had to leave their homes, not because there were no industrial work opportunities, but because in the arable regions the way to industrialisation was barred from within. In the Oberland and the other industrial regions, however, the legal, economic and social preconditions for intensive industrialisation did exist.

We have outlined many problems in this first chapter, which we will

number of	10	50	100	500
cotton spinners	.	▪	■	▣
looms for				
muslin weaving	∘	○	○	
Indian weaving (cotton)	•	●	●	

The cottage industry at the end of the eighteenth century
Source: Paul Kläui and Edward Imhof, eds., *Atlas zur Geschichte des Kantons Zürich*, Zurich 1951, Plate 35

investigate further as our thesis is developed. It is to be hoped that we have answered the question as to why the Oberland, and other parts of the Zurich territory under the Ancien Régime, turned into industrial areas, while the other regions of the territory were hardly, if at all, affected by this profound transformation of their environment and economy.

J.C. Hirzel formulated the sentence with which we close this chapter: 'it seems as if the factory hands had climbed down from the mountains, and that the closer these lie, the more factory hands there are'.[71]

2 ✣ Changes to the structure of family and population in the industrial regions

In the last chapter we learnt about people who were ostensibly born into a peasant community and culture, but who remained in reality cut off and excluded from it. If we are to investigate the specifically folklorist question of how traditional ways of life and their manifestations in the popular culture of the Oberland changed with the advent of industrialisation, we must be fully aware that the innovations arose only partly out of a peasant world. We will find the purest and most clearly defined forms of a new 'industrial' possibility of existence, with its appropriate cultural expressions, among those sectors of the population which were never able to become rooted in an agricultural community.[1]

We can formulate our question even more precisely, and thus on a more theoretical level: in the following pages we want to find out whether and how the basic conditions of human society were changed when the Oberland was industrialised. The most disparate areas of human life can reveal how industrialisation created new possibilities for existence, giving rise to new forms of community and a new popular culture.

This sort of question gives rise to a few methodological difficulties: first of all, our enquiry into the emergence of new ways of life needs to be treated historically, meaning that attention must be paid to the period and the mentality which provided the historical background. For these reasons we have limited ourselves to the period before 1800, a time when the Oberland relied chiefly on domestic spinning. The collapse of hand spinning and the great transition to domestic weaving and machine spinning in the Oberland can only be briefly scanned at the close of this work. As mentioned above, this epoch-making upheaval belongs historically and technically to Part two of this thesis.

However, our enquiry demands besides the historical treatment a fundamental approach, in so far as we understand that cottage work provided a means of existence, with a way of life peculiar to itself. Such a view requires that we look constantly beyond the limits of our period, so as to address the general nature of the topic. Both these aspects will have to be taken into account in the course of our treatise, without referring to them specifically. For

37

this reason many of our primary sources extend beyond the limits of the Ancien Régime, our period.

Our enquiry begins with the smallest and most natural human community, the family. This immediately presents the question of how the preconditions for getting married and starting a family changed with the advent of industrialisation.

The works of Gotthelf have taught us that marriage vows in peasant circles did not constitute an intimate private agreement between two lovers. In a peasant marriage, it was the farm with its human and material assets which mattered. Claims of an individual and personal nature had to give way to the objective of maintaining the organic unit of the farm and preserving the fragile equilibrium between the number of workers and consumers in a peasant family and the size of their property. Such conditions led to peasant marriage customs,[2] in which individual family members were obliged to acquiesce.

So it became the custom [wrote J.C. Hirzel in 1792] to leave the properties together and only to the sons, who also refrained from marriage, that the farm might always remain capable of providing for the household . . . this also happened in the various regions of our country [he means the canton of Zurich] in which only arable farming was practised. Whence we observe that the fertile Wehn Valley has, with regard to its population, only slightly increased. A farmer calculates as follows: my farm can feed no more than one, at most two sons. The others can remain single or seek their fortune elsewhere.[3]

Hirzel is here describing a system of impartible inheritance, or the right to designate individual family members as heirs. This practice did not just affect the Oberland, but the whole countryside of Zurich. The tendency to designate one heir and to limit subdivision of the property was reinforced in the Zurich territory by the development of communal rights, including those concerning the use of common lands, in the seventeenth century. Use of the common lands was a major part of the peasant farming economy and the aforementioned material form of commonage rights had a direct effect on peasant inheritance.[4] In the Oberland, as we have seen, this factor was not much in evidence. Although the Oberland is a countryside of single farmsteads, strict peasant marriage customs like those shaped by impartible inheritance must have already been lacking before industrialisation. Such customs did indeed exist there, but not as exclusively as in the arable regions of the Zurich countryside. The Oberland's large share of the economically weak had a splintering effect.

A whole new situation was created by the possibility of earning a living in the Zurich putting-out industry. For those people whose basis of existence stretched beyond an agricultural community (and upon whom we will focus at the present moment) a completely new set of requirements for marriage and setting up a household were established. The industrial source of earnings made it possible to support peasant farms on non-agricultural foundations. This change in the peasants' existence basis also changed the conditions governing inheritance. Hirzel recognised this change clearly, writing that in the places where factory wages were available, the peasant altered his previous 'calculation' to:

'I have three or four sons, each will get some meadowland, enough for one cow at least, some ploughland etc. This should make a fine contribution towards the family's keep, and working their little property leaves them with enough time on their hands to acquire the rest in factory earnings.' At the final count, people also considered it acceptable to own just a corner of the house in which to set up a spinning wheel or loom, and room for a garden for planting vegetables.

The author tells us of an 'upright farmer' whom he encountered in 1792, 'who was farming only 1/8 of his deceased grandfather's farm and was living happily and contendedly on this'.[5] C. Meiners wrote in his *Letters about Switzerland* that

the increased and secure earnings produced by combining factory work with working in the fields enabled marriages to take place sooner and in greater number, thereby increasing the subdivision and the value of the farms, as well as enlarging and improving the houses and villages. On account of the prospects opened to the countryman and his children by their industry, he was no longer anxious to limit the size of his family early on. Fathers and sons had previously shied away from dividing up their larger and accumulated holdings because they feared that individual shares would be inadequate for feeding their owners. This fear disappeared completely after the expansion of factories and factory workers and now the sons insist on subdividing their fathers' inheritance, which had perhaps already been split up many times previously, because they are convinced that even a small piece of ploughland is enough to feed its hardworking owner, with wife and child.[6]

It is obvious that marriages increased in frequency and were entered into at an earlier age in peasant circles when the putting-out industry managed to penetrate them. J.C. Hirzel has measured this phenomenon statistically. He chose the parish of Fischenthal as his example. According to his figures the average number of marriages in the space of a decade changed as follows:

> 1641–70 42 marriages took place on average over the decades;
> 1671–1700 81 marriages took place on average over the decades;
> 1701–50 113 marriages took place on average over the decades;
> 1750–60 165 marriages took place on average over the decade.[7]

At this point it must be emphasised that such marriages could no longer be called peasant marriages, since they would never have taken place had there been no possibility of industrial work. We have got to destroy the genre picture so rigidly preserved in the literature of the contented farmer tilling his acre, milking his cow and, as a sideline, engaging in a cottage industry with his family.[8] This scenario did not apply to the Oberland, and indeed would present a wholly mistaken and false picture of the industrial landscape. The putting-out industry was a sideline for only the very smallest section of the Oberland farmers (and certainly not for the unpropertied outworkers), but it was the basis and means for these peasants get to be able to married at all and to work their portion of farm with their families. This is clearly indicated in the synodal speech made by Salomon Schinz, minister of Fischenthal:

Never would such a crowd of people have arisen in this harsh region, had the ample factory wages not made it easier for them to feed themselves and encouraged them to increase, so that within half a century the population has doubled. Even the farm owners of the middle class could not subsist without such earnings, since big debts have been amassed on many pieces of land as a result of buying in at high prices, or by frequently splitting up properties, which necessitates building new dwellings, or by buying out – debts which cannot possibly be offset from the farm produce, but only from the owner's earnings with the spinning wheel or the weaver's shuttle. Which has led inevitably to many disasters; as earnings from cotton dwindled, the false appearance of prosperity has faded from these regions. There are actually very few prosperous farm owners in my parish, as also in Bäretschweil, Bauma and Sternenberg; also only a small number of those, who have to pay out only half the value of their farms in interest. Anyone who has to pay only 4 *Gulden* interest on a little property, enough to feed a cow through winter and summer, can still survive. But every significant accident to his cattle or his property etc. can precipitate him into the class of the poor, and if he has a relentless creditor, into the class of the homeless. And such people are terribly numerous. More than 1,360 people of my parish are forced to live solely from factory earnings and about 200 households own no movable or immovable property of any kind, apart from their spinning wheel, loom, domestic essentials and clothes, and the very poorest lack even these last.[9]

We must be aware of the social and economic effects of such changes. There grew up out of the peasant world households which could only keep their farms with the help of the putting-out industry. Johann Hirzel, minister of Wildberg, also mentioned this relationship in a synodal speech. He stressed that the owner could not pay his interest from the produce of his land, but only from what he earned by spinning and weaving: 'The original reason for the present condition of the mountain folk must be sought for in earlier times. First in the unlimited credit, which the land owners were granted previously.'[10] The same phenomenon is reported by an anonymous person concerning Appenzell. In his treatise he describes in a tersely stylised manner the subsistence basis on which a new type of mountain farming could develop.

What has to a certain degree impeded the improvement of cultivation has for many years been the harmful use of *Vollzedeln* (credit notes) on our *Heymathen* (farms). Anyone was able to buy such a farm with an appropriate note of credit and the interest payments, without having two pennies of his own to rub together: a couple of cows provided his family with their basic subsistence and his loom secured him an easy means of earning the interest on the property and other needs.[11]

At this stage we require only a limited view of the phenomenon of a new mountain peasantry, which developed around the non-agricultural putting-out industry. We have enquired into the new requirements for founding a peasant family which emerged with industrialisation. We have seen how the former customary right of inheritance was undermined by the source of industrial earnings. Marriages in peasant circles occurred more frequently and earlier. During the course of the eighteenth century the subdivision of farms put increased pressure on the authorities to 'loosen the belt',[12] i.e. to allow people to subdivide rights and houses and to build new dwellings, rooms and ovens.

This will be discussed more extensively in Chapter 4, where we will learn about the destruction of the traditional right of inheritance, the division of farms and houses as well as the changes to the ground rights and ways of using the soil, and also to peasant farming methods.

The changes brought a whole range of traditional ways of life into flux again. A new attitude to marriage developed hand in hand with the altered right of inheritance. Material considerations were no longer central to marriage. The farm and property could now, with the help of industrial earnings, be divided without loss of income. People found that their family bonds and responsibilities were less important. A marriage could no longer threaten the survival basis of the other family members. Marriage was no longer a contract affecting the outcome of a community and its economy down to the last detail. For the marriageable sons and daughters of peasants this shift allowed them greater latitude for following their own inclinations. Drawing up a marriage contract became a more intimate affair: it became a promise between two persons, who hoped thereby to realise happiness for themselves as individuals. Both courtship and marriage were individualised.

Let us now take a look at this trend in that sector of the population which did not grow out of the secure peasant world. It consisted of those economically unviable inhabitants of the Oberland, whom we met in Chapter 1, at the dawn of industrialisation. We stressed the significance of industrial earnings to these people; the demand for labour in the Zurich putting-out industry had grown steadily from the middle of the seventeenth century onwards. The bulk of the Oberland population placed their lives in the hands of the putting-out masters, blindly trusting in the 'mysterious play of economic laws'.[13] Trusting blindly, they married. Being used to spinning work from earliest childhood, and in part to weaving work, they believed that this provided them with all they needed to get married: 'Marriages were entered into recklessly, without considering whether it would be possible to provide for wife and child, in the firm but blind faith that the good factory earnings would go on for ever.'[14] Minister Salomon Schinz described indignantly how a girl from the outworkers' circle in Fischenbach would enter into marriage:

Brought up alongside the spinning wheel or the loom, ignorant of other domestic and farming work; keeping wanton company deep into the night almost every day, and when her work is done, she spends her day's earnings or a part thereof on fripperies or brandy, indulging in every form of sensuality and making use of the most shameful methods, even stealing the stuff given her to work, or removing wares from her parents' house is not too shameful, and then getting married, when her circumstances force her to it, often joined to an equally thoughtless and equally poor youth, with neither bed nor household goods among their possessions . . . what are the consequences of such destitute marriages, when they often owe even the few clothes they have to the tradesman?[15]

We shall see later on that the outworkers' life style, so clearly condemned by Schinz, can also be judged differently and positively. In any case, the fact remains that in these circles, marriages could be entered into without any material support. 'Early marriages between two persons, who bring two spinning wheels but no bed with them, occur fairly frequently among these people',[16] wrote the minister of Wildberg. Such marriages, based on spinning wheel and loom, are commonly referred to as 'beggars' weddings' in the sources. A formula indicative not only of the pride and scorn of the propertied, but which also exposes their inability to perceive and acknowledge novel elements, as instanced by these marriages. They could not understand this freer and looser behaviour vis-à-vis the material culture. To enter into a marriage without enough household goods, bedclothes, for instance, to last for the rest of one's life, was, they believed, an outrageous venture, quite out of the question. Johannes Schulthess demanded with holy zeal that beggars' weddings be straightaway prohibited by State and Church. As Canon and Professor of Theology and member of the Council for Church and Education, he also found biblical confirmation of this proposition: ' "He who fails to provide for his relations, and especially those dwelling in his house", says the Apostle, "has denied the Faith; yea, he is worse than the heathen." '[17] Schulthess was definitely not alone in his condemnation. People in many places were trying to establish a legal basis for preventing early marriages and beggars' weddings. Johann Hirzel believed that

only by tightening up the law, by harsh punishments and limiting [the number of] *Pintenschenken* (taverns), where the thoughtless inhabitants indulge without any embarrassment in loose behaviour and which can provide occasion for such beggars' weddings, can this rapidly increasing evil [early marriages without household goods or property] be averted and this source of poverty and multiple misery be stopped . . . and how natural too is the wish and entreaty, which I here dare to express, that these early beggars' weddings be prevented by legal means, by establishing in law a certain minimum age and property. People's freedom would not be overly impaired by this, and the number of illegitimate children would not be any greater as a result.[18]

In April 1813 the Wetzikon elders decided that 'The early marriage of poor persons shall where possible be prevented by the minister's intervention, and any burgeoning friendships shall be reported by the elders to the minister.' Minister Nägeli wrote resignedly and knowingly in the minutes: 'Who is going to supervise a sieve full of fleas?'[19]

It is in the nature of our sources that the new practices surrounding courtship and marriage should be condemned throughout. We are obliged to follow up these sources, but we must try to free ourselves from the subjective valuations they make.

We have seen how people's willingness and ability to marry increased when the putting-out industry managed to gain a foothold in their peasant circle. Courtship and marriage were de-materialised. Marriage contracts became far more intimate and personal agreements when both partners built their marriage exclusively on the putting-out industry. As long as industrial earnings flowed smoothly, material considerations receded, allowing people room to deploy their intellectual and spiritual potential. Our critics, aware of their local responsibilities, took into account only the material aspect of the beggars' weddings. Their harsh condemnation of the new marriage practices was determined by this consideration, with particular reference to their experience of the years of crisis and shortage. We can take advantage of our distance in time and our awareness of history to set the personal and human aspect to the forefront. This not only allows the changes to their way of life to be seen more clearly, but makes us (as opposed to the sources) judge these trail-blazing innovations differently and more positively.

Before approaching this problem, it must be stressed that it was not industrialisation which changed the practices and customs surrounding marriage – life's most important rite of passage. Such an assumption would require a wholly materialistic perception of history, one we cannot share. Industrialisation merely brought to a large section of the rural population the material possibility of copying new ways of life and behaviour from other sectors of society, or of developing their own. Industrialisation enabled these people to individualise courtship and marriage; a development which must be viewed against the background of the trend towards individualisation in Western Europe, which was given a decisive impulse during the late Renaissance and Reformation. This development included the transformation of the erotic world of emotion, when a privileged class of city-dwellers copied and assimilated the sophisticated forms of the courtly and aristocratic life style. With the destruction of the unity of baroque life the whole gamut of erotic emotions was released from its ivory tower: pietism, loaded with a new inwardness, gave rise to a secularised and self-orientated Eros, announcing the arrival of Werther. Bourgeois love found its outward and inward expression in the Biedermeier style, a style we still encounter nowadays in debased and drooling 'dream boat' form, being droned out of every radio and juke-box. It is in the context of the development sketched above that we must see the change to the marriage practices in the Zurich countryside, which was unleashed by the possibility of industrial earnings. As urban fashion and the urban need for luxury penetrated those sectors of the rural population of Zurich employed in industry, they brought a new intellectual and spiritual attitude and its outward manifestations with them.

The putting-out industry provided girls and boys with the material preconditions for getting married, thereby sweeping away all the young people's reservations and fears about getting to know and love one another.

Unrestrained by material considerations, their desire for the opposite sex could be fulfilled. Johann Schulthess wrote that 'As soon as a young lad is confirmed, he starts making up to one or more girls, as if the ceremony was for this purpose.' He went on to write that the daughters, however, 'knowing that they will otherwise never get a husband, open their bedrooms to the night prowlers and allow them access, in the certain or uncertain hope that, should they get pregnant, they will not be abandoned to their disgrace'. Schulthess wrote sadly that this vignette was no 'bookworm's fantasy, ach no, but was drawn from life'. As a young boy he had unfortunately seen many instances of this evil with his own eyes, and over the last four decades it had become much more prevalent and general, and anyone would be able to bear witness to his judgement who 'has opportunity to observe this behaviour, when indulged in openly and immodestly'. Schulthess refers to the country ministers' visitation notices and quotes a report in them, which says 'The so-called *zu Licht gehen* (going to the light) is considered a right and a freedom and not as anything sinful. Weddings always come after pregnancy.'[20]

It would be mistaken to see the *Kiltgang*'s form of nocturnal courtship, called *z'Licht go* in the Zurich countryside, as a consequence of people basing their existence on the putting-out industry.[21] This form of courtship went back to pre-industrial times and originated from the living conditions in farmsteads and villages. Cottage industry simply allowed this form of courtship to be adopted by a wider section of the population. The rising number of people wanting to get married made use of thoroughly traditional forms of courtship, although their attitude to these forms changed, with the emergence of a new industrial working class.

By *z'Licht go* and *Lichtstubeten* was meant not just social gatherings involving unmarried girls and lads (which we will discuss later on) but also nightly encounters between two lovers, with lads climbing into the daughters' and maids' chambers.[22] The mandate of 7 July 1658 commented that

we have uncovered a profound and widespread evil: the *Lichtstubeten* and *Waidstubeten*, as well as the young lads' nightly encounters, slipping in and climbing up to the daughters and maids in their bedrooms and chambers, item, in other corners too, yea even close up to them and into their beds, should all be most strenuously forbidden with due authority.[23]

But the authorities' edicts and the Church's admonitions were all ineffectual. In spite of the prohibition, the country-dwellers clung firmly to this form of courtship. The era of the Helvetic Republic (1798–1803) had a liberating effect here too. The prohibitions were lifted and the authorities turned a blind eye to nocturnal courtships.[24] In a treatise *About the Revision of Matrimonial Laws in the Canton of Zurich*[25] J.C. Nüscheler demanded that 'these wicked practices of going to the light and the *Lichtstubeten* should be forbidden by means of fines or emprisonment'.[26] Nüscheler's pronouncements have particular weight, given that he was president of the matrimonial law courts for seventeen years. He writes that

through misuse it has here and there become the custom for an engaged man to think that as soon as he has given his fiancée a marriage writ and a pledge, he is entitled to demand that she allow him his so-called marital rights . . . From the first Revolution [1798] onwards, however, going to the light, which in 1786 was still prohibited by means of a specific fine, had spread beyond all bounds, with the result that it was not only engaged couples, wanting to get married as formerly, who went to the light, but also those who had no intention of getting married, but only wanted to enjoy forbidden fruits.[27]

J.C. Hirzel wrote that it had become the practice in the Knonau parish among engaged couples 'to remain unmarried until they are forced to wed on account of no longer being able to avoid pregnancy'.[28]

Marital vows had clearly been secularised and individualised – becoming a secret contract between two persons. It was not the holy sacrament of the Church but the marriage certificate or pledge which was binding.[29]

It was usual with such marriage practices for extra-marital pregnancies to impose their own necessary rules: a pregnant girl was able to demand satisfaction from her fiancé (*zu Ehren ziehen*) and to force him to marry her on moral grounds. For Nüscheler, these enforced weddings were one of the main reasons behind the many divorces:

More than half of the many divorces in our canton are due to the above reasons – especially on account of the enforced marriages (*zu Ehrenziehens and gezogen werden müssens*) . . . Marital fidelity is all too often seen merely as a side issue, and the enforced marriage as the main business – in these cases the thought is often present in parents and children: should the marriage work out happily, well and good, and may the marriage prosper – and her honour is at least preserved; but if it does not work out well, they can always get a divorce from the judge.

Nüscheler saw these marital practices, which had been adopted and developed by the working population, as the primary reason for the moral breakdown of the family. 'In most cases the happiness of such heedlessly contracted marriages does not last long, since once they are married everything appears to them in quite a different light than previously.'[30] Johann Schulthess even knew about regional variations in marital practices and morality. The author asks us petulantly

How is it that it is precisely in those regions where the most thoughtless marriages and the beggars' weddings take place that year after year all forms of extra-marital fornication, adultery, prostitution and divorce become more prevalent? That in the areas, on the other hand, where the old practices are adhered to, only the one son among three or more will get married, who will inherit the paternal house and property, unless one or the other moves in with a wife somewhere, or otherwise finds a house and a homeland along with a decent livelihood – that, say I, among such people there is the most chastity and clean living to be found? And how is it that the population, as far back as anyone can remember, has only grown insignificantly or has fallen in the latter areas, but has swollen up three or fourfold since the middle of the seventeenth century in the former regions?'[31]

We must break in at this point with our comments and assessments, thus moving on to the next section.

We have already mentioned that the young persons working in industry, unhampered by material considerations, could follow their inclination regarding the opposite sex. But their freer association did not mean that they had no ethical or moral principles. Demanding satisfaction, *zu Ehren ziehen*, was in itself proof that the necessary outcome of these forms of courtship, which contemporaries considered new, was determined by force of custom. *Zu Ehren ziehen* would quite simply have been unthinkable in a peasant economy with its harsh inheritance laws, and the statistics for extra-marital births in such areas show that 'chastity and clean living' were not their only attributes.[32] In any case, the moral values of the industrial working population were different and new. They had to be different when they no longer had to take a whole series of material and human requirements into account before getting married, and only the personal, 'me and you' related claims of the marriage partners counted. Industrial earnings made it possible for individuals to be released from the inflexible order of things.[33] But this freedom meant that moral responsibility was laid on each individual; he was no longer encompassed by an economic association and its particular human and material order, which obliged each member to conform to its ethical and customary norms of behaviour. It is not surprising that people broke out and went astray when they had the freedom to indulge the most elementary and human desires. Nor should we be surprised or even annoyed by contemporaries' damning reports condemning the immoral behaviour of the outworker population, since they came from a social circle where this new situation did not apply.

It is from this point of view that we should look at the other matters for complaint listed by Johann Schulthess and which have been raised by many other critics: 'extra-marital fornication, adultery, prostitution and divorce'.[34] Nüscheler and the others were mistaken in their belief that 'the divorces would at least be reduced by half' by forbidding the *zu Licht gehen*.[35] Going to the light was only the traditional cover, which could certainly be prohibited, behind which lay a reality stronger than the force of the law: a new function of marriage. People no longer got married (or refrained from marriage) for the sake of the farm, as in peasant circles, but because they saw marriage as a means of fulfilling their hopes of individual happiness. Marriages were now the result of pairing off. This applied especially to those illegitimate 'marriages' which were only given public sanction in church when honour had to be maintained by the *zu Ehren ziehen*. The result of these new values, along with the removal of material considerations in courtship and marriage, was that marriage itself became more fragile. Seen in positive terms, people's demands on marriage and married life together became, in human terms, more varied and intimate. This did not, however, mean that marriage became in itself capable of satisfying these demands. Which explains the many divorces among workers in the putting-out industry and their corollaries: extra-marital fornication, adultery and prostitution. The danger of destroying a marriage was all the more acute the less a marriage was maintained by material bonds, the less it was anchored in a unit of production.

We shall not follow up these particular problems here, since they belong to an aspect of life which we shall examine further on. This section simply asks the question of how the preconditions for getting married and starting a family were changed by industrialisation. An attempt will be made to provide a broad outline of the general situation. This involves recognising the reciprocal relationship between marriage and industrialisation. The new intellectual and spiritual attitude of the outworker population towards marriage affected industrialisation in its turn. The rise in people's willingness to get married and the rise in the number of weddings drove industrialisation onwards.

Both academic and popular books on the subject have widely publicised the view that family cohesion was weakened as a direct consequence of industrialisation. We shall investigate this problem, with its important social implications, in the following sections.

Let us begin with a surprising observation: that the outward conditions of industrial existence did not have to result in the family unit being weakened. This fact has an important bearing on the problem of causality.

We must start by referring back to the findings in Chapter 1. We have seen how the putting-out industry was able to set foot in and spread out in every region of the Zurich Canton which did not have any effective means of restricting immigration, and which possessed no (or insufficient) laws against subdividing houses and setting up new ones. We have pointed out that these conditions led to the Oberland becoming an industrial landscape, and how a growing number of economically weaker, landless persons were able to establish themselves and make a living in the country. Further, in the peasant regions of the Zurich territory, many unmarried sons and daughters were obliged to seek their livelihoods by serving in foreign parts and outside their area. If we had maps showing in what density servants, farmhands and maids were recruited in each region over comparable periods, they would illustrate these conditions clearly.[36]

Let us now pick up again where we left off in the foregoing section; we will take a look at the marriages contracted with the help of the industrial basis of existence. Let us begin with the outward preconditions: Where did the newly married couple find a lodging?

We have heard how it became the norm in the industrial regions of the canton of Zurich for families with several sons and daughters to divide amongst themselves the property, house and parish right. This consequence of industrial employment did not loosen the patterns of residence at all. On the contrary, it kept the family together, at least in residential terms, a qualification we must emphasise. The family unit grew larger and could extend over several households, since the grown-up children were no longer obliged to remain single or to set up their own household somewhere else. In the Oberland, where there were fewer large farms and properties and the little cottages were soon incapable of being divided up any more, a particular form of communal existence developed which is still clearly reflected in the settlement pattern of the countryside. It involved living in rows of attached cottages, known as *Flarz* houses, which we will discuss in greater depth in Chapter 4. They were typical of peasant homes in areas of cottage industry, and their numbers increased during the eighteenth century with the advance of industrialisation. These rows of houses were characteristic and should be viewed against the background of the organisational and formal family and kinship structure of their inhabitants. Let us take the question of the formal structure first. The increased number of families was expressed formally by the changes to the settlement pattern of the countryside. The rows of *Flarz* houses multiplied; single farmsteads grew into hamlets; hamlets developed into villages. C. Meiners wrote that

as the number of marriages and people increased, the number of houses and the size of the villages and hamlets naturally increased at the same rate. Where only a generation ago there had been one, or a few haphazard and scattered, dwellings, there can now be seen imposing villages, and little scruffy villages have grown into extensive and urban settlements. Even the bare and chilly mountain slopes, which are otherwise visited only by herdsmen, and the eroded patches at the edge of cleared woods are being covered, increasingly as times goes by, with the new dwellings of fortunate people.[37]

If we follow the development of such hamlets using population registers, these sources provide us with a picture (albeit rough and in parts unclear) of the formal cohesion of family and kinship. Families employed in industry and living in common became more visible as their numbers expanded. In 1634 the inhabitants of the Heferen (Wald parish) consisted of Hans Egli with his wife Barbel, Jagli Hess with his wife Aneli and Christen Hess with his wife Aneli and his two-year-old daughter Aneli.[38] By 1739 the parish roll of Wald provided the following picture of the residential pattern in the Heferen. Minister Heinrich Rahn's register gives their names as follows:

1. Hans Krauer's, deceased, widow, Anna Kunz (born 1666). Child: Heinrich 1693.
2. Hermann Ulrich Krauer 1699, Barbara Kindlimann 1707. Children: Hans Jakob 1731, Dorothea 1733, Regula 1738.
3. Johanes Krauer 1710, Barbara Schnyder 1709. Children: Susanna 1734, Hans 1736, Elsbeth 1738.
4. Jakob Krauer's, deceased, children, Emma Margaretha 1728, Susanna 1732.

5. Heinrich Rordorfer's, deceased, widow, Regula 1673. Children: Hans 1703, Maria 1708, Susanna 1711, Johann 1716.
6. Jakob Hess's, deceased, widow, Lisenbetha Kindlimann 1677. Children: Margaretha 1707, Hans Jakob 1713, Maria 1715, Hans Heinrich 1719.
7. Rudolf Hess's, deceased, widow, Anna Brunner 1680. Children: Max 1708, Elsbetha 1714, Barbara 1719, Anna Maria 1723.
8. Hans Conrad Hess's, deceased, widow, Elsbeth Krauer 1654. Child: Rudolf Hess 1704.
9. Domestica Hans Brändli's, deceased, child, Anna, 1697.
10. Hans Egli 1682, Barbara Homberger 1700. Children: Susanna 1711, Elsbetha 1716, Hans Jakob 1723, Anna Dorothea 1730, Hans 1733, Hans Rudolf 1736.
11. Hans Jacob Egli fil. 1703. Catharina Hourgger 1713. Child: Margaretha 1733.
12. Caspar Lätsch 1680, Dorothea Egli 1685. Children: Regula 1736, Elsbetha 1737.
13. Caspar Hess 1682, Maria Krauer 1692. Children: Barbara 1718, Hans Jacob 1723, Elisabetha 1726, Maria 1730.[39]

We can see how the three households (two Hess, one Egli) of seven persons living together in the hamlet Heferen had over a century grown into thirteen households of fifty-three persons. The original Egli and Hess households had now increased two and fourfold, comprising eleven and eighteen persons respectively. The Krauer family had settled in Heferen with four households and fourteen persons. We also find two Krauer daughters married into the Hess family. Dorothea Egli had married Caspar Lätsch and they too were still living in the hamlet.

In the hamlet Aathal in 1634 there were also three households of fourteen persons altogether. Two Strehler families and the households of Uli Reymann and Anna Eglin, with their children: Hans (twelve), Barbeli (eleven), Anneli (ten), Heinrich (three), Uli (two) and Elsbeth (one).[40] A century later (1739) we discover six or seven households there with thirty-four (thirty-eight) members. The Strehler family was no longer living in the hamlet, nor were any married daughters. The Reymann family on the other hand had remained in Aathal and had branched out. A few details of the structure of this kinship group can be found in the sources:

1. Heinrich Reymann's, deceased, children, Rudolf? Margartha?
2. Hans Bernhard fil. 1668, Maria Pfenninger? Child: Verena 1718.
3. Heinrich Reymann 1687, Verena Schroff 1691. Children: Heinrich 1715, Elsbetha 1718, Hans Jacob 1724, Hans Heinrich 1726. Hans Reymann frat. 1691, Barbara Oberholzer 1690.

4. Jacob Reymann 1694, Offra Hammerli 1695. Children: Margaretha 1726, Hans Erhardt 1739.
5. Hans Bernhard Reymann's, deceased, child, Barbara? Hans Reymann 1685, Esther Sperger, 1678. Children (of first marriage): Anna 1686, Maria 1692, Dorothea 1696, Hans Jacob 1698.
6. Heinrich Reymann fil. 1669, Susanna Hotz 1695. Children: Margaretha? Rudolph? This particular family is described as 'not in the parish' – whether temporarily or permanently we do not know.[41]

Alongside all these Reymann households there were in 1739 only the Hüsser household consisting of two families (nine persons) and one further family with six children.

Both these examples from the Wald parish illustrate the structure of population and its growth in two hamlets around 1740. They represent many similar cases, and apply to the whole of the Oberland. Industrial earnings obviously extended the living space in the hamlets and single farmsteads and indirectly also broadened their subsistence base, since the cash earned by spinning and weaving could be spent on acquiring new fields and on clearing new tracts of woodland.[42]

This brings us to the problem of the formal structure of the family. Both our examples show how the introduction of the putting-out industry into the Oberland countryside of single farmsteads and hamlets enabled extended families and whole kinship groups to live together in a community; not under one roof but in a small isolated settlement area. Individual households could also grow into their own extended families. In Hinderburg (parish of Bäretswil) in 1723 there lived eight households with forty-nine members of the Spörri family in 1723. Hans Jacob Spörri's household consisted of the following persons:[43]

> Hans Jacob Spörri, sixty-six years; Anna, his wife, sixty-five years
>   their first son, Hans Jakob Spörri, thirty-nine years; Anna, his wife, thirty-eight years;
>   their child: Hans Jakob, six years
>   their second son, Marx Spörri, thirty-six years; Anna, his wife, thirty-five years;
>   their children: Anna, twelve years, Barbara, ten years, Conradt, three years
>   their third son, Heinrich Spörri, thirty years; Regula, his wife
>   their fourth son, Hans Spörri, twenty-eight years; Anna, his wife, thirty-six years.

We have been guided so far by the general question: where could a newly married couple find to live? The question as to how the conditions of settlement in the Oberland gave rise to a specific pattern of industrial settlement will be discussed in Chapter 4.

In the villages the conditions were different. Here the parishioners could make it difficult to build and divide up houses, and even entirely forbid it. They could also forbid stoves and ovens and chimneys from being installed, and so prevent building.[44] This situation produced not only peculiar forms of communal living, but also equally peculiar subdivisions of houses. As Johann Conrad Nüscheler wrote in 1786, 'this results in the unpleasant consequence that in most villages in almost every house there are two or three rooms, and in each room, three to four households'.[45] J.C. Hirzel writes: 'One often sees three to four households squeezed together in one chamber, related in the second, third or often even remoter degree.'[46] We will discuss these residential patterns and their social effects later on. To come back to our original question, we can already establish that from the point of view of residential patterns industrialisation had not broken up familial co-residence, even in the villages. But, needless to say, these residential patterns, imposed by the economic imperatives of peasant life, and sanctioned by the authorities, were designed to destroy the structure of the family from within. There could have been no question of an intimate family life, when several families were living together in one room. Such a shortage of living space must have made the parents dread the birth of every new child. The children were brought up to move away and live and work elsewhere. Pre-industrial conditions of a legal, social and economic nature affected and influenced in various ways the cohesion of the families employed in industry.

Childbirth brings us to another aspect of formal family structure, to the problem of demographic growth. We begin with the rise in population, a phenomenon which the economists of the nineteenth century were not the first to attempt to grasp and explain. Already in the eighteenth century concerned men, aware of their responsibilities, were writing treatises about it. They were generally aware that the staggering increase in the birth rate was a direct consequence of industrialisation. We have already heard Salomon Schinz's opinion, that industrial earnings had 'straightaway planted'[47] hordes of people in the mountains. Johann Schulthess spoke of a 'torrent of people' and quoted a deceased pastor as saying: 'these people came with the cotton, and will have to leave with it'.[48] A rich farmer and village official put it, while talking to Uli Brägger in 1793, even more strongly: 'The cotton louts, like a rotten dungheap, have given birth to and raised all that rabble, that creeping, strutting pack of beggars.'[49] Behind all these descriptions lay the same awareness that the putting-out industry had altered the conditions of existence in the Zurich countryside. J.C. Hirzel tried to analyse these changes using statistical and scientific methods. On several occasions he compared the industrialised domain of Wädenswil with the predominantly agrarian domain of Regensberg. According to the register of cotton spinners and weavers (1787) there were 1,965 outworkers in Wädenswil and 176 in Regensberg, forty-four of whom had only turned to this work during the last two years. This meant that 1/4 of the inhabitants of Wädenswil and 1/20 in Regensberg were employed in manufacturing. Hirzel drew up a chart of the population growth in both these domains, which he attributed to 'unhappy Waser'. Hirzel interpreted these figures as follows:

Year	Wädenswil	Regensberg
1469	31	599
1529	1,526	2,890
1588	3,060	3,360
1610	4,039	4,290
1634	2,829	2,840
1671	4,421	4,064
1678	4,730	4,090
1700	3,997	4,280
1748	5,931	3,609
1762	6,474	5,031
1771	7,675	4,057
1773	7,415	3,949

One can see that around the middle of the seventeenth century Regensberg had more people than Wädenschwil, but that since then and especially since the beginning of this century, during which time cotton factories have grown very numerous and have mostly fallen into the hands of the clothiers, one discovers an astonishing rise in the population of Wädenschwil, which proves beyond doubt that the factories encourage population growth.[50]

Gerold Meyer of Knonau wrote in 1837 that the industry called in an 'artificial population'. He also compared two regions, in the first of which industry was generally dominant, in the second of which farming was almost the only activity. We have included his figures since they concern the Oberland.[51]

District of Hinwil

	1634	1836
Bärtentschweil	484	3,462
Bubikon	262	1,583
Fischenthal	466	2,814
Gossau	859	3,118
Grüningen	674	1,583
Rüti	139	1,112
Wald	570	3,895
Wetzikon	887	3,664

District of Bülach

	1634	1836
Bassersdorf	742	1,792
Bülach	1,779	3,400
Dietlikon	215	704
Eglisau	998	1,608
Embrach	1,100	2. 012
Glattfelden	593	1,098
Kloten	1,082	2,068
Lufingen	148	262
Rafz	412	1,337
Rorbas	688	1,424
Wallisellen	149	553
Wyl	1,056	1,803

An article entitled 'From the Early Industrial History of Wald'[52] provides us with a detailed history of how the population of this parish developed. Between 1634 and 1792 the population grew by almost five and a half. H. Krebser writes that 'These figures are the more impressive when we learn that the population of the city of Zurich grew from 9,122 to only 10,579 during the hundred years between 1671 and 1769.' The parish of Fischenthal numbered 3,400 souls in 1817; twice as many inhabitants as in 1949.

These numbers and comparisons are astonishing. The enlargement of the living space through the putting-out industry can be perceived when we compare the population density in individual districts in 1836, using Gerold Meyer's figures.[53]

District	Inhabitants per square mile
Zurich	9,620
Hinwil	9,120
Bülach	5,030
Regensberg	5,015

They show that the remote region of Hinwil was almost as densely populated as the fertile regions of Bülach and Regensberg.

This is where we asked ourselves about the formal structure of the family and its organisational and emotional cohesion. The fact that the birth rate and the population increased did not mean that marriages had become more fertile. We have quoted J.C. Hirzel's statistics for the parish of Fischenthal relating to the phenomenon of the increased frequency of marriage; 'according to these [statistics] the population has more than doubled within a hundred years. Marriages have increased by a factor of four and baptisms from 51 to 131, a ratio of 10:24.' The overall result was, however, that marriages had become less fertile, which Hirzel found so surprising that he did not believe it and assumed his sums were faulty: 'It could be, however, that previously not all marriages were registered. Maybe only those celebrated in the village church.'[54] In fact one would expect a different result, according to C. Meiners' simple reckoning, which has already been quoted: 'On account of the prospects opened to the countryman and his children by their industry [he means cottage industry], he was not anxious to limit the size of his family early on.'[55] But if one digs deeper into the living conditions of the putting-out industry, it is no longer suprising that the fertility of marriages declined. This many-faceted problem has to be explained by a new approach to birth and the child itself. We are dealing here with an intellectual and spiritual attitude, and especially with the basis of everyday Christian beliefs. The industrial population cannot be viewed as a whole here, without distorting the picture. We must undertake to make distinctions.

In places where the population engaged in industry was still able to retain a bit of farmland, or – as was especially the case in the Oberland – acquire new lands, they enjoyed different conditions to those experienced by the landless cottagers. It is remarkable how ownership of land, even in cottage industry circles, helped keep the family members together. The practice of *Rast*-giving, which will be discussed in the next section, could not assume the same importance among propertied families as among the landless families employed in cottage industry. In places where industrial earnings had given rise to a mountain peasantry, a child would be obliged to contribute to the family budget. He would not be able to avoid his duty of earning the rent for the property by spinning and weaving. We have become conscious of how much this customary obligation determined the fate of daughters in particular, from the stories told us by an old silk weaver.[56] She tells how her family counted on her earning power as a matter of course. 'Just wait until your daughters are big', the neighbours told their father, 'then you will be able to put by some money.' They handed the money over quite as a matter of course and it was used for their own little home or for that of their brothers. The narrator's sister wove at home until she was forty and handed all her earnings over. In such a family-orientated economic unit, the bonds between parents and children would be very strong, due to material considerations, and no limits would be set on the fertility of the marriage. People wanted children, especially daughters. Our narrator's neighbour had seven daughters.

Material considerations represented only one aspect and must be linked to others, bringing us to the heart of our folklorist enquiry, which attempts to understand ways of life and conditions of existence by looking at the triangle of

I, you and object, that is, the way individuals relate with one another and with the material world. We will analyse these connections elsewhere.

While one might expect that the fertility of propertied marriages would at least remain constant, this did not apply to the landless cottager marriages. Children were rather unwelcome in circles employed in the putting-out industry, in spite of being able to earn their own keep at a very early age. Their parents were not unhappy when they moved away from home and were taken in by strangers. However harsh and 'inhuman' the parents' attitude may seem to us, they were not too unhappy either when their children died. When Uli Brägger recovered from a dangerous illness, his father said to him: 'God has heard your entreaties . . . but I want you to know that I did not think like you, Uli, and I would have considered myself and you happy if you had departed hence.'[57] Johann Schulthess wrote:

This is why so many parents did not just think it, but wished out loud and openly for their children's death. One would hear – and I witnessed this myself – a poor woman railing at Heaven, when the child of a well-off neighbour died, saying I am not so happy. If one of my children were to fall off the bench, I would more likely have two of them get up off the ground again, rather than him break his neck. And another woman, a poor person walking along the street with the minister, holding hands with a jolly child just recovered from smallpox, says brazenly before both of them: 'If only he had died from the pox!'.[58]

This attitude to child bearing and children was determined on the one hand by the straightforward reason that a baby kept his mother away from working at the cottage industry. Time meant money to her. If the child grew up, it would step into the customary *Rast* relationship. A further reason was the unimaginable shortage of accommodation. The rapid growth in population together with the local laws against building created living conditions in which every increase to the household was an unbearable burden. We will learn even more about these living conditions.

The attitude of the outworkers to birth and children cannot be explained only in terms of living or material conditions. Undoubtedly the changes involved, which penetrated large areas of the life of the common people, have to be understood in relation to the changes to the organisational and emotional structure of the family. We recognise that our attempt to differentiate between propertied and landless families can give rise to false conclusions. Owning property is on the one hand a question of birth, but on the other the symptom of an intellectual and spiritual attitude. The putting-out industry and the work it offered brought both the possibility of acquiring land and the other possibility of discovering self-awareness and satisfaction by developing greater needs.[59]

Consequently, we must examine the structure of the family from inside, and will attempt to do this by taking *Rast*-giving as our example, paying particular attention to family cohesion.

Rast means in this context no more than a task, performed over a specific period.[60] Stutz uses the term in this sense when he says of a spinner:

Der Segen war gross by ihrer Arbeit.
Der Rast hat ihr kein Mol versait.

The blessing of her work was great.
She did not fall short of the *Rast* even once.[61]

The purely technical meaning of this term was given a broader sense in the industrial regions around Zurich. Parents or providers would assign a daily or weekly task – the *Rast* – to their children, which they had to complete in return for their keep. The children were not obliged to do any work in excess of the *Rast* and they could keep their excess earnings. The term *Rast* expanded to mean not just the task but also the money the task was worth, which gave rise of the expressions *Rastgeben* (*Rast*-giving), *Rastnehmen* (*Rast*-taking) and *Rast-machen* (*Rast*-making).

This introductory definition is generalised and stylised. We are aware that the whole question of this practice in the putting-out industry cannot be isolated from the work and the work practices which appeared with cottage industry. This aspect will be discussed further on.

The brief genesis of *Rast*-giving and *Rast*-taking already demonstrates how the practice (which has often been fiercely condemned) had its roots in the living conditions of the putting-out industry. One might be inclined to hold industrialisation responsible for the manifold and indubitably catastrophic consequences of this practice, and thereby to assess its influence on the life of the common people as completely negative. But this was not the case. While industrial earnings had provided the opportunity to develop this practice, by creating the material preconditions for it, other causal connections must be held responsible for this development. When Jakob Stutz describes it as a thoroughly good and beneficial custom, which in no way needs to loosen the bonds between parents and children, this is evidence enough that industrial earnings provided both positive and negative opportunities for change. Stutz's story *Lise and Salome* tells a black-and-white tale of two weaving girls. Lazy, work-shy Lise goes to the bad, but poor, virtuous Salome achieves riches and respect. Salome's mother, Stutz writes, made her daughter's work easy and enjoyable, and gave her only reasonable *Rast* tasks to do. Anything this virtuous girl was able to earn on top of this was carefully put away in her savings box. When naughty Lise came to her and tried to lead her astray she would reply good-naturedly that she did not have the time to go to the *Stubeten* (gatherings in people's houses) since she had to keep on weaving so as not to neglect her weekly *Rast*.[62]

We have begun by presenting the 'ruinous *Rast*-giving'[63] in a positive light on purpose, and will now follow up the development and consequences of this practice. It has already been stressed that *Rast* was not practised among families which were still firmly established on their own land. Their children would contribute their earnings to the family concern as a matter of course, since maintaining the property took precedence over individual happiness. The sister of the woman mentioned above, who stayed at home until she was forty, did not have any savings of her own.

But as soon as this mental and spiritual attitude to peasant property and land altered, *Rast*-giving had to develop; and the danger of such developments inevitably grew acuter as the countryside became increasingly industrialised. The question of causality cannot be wholly solved but remains dependent on the existing conditions. Johann Conrad Nüscheler quotes a very instructive example. His question about the origin of the unused and neglected farmland generally received an answer of the following kind:

My wife and I are growing old. So we are not able to work as much as before. We also have three children, two of whom pay us a *Rast* of 30 *Batzen* every week. Only one of our daughters still helps us with the work. We only do as much work as we can and need to do and we live from what the other children give us. It would be difficult for us to find day-labourers and workers or to employ a farmhand and a maid, since their pay and keep would be too expensive. We can, thanks be to God, do very well on what the children give us.[64]

This example demonstrates how the practice had developed within one generation. It was not just the children who had lost interest in the farm, but their parents' resignation shows us that their pride in their own farm was destroyed. This source informs us about the inner cohesion of the family; the daughter who was still working with her parents felt most strongly bound to them and to the farm. The other children were involved in a pure *Rast* relationship, which meant paying their contribution of 30 *Batzen* and not having to do any other work. They had become boarders in their own family. If within one generation the changes had been able to take hold to such an extent in this family, which was after all still partly engaged in farming, we should not be surprised at the forms taken by the practice of giving *Rast* among those people who had owned no land for generations. A hundred years had passed since the 'Description of the Poor in the Whole Countryside' and the growing number of such landless persons had found sustenance and living space in the Oberland. Let us recall how it became the custom in those circles to marry young and without possessions. These people had never learnt what it meant to dedicate one's life to working on one's own farm and to derive one's self-confidence and assertiveness from ownership of land. If they were lucky, they grew up in their own share of a house, otherwise in rented accommodation. The began earning their own living when very young, at five or six years old. In these circumstances it is not surprising that forms of *Rast*-giving developed, against which the authorities had to intervene. In these circles it became usual not just for the children to pay their parents a weekly *Rast* 'thereby believing that they had purchased their complete independence',[65] but even these extremely loose family ties could be cut and the children would move out and earn their keep with strangers. Johann Hirzel used the term *Rastgeben* in this extreme sense alone:

As people's fear of the All-Knowing diminished so did the children's duty towards their parents remain unfulfilled. This led to *Rast*-giving, whereby the children leave the parental house and earn their keep in other parishes, preferably in distant places, in order to be able to keep for themselves what they earned over and above the weekly pay for their board, and to pay many dues to frivolity, thoughtlessness and loose morals, and so to escape entirely all supervision, especially from the obedience due to their parents.[66]

The mandate of 25 March 1779 provides us with more information about *Rast* relationships.

The Mayor and council of the town of Zurich must hear and agree with deep-felt regret that the practice of giving *Rast* to children in the countryside has over the last few years increased out of all proportion, leading to the collapse of the discipline and order which are indispensable to social and domestic existence, and could easily deteriorate into a dangerous evil. Consequently all children in the countryside are absolutely forbidden from being given *Rast* until they have grown old enough to be allowed to leave school, according to the school ordinance instituted shortly beforehand;[67] since these childrens' sorely needed instruction has been neglected on account of giving them *Rast* too early on, and since people's attention is directed simply and solely at earning money.

From the time when children are allowed to leave school until the time when they are permitted to partake of the Lord's Supper, they are to be allowed to give *Rast*, on condition that they remain in their parish and do not give *Rast* without the knowledge of their parents, the minister and the parish elders, and that they should be told by every form of official remonstrance to give their *Rast* to their parents and to be directed by the minister's most pressing reminders to obey their parents willingly and to live a Christian and upright life at all times. But should a child of that age want to move away from his parents for justifiable reasons, he should be allowed to give *Rast* to honest decent people in his parish, but only with the consent of his parents, his minister etc. . . ., and to have the observance of the duties he owes his parents most forcibly instilled in him. In every case the children are bound to attend religious instruction and coaching assiduously and nobody is to keep them away from it. Thirdly and finally those children who have already been admitted to the Lord's Supper, should, in case the manner of their employment requires that they go outside their parish, be allowed to do so; but beforehand they should report to the minister of their parish and may only move away with the consent of their parents and the parish elders, armed with a certificate of good conduct and a letter of recommendation to the minister of the other parish for their necessary care and supervision.[68]

Contemporaries all view the consequences of *Rast*-giving in the same way: the 'natural relationship between parents and their children' was 'destroyed, or to a great extent impaired'.[69] In many places *Rast* was preventing children from being educated properly.[70] 'The bond between parents and children was loose everywhere in the country.'[71] 'The sacred duties towards the parents were being neglected.'[72] 'How could children be brought up properly by parents who themselves had only just left childhood behind them, who were not used to any discipline on account of the unholy *Rastgeben* and had themselves not learnt to accord their parents any respect?'.[73] A pastoral letter of 1777 admonished:

the so-called *Rastgeben* is to be banned from your households. You make your children independent of you and you remove the duty which is incumbent on you, whereby God's law requires that a child should stand by his parents, when you come to an agreement that the child should pay you a certain sum for his keep, and keep the rest of his earnings for himself. You can see already how such *Rast* children turn against their parents and how reluctant the parents become to give them any orders so as not to have to hear their answer: I have my own work to do. Let holding everything in common remain the cement of your households.[74]

The social consequences of *Rast*-giving were obvious: although building regulations and lack of freedom of movement might hold families in the putting-out industry together physically, the cohesion of such families was weakened from within. One is tempted to assign all the blame for the abuses to industrialisation, since the material possibility of loosening the family bonds only came with the new work opportunities. But one must remember where these sections of the population had to seek their livelihood before industrialisation. The father might be in Swabia, earning his own and his family's keep, and his daughter might be in service in Zurich, his oldest son might be fighting in Dalmatia and his mother spinning along with the rest of the family in Fischental, so one really could not talk of an organisational and formal family cohesion. This was the fate of poor peasant families: day-labourers, cottagers and villeins. What about the propertied? The younger children, who would not inherit, either renounced starting families of their own and stayed on the farm as hands and maids, or they were forced to move away and seek their fortunes elsewhere. The critics of the eighteenth and twentieth centuries forgot these conditions of pre-industrial peasant life only too easily, because the fates of those affected were mostly played out off-stage in distant parts. They judged the social consequences of industrialisation only negatively and they sang the praises of the peaceful life of the country. They did not want to take into account the many people who were able to settle in their own homeland only as a result of industrialisation. This does not mean we want to trivialise or contest the social consequences of the *Rastgeben* practice, but simply to try to distinguish the sunny and the shady sides of industrialisation clearly.

In our attempt to grasp the changes to ways of life under the influence of the putting-out industry, we began by looking at the family. The putting-out system with its employment possibilities tied countless people to their homeland, who were previously forced to seek their livings among strangers and out of the country. For countless people the putting-out system provided the material conditions which allowed them to get married and to found their own households. This led to the de-materialisation of marriage and the traditional peasant inheritance customs were changed. The way was open for individuals to choose their own life partners. Industrial regions were distinguished by a higher rate of marriage and a strong natural population growth. These are the visible signs of altered human behaviour and altered inter-personal relations. The structure and internal cohesion of the family also changed. Families were obliged by lack of freedom of movement, along with legal and economic restrictions, to go on living together, and the population growth led to an expansion of co-residing groups. The material preconditions which had chained the members of peasant kin groups together in a common destiny no longer applied, however. This led to the emergence of the nuclear family. The more a family could rely on its farm alongside cottage industry, the stronger were the bonds holding the family together. Landless outworker families, who did not experience this type of material compulsion, fell apart earlier, as was manifested in the traditional practice of *Rastgeben* and the early marriages (beggars' weddings).

All these changes to the structure of society and population went hand in hand with a new attitude by the population engaged in industry towards life and society. We will tackle this line of enquiry in the next chapter.

3 ♣ Life and society of the population engaged in industry

The remarkable population increase which occurred in the eighteenth century in the industrial regions of the Zurich territory had unavoidable consequences for the life of all the common people. This demographic surge was felt in all spheres of everyday life and society. The movement had some of the frenzied power of a natural phenomenon. We have heard the voices of those who were horrified by this phenomenon and it is understandable that such voices became more frequent in times of hardship and crises. But in many places there also arose, alongside the horror, concern and the desire to understand the origins of the population growth, to identify its manifold effects and by so doing also to accept its trail-blazing innovations. Johann Conrad Nüscheler summed up this patriarchal awareness of responsibility in a chapter-heading in his *Beobachtungen eines redlichen Schweizers* (*Observations of an Honest Swiss*) (1786): 'The population increase, which it is imperative to know and learn about beforehand'.[1]

There was no shortage of minds capable of recognising the extent to which industrialisation built up pressure within the closed sphere of a legal and economic order, within the rigid constraints of the social structure and the dogmatic stranglehold of the ecclesiastical authorities' moral legislation; but the Helvetic Revolution (1798) had to occur before the pressure could be released. J.C. Hirzel spoke in 1792 of 'the belt which the authorites were obliged to loosen'.[2] In the event, to extend Hirzel's metaphor, the citizens/subjects had long ago grown out of the clothes offered them by the authorities. The following example is intended to introduce us to this chapter's line of enquiry.

The records of the parish supervisory boards in the industrial regions are full of complaints and arguments about the sittings in church, called *kirchenörter*. When people entered a church, their primary concern was not to meditate and concentrate on the word of God but to concentrate their forces in the struggle for the disputed church bench. The record of Wald reports on 7 March 1756 the complaint 'that those in the Mettlen and from Unterbach, who claim to sit in what is called the *Heusser* seat push each other a lot and create a great disturbance in the church'. The Church elders from those places were directed to stop the people creating this disturbance and to denounce those 'who push so insistently'.[3]

The connection between these disputes over church sittings and our enquiry is obvious when we know that the right to the sittings in a church was linked to house ownership.[4] The disruptions to church services were a direct result of the conditions of existence arising from the movement of populations which accompanied the process of industrialisation. Hamlets, farmsteads and villages, like the settlements of Mettlen and Unterbach in our example, were growing bigger. This development inevitably gave rise to disputes about entitlement to church sittings, which impaired church services and religious life as a whole.

Irrelevant as this example may seem at first glance, it does in fact relate to the question addressed in this chapter. If we want to understand the life and society of the industrial landscape of the Oberland, we can no longer perceive the changes simply as a consequence of industrialisation. Our task is rather to observe the conditions of existence as they emerge from the tension between industrialisation and the prevailing order.

We are not able to convey the whole picture, but have selected a range of examples from the most varied spheres of everyday life in order to demonstrate how the basic conditions of human life and society change.

Let us begin with the most immediate necessity, food, which is 'tradition-ally considered to serve not just as provision for our bodily needs but also as the mainstay of our whole being'.[5] By considering and assessing food we are taking a fundamentally important aspect into account. The putting-out industry was built up on a money economy. Those people who had fallen into industrial dependence saw their lives bound to this rationally organised economic and wage system. They procured most of their daily needs by means of a non-agricultural foreign medium. This medium, money, once introduced into the original framework of their lives and subsistence economy, flowed more and more strongly into the Oberland with the growth of industrialisation, and changed the traditional diet. In Chapter 1 we saw how the possibility of living in the Oberland was extended from outside by the industrial work opportuni-ties, and in Chapter 2 we saw how a population grew up with the putting-out industry which could no longer possibly be fed off the land.[6] The less the Oberland was able to supply its inhabitants with the food they needed, the more they were obliged and able to alter their local eating habits.

The subject of diet is significant when we come to differentiate between the property-owning and the landless members of the population engaged in industry. We have learnt about mountain peasants who were able to cover their farms' rents and running costs with the help of industrial earnings. Such families would derive most of their nourishment from a couple of cows (according to *Memories of the Fatherland*) and their looms enabled them to earn their rent and other needs with ease.[7] Such a symbiosis between smallholdings and cottage industry scarcely altered the traditional diet, in so far as cottage industry did not entail a transformation of land use and of farming methods.[8] People's food requirements were generally met from their own farm produce, and depended on the seasonal harvest and slaughtering times in the agricultural year. Milk and flour soups, oatmeal gruel and dried fruit formed the basic diet along with the few vegetables, turnips, peas, beans and cabbage. Bread was not an everyday staple for the Oberland peasants. Meat was a rarity, and most mountain peasants only tasted it when an animal had to be slaughtered. Potatoes will be discussed later on. We find more precise details about peasant menus in the more level regions of the canton: the peasants of Lufingen near Embrach ate barley soup, milk, dried or raw pears for breakfast, pease pudding and a few vegetables at midday and evening. Most of them had to buy meat and wine, which is why these were feast-day foods. Minister J.C. Sulzer noticed that the peasants of Seuzach 'eat peas, barley soup and vegetables all week'.[9] Without being able to go thoroughly into the feeding habits of previous centuries, these meagre menus remind us that we have not yet reached the well-fed era of minimum wages and calorie counting. World trade and its exchange of goods only emerged in the nineteenth century. Starvation years were a normal feature of life and no one expected to be able to eat their fill.[10] One could sum up the whole diet of those days under the words 'gruel and broth' (*Mus und Brei*).[11]

These feeding habits applied to those members of the population engaged in industry who derived outer and inner support from farming their own land.[12] They represented a way of life which persisted in this form into the twentieth century. The latter-day industrialist Jakob Oberholzer came from a family which derived its livelihood in As-Hübli from domestic weaving and farming. Jakob tells us himself how he carried his wares to Winterthur every week in the 1840s, taking just some dried fruit to eat on the way.[13] The following life-like vignette is taken from the life of Elisabeth Hess (née Brändli):[14]

Besides the cloth trade my parents and grandparents also ran a small farm. We owned a cow, a goat and a pig. We had our own milk, butter, potatoes and fruit for the household. Our food was simple . . . Each year a pig would be slaughtered and its meat salted down for the winter, which then gave us something nice to eat every Sunday. All year round we had to buy meat from farmers who had to kill off their cattle. That always provided a little variety in what we ate. We also sowed wheat, oats and barley, which we had ground for us. In wintertime we baked bread and good cakes every month. This work was always done by my grandfather . . . At New Year he would bring us children loaves, as well as men and women and all sorts of shapes made out of short pastry.

Senator Heinrich Hess[15] has said that when he was young 'throughout the year meat appeared only very seldom on the table, during the fair and at Christmas . . .'

. . . in those days [*c.* 1890] sugar, chocolate and jam still belonged to the realm of luxuries. Bread, flour, maize, potatoes, turnips, cabbages and fruit, both dried and fresh, were the foods which appeared on every table. Meat and sausage turned up only seldom, not even every Sunday. There were even families who could not afford meat at any time of the year, although the prices were low.[16]

The outward self-sufficiency of a farm in which outwork and agriculture complemented one another reflected its inner structure. Tenacious and traditionalist forces were inherent in it. An anonymous author wrote in 1811 that

it is a fact generally observed and which certainly also applies to their canton that the land owner, principally the actual farmer, who is concerned with nothing other than working his land, remains far more loyal to his father's way of life in his habits and morals, both under similar as well as under far better financial circumstances, than he who is almost exclusively employed in urban and especially in manufacturing trades.[17]

And yet we have seen how other needs infiltrated even the mountain peasants' households along with industrial earnings: 'A series of pretentious needs',[18] as the anonymous author called them elsewhere. The more people were being severed from the land with their lives 'hanging only by threads of cotton, which they spin or weave',[19] the more freedom they acquired to choose the food they wanted. They no longer belonged to the class of primary producers. Money interposed itself between their work and their daily nourishment. Their menu was no longer dictated by their own harvest produce. Food had to be bought, thus providing the freedom to select foodstuffs both from within and without their economic sphere. The way was open to satisfying 'pretentious' needs. It seems important at this point to stress how much the freedom of the population engaged in industry to determine their diet as they wanted affected the local peasant economy. When the majority of the population within a rural economic area becomes consumers, these consumers' demands determine the type and quality of agricultural produce, leading to the commercialisation of agriculture.

By comparing a few statistics, one can get an idea of how many Oberland inhabitants owned no land or property, apart from a vegetable patch, and lived entirely on their factory earnings. The list of factory workers in the Grüningen district in 1789 contains the following comment: 'According to the unanimous reports of the officials it can be estimated that at least a quarter of the 8,992 spinners are employed in farm work during the summer.'[20] Minister Schinz informs us that in 1918, 1,360 of the 3,400 inhabitants of the parish of Fischenthal 'lived exclusively on their factory earnings, and around 200 households' owned no immovable property of their own.[21] A century earlier (1702) this parish had numbered 957 inhabitants; of whom '657 persons have grown fruit, and 300 persons have grown no fruit'.[22]

Contemporary reports and complaints confirm that the range of food in factory worker circles had changed and extended beyond the staple foods, gruel and broth. J.C. Hirzel reported that 'coffee is almost generally drunk for breakfast, particularly among the factory workers'.[23] 'Coffee and meat are very common, especially among the class of factory workers.'[24] 'The morals of these people [meaning the inhabitants of the Oberland] have much deteriorated as a result of the good factory earnings: large sums go on imported wine and brandy, and coffee is also a very common drink now.' All these needs had become so prevalent that the writer doubted whether the supply could meet the demand any more: 'a circumstance which casts a doubt on factory earnings, on account of the increased population they lead to, is the lack of an easy supply of the goods we need. These are in fact many; bread, butter, meat, timber and logs for burning, all the linen and woollen cloth required for clothes, and the stimulants which have become necessities: tobacco, tea, coffee, sugar.'[25] C. Meiners makes a connection between the factory workers' diet and their work: 'since the factory workers are employed at lighter work and spend their lives sitting down, it is natural that they cannot enjoy the rough and partly indigestible food eaten by the countryman, whose work is harder and done in the open air'. The writer, however, perceived that this explanation was not good enough and pointed to the urban influence to which the putting-out workers were exposed:

Most factory workers are not satisfied with nourishing and digestible, though cheap and simple, meals: but they yearn for the tasty foods of the towns, with which they have opportunity to become familiar. Coffee with the richest cream is drunk every day by all the factory workers, who eat meat every day as well, and indeed often the most tender and expensive meat available too. It can happen fairly often that factory workers living away will send someone to town to fetch veal at times when it is in most short supply and most expensive.[26]

Meiners' account illustrates our earlier statement that the diet of manufacturing people was no longer bound exclusively to local and regional harvest produce. Meat, white bread, cakes, coffee, sugar, wine, brandy, etc., enlarged the traditional diet. They did not just enlarge it, they also replaced it, since the new necessities were not just seen as extras and treats: 'in the mountainous part, where field work has been exchanged for spinning and weaving work, harmful coffee and even more harmful brandy' serve as food, wrote minister Holzhalb in 1788.[27] The factory population's diet during times of unemployment is a measure of how much they had grown accustomed to these new needs and how unable they were to return to gruel and broth. Minister Escher in Weisslingen wrote in 1792 that their food consisted solely of potatoes and root coffee over a long period.[28] 'Many of the poor people do not cook anything for a few days at a time, but they keep going on bread and wine, or bread and fire water.'[29] 'In good times', Johann Schulthess wrote, 'freshly baked white bread, cakes and whatever else they took a fancy to' made up the factory workers' diet, but in bad times 'their meals consisted of potatoes, which they stuffed themselves on, their drink was coffee or chicory-water, which unsettles the stomach, and brandy, which unsettles the nerves'.[30]

The aspects considered so far are not enough for understanding the factory workers' altered dietary habits. Let us tackle Meiners' point about the technical aspect of the work again. The monotonous work of spinning or weaving aroused to a considerable degree the desire to interrupt the monotony of the work with little gastronomic treats. The outworker's appetite was not stimulated by any physical exercise, which was why his boring work made him all the keener on tasty titbits. In *7×7 Years*, Jakob Stutz describes how he and his sisters would long for the taste of food and dainties even while they were spinning: 'and all at once we would turn choosy, saying we wanted to eat bread (*Brödle*) too, like the people in the *Spinnstuben* normally used to do, since we were not peasants any more, but we belonged to the class of poor people'. A newly baked, two-pound loaf of white bread would turn up, and, enlivened by this gastronomic treat, they would continue their work cheerfully.[31]

The outworkers' notorious *Leckerhaftigkeit*[32] (sweet tooth) is understandable. Their working day was different to that of the agricultural workers, and they could also arrange their meal times to suit the rhythm of the work. This had broader implications. In an outworker family the woman's sphere was not primarily that of kitchen and stove, but of spinning wheel or loom. Her time was money and cooking had to be done quickly. What was more, the daughters of outworker families, especially in places where the practice of *Rast*-giving was well established, did not learn cooking or household skills any more.[33] We will have more to say about this later on.

The potato made much the deepest and most lasting impact on the traditional menu. It is revealing that this new tuber was first planted in the industrial regions. Peasants engaged in industrial work were not only the first to change to clover cultivation, and to using manure to intensify yields, but they also planted potatoes earlier and more intensively than anyone else, at a time when 'in other places the peasants viewed this new fruit with extreme suspicion'.[34] J.C. Hirzel writes that

necessity had taught them long ago to consider how to make the most advantageous use of their property. As, for instance, when the numbers of factory workers increased, so too was potato-planting, this insufficiently recognised and honoured Gift of Providence for the prevention of starvation, first generally introduced in the parishes of Wald and Fischenthal.[35]

The Oberland was vitally affected by its inhabitants' change of diet, and it is so significant for us because it highlights the causal connections between the process of industrialisation and the existing order. Under the Ancien Régime ministers were paid by means of tithes. Only primary produce was taxed, and non-agricultural cottage industry was not affected, so the Oberlanders tried to avoid paying tithes by turning more and more of their land over to potatoes. Their traditional field system being one of individual land use made it possible for them to change over like this, since it was not tied to the compulsory crop rotation of the three-field system.[36] More precise information about the parish of Wald has been provided by Heinrich Krebser's research; in 1751 the minister of Wald, Johann Ludwig Meier complained that during his predecessor's ministry

not only has a large part of the pasture and ploughland and cleared ground been laid to grass and the owners make use of it without paying tithes, but also a large quantity of potatoes have been increasingly planted, partly in tithe-paying meadows, which have been dug over, and partly in pasture and ploughland, without paying the tithes on them.

When the peasants of Wald had to account for themselves to the authorities in 1753–4 they claimed that in their parish for the last fifty years and more, potatoes had been planted and that no minister had ever demanded his tithe on them. Potatoes were not mentioned in the old tithe documents. It was finally agreed that potatoes could be grown in vegetable gardens without tithes being paid on the produce.[37]

Convincing as the legal and economic considerations may be in explaining the introduction of the potato into the Oberland, other aspects must be taken into account as well. Economic attitudes changed in line with the growth of cottage industry. The peasant acquired something of the nature of the putting-out industry when he placed his own farm on the non-agricultural basis of industrial earnings. He underwent an intellectual upheaval: the rigid fetters of tradition, which bound him to the working and farming methods of his father and grandfather were sprung and the way was open to introducing new methods and crops. This new rural and cottage industrial economic thinking was manifest in a rationalisation and intensification of farming methods, primarily in a shift to labour-saving potatoes and pastoral farming.[38] Potatoes and milk products thus became the Oberland mountain farmers' favourite food. They often ate potatoes three times a day, and an Oberland saying runs: 'Am Morge sur, z'Imbig i der Mondur und z'Nacht geschwellt und angestellt' ('In the morning sour, at lunch in their skins and at night boiled and dressed').[39] Potatoes formed an important basis of the diet not only of land owners but also of the landless outworkers. Many families were given small allotments by the land owners, on which they could grow potatoes for the winter.[40] In years of starvation and hardship they were grateful for this new crop. J.C. Hirzel writes:

In the starvation years [of 1770 and 1771] people began planting potatoes frequently, but once bread had become cheaper, their enthusiasm began to wane. Factory workers prefer bread, coffee and meat to potatoes and prefer to run the risk of starving to death in periods of unemployment to putting something aside against leaner times by their thrift during the good times.[41]

To explain the introduction of the potato we have listed the wish to avoid paying tithes, the ability of the Oberland small farm economy and the readiness of the outworker peasants to change. But how and why did the potato become a common food? J.C. Hirzel has provided the decisive answer:

1770 and 1771 were years of starvation and crises which allowed the potato to become generally accepted, if somewhat slowly. As later on with maize, the potato was introduced throughout the population during times of need. The significance of industrialisation in this process is striking. It unleashed the strong demographic growth by making it possible for people with little or no landed property to settle down. These people were most severely affected by the years of hardship and the crises of 1770–1 (and at the turn of the century), and it is only when set against this gloomy background that J.C. Hirzel's words can be fully understood: potatoes became a 'gift of Providence' for the industrial population.

Hirzel's remarks about the lack of thrift among the industrial population lead us to a whole series of problems, which include the question of diet, but also point to clothes, the need for luxuries and especially the outward trappings of life.

In the last chapter we saw how people in outworker circles got married without any possessions or land, trusting blindly to 'their old friend cotton'.[42] The same trust determined the way these people organised their lives. Whenever factory people are mentioned in contemporary accounts, there are complaints about their spendthrift ways. C. Meiners wrote: 'It is true that the largest or at any rate a large proportion of the factory workers spend everything they have earned in the week, and so when their former earnings are stopped for only a few weeks, this necessarily leads to oppressive poverty.'[43] The rule became 'living from day to day, hand to mouth',[44] and 'that for every one who has raised himself up there are twenty who live from one day to the next like the birds of the air,' and at every brief work stoppage they are reduced to begging, scarcity, destitution or oppression by hard-hearted speculators'.[45] Salomon Schinz provides an even more telling and general characterisation: 'Indeed there is very little to be said in favour of the actual factory workers. They seem to be very much alike in all the regions of our part of the world. Thoughtless frivolity, never thinking of the future, but spending their abundant daily earnings on riotous living was natural to this depraved class of person.'[46]

How are we to understand the new attitude to life adopted by the outworkers, and how are we to explain the fact that large sections of the country population tied their lives unthinkingly and carelessly to the cotton industry, described by Uli Brägger as 'like a bird on the bough, like showers in April'.[47]

We have seen how the outworkers met their essential needs out of their intermittent wages. The agricultural year and the necessity to build up reserves no longer applied to them. They were no longer obliged to calculate and save up for the months and seasons ahead. Outworker households got used to an artificial rhythm and only had to cope with short time intervals. They adjusted their standard of living according to their chancy and variable incomes, since they, unlike the peasant farmers, required no economic safeguards. Failed or faulty crops did not affect them directly. They believed they held the threads of their fate in their own hands, although the fluctuations in wages, market saturation and escalating prices should have taught them better. They absorbed these shocks as if they were natural disasters, being incapable of seeing through the 'mysterious play of economic laws' and incapable too of recognising how shaky were the foundations on which their existence rested. The bitter experiences of the collapse of the domestic spinning industry lay ahead. They could not understand the trade and customs policies of foreign rulers. But when a neighbouring farmer's harvest was destroyed by frost and hail, the outworkers reckoned that their livelihood was secure. Johann Hirzel provides us with an instance of their beliefs in this regard: spinners and weavers were of the opinion that they were not like farmers, who 'received their bread from the hand of the Lord'. This meant that their own 'feeling of dependence on God was weaker'.[48] Jakob Stutz's grandfather taught him his attitude to life and security, which is characteristic of the attitude of the common people in wider circles: 'One should enjoy it when one has it, and when it is no longer there, one can still praise almighty God'.[49] In so far as the outworker was able to envisage putting his life on a secure basis, he was nourished by sources different to the farmers'. The non-agricultural basis of existence entailed taking a new attitude towards the material and intellectual things of life.

The factory population's new attitude to life was documented outwardly by their clothes. Traditional clothes performed various functions over and above keeping out the cold. They expressed the class and professional status of the wearer and distinguished between sexes, ages and civil status. By considering the function of clothes, one can reach conclusions about their wearer's way of life.[50]

Traditional clothes had to change along with the new ways of working and living of the factory population. The outworkers' demands on their everyday and working clothes differed from the peasants'. Spinners were no longer exposed to wind and rain and the changing seasons, but were able to do their work in the shelter of their cottages or out in the open, enjoying the sun's warmth or the cool shade. Their work did not wear out their clothes, allowing them to use better and finer cloth for everyday wear. There was plenty of reason for so doing, since spinning work was done in company.[51] People dressed and adorned themselves with care, mindful of their surroundings.

A further outward factor determined the clothes of the factory workers. Whereas the countryman was still able to provide his most essential clothing requirements from his own farm, the majority of outworkers was forced to buy every little item. Our remarks concerning the self-sufficiency of the peasant class in the matter of food also applied to their clothes. But even if a propertied outworker could still call a hemp or flax field his own, his putting-out work obliged him to calculate whether it was worthwhile for him to spend time on turning his harvested crops into his own yarn, cloth and clothes. Minister Brennwald of Maschwanden reported in 1797 that 'Many outworkers are so enamoured of their work, on account of the daily shillings which they can earn with it . . . that many of them even allow their own hemp to be processed by other spinners and instead remain seated at their cotton wheel'.[52] All sorts of external circumstances were proposed as reasons for the factory population's new way of dressing, but they do little to explain it. Of far greater importance to us is the inner attitude to traditional clothes of country people employed in industry.

Under the Ancien Régime the State directly controlled the traditional manner of dressing by means of regulations about morals and clothes. The State Church of the seventeenth century, with its strict dogma and its rigid puritanical spirit, determined – in alliance with the lay authorities – the outward appearance of their country subjects. Official rejection of the world as a vale of tears, through which one must walk to reach eternal life, was to be expressed by a plain appearance. Every form of luxury was to be avoided as bodily temptation. This strict spirit of renunciation of the world reached its high point in the seventeenth century. It is well known how enduring its mark on the traditional attitude of the population of town and country has been.[53] Alongside the ecclesiastical and religious connotations of the regulations about morals and clothes, which reflected the *Zeitgeist*,[54] we may distinguish a further and notorious intention, a survival from the high and late Middle Ages, to determine clothing according to social standing. The two functions are intertwined: while the prohibitions were indeed directed against luxury as such, they contained the elements of social differentiation. The Sabbath and Moral mandates for town and country of 1650, for instance, stipulate (regarding ostentation) that every country-dweller should 'make sure he has a decent, suitable dress according to the custom of each village and styled in a manner appropriate to each person's standing'.[55] While town burghers were allowed only a limited individual range of choice in their clothing, the country-dwellers were restricted even more by the government regulations. Johann Kaspar Escher, governor of Kyburg (1717–23) wrote:

the two big Penance Ordinances (*Buss-Mandate*) issued in August 1722, the first for the town and burghers, the other for the country and countryfolk, draw in the Article about haughty dressing (*Kleider-Hoffart*) a clear distinction between burghers and peasants, forbidding the latter very many things, which are permitted the burghers; strangely enough the women of the countryfolk are obliged to wear a truly ridiculous dress.[56]

Countryfolk were supposed to be distinguished from townfolk by their outward appearance.

Legal requirements of this kind were reinforced by the traditional demands of the local community. 'Nobody pretends to be a gentleman or ever to become one', wrote minister Burkhart about the peasants of Lufingen. 'Nobody can acquire or assume any outward privileges over the others, without being ridiculed by the whole village.'[57] Of Otelfingen he recorded that

anyone who did not know the place would think I was pulling his leg if I were to tell him: There is a place in my gracious masters' region where the poisonous snake of luxury is unknown, although nearly everyone living there is rich, as rich indeed as those who own more than a ton of gold . . . The richest among them goes about like the poorest in his baggy trousers and rough twill coat, which they make themselves.[58]

These few remarks illustrate how important was the function of clothes in determining the status of the members of the community and for deducing an individual's sense of status and community and his attitude to life in general, from his manner and way of dressing. Having just looked at examples from the local peasant communities the question now arises: how did the factory population react to traditional ways of dressing?

The sources speak out clearly. The country-dwellers employed in industry attempted to distance themselves from their peasant environment by the way they dressed. The anonymous author of *Contemporary Remarks about the Swiss Cotton Manufacture* points out that

their income from their abundant earnings gave rise among many of them to expenditure unsuited to their means and which in many respects overstepped them. The food and clothes of those who lived from hand to mouth were more expensive than those of the propertied country people . . . The females vied against each other in exaggerated and unseemly adornment. Whereas the female inhabitants of the Berne canton, whose wealth was far more solidly established, remained faithful to their lovely and flattering country costumes, in the manufacturing cantons of eastern Switzerland a way of dressing was introduced which was as unsuitable to the country as it was tasteless, and which bore the marks of decadence. Can this approximation to urban clothing, life style and morals really be desirable?[59]

As an 'old, experienced countryman' said to a 'young peasant lad': 'But it is, unfortunately, only too true that in some places there are simply too many people who prefer spinning, weaving and knitting to working in the fields', because 'they earn a fair bit of money every week in the good times and since, as they say, they want to enjoy themselves, they buy themselves lovely though useless clothes and often marry early'.[60] Meiners pointed out that 'sadly the factory worker's sweet tooth emerges almost at the same time as his vanity and desire for admiration. He spends on expensive clothes and fashionable adornments money which could be spent on the meadows, fields and gardens, or put aside against hard times.'[61] The factory population was given over to 'a state of frivolity',[62] wrote Johann Hirzel, and minister Schweizer, like so many others, denounced their *Kleiderpracht* (splendid clothes).[63] For the industrial regions around the lakes, which (as we will see) played a decisive role in the transmission of urban luxury and cultural goods into the Oberland, we have Salomon von Orelli's account:

This peasant arrogance [peasant is used here in the sense of country subject as opposed to town burgher] had evil consequences; it aroused almost irresistibly the country peoples' desires . . . Very few of them were acute enough to invest the bulk of their earnings [from industry] either in ground rents or in capital assets . . ., the majority spent their earnings on pretty clothes and squandered the rest. On Monday morning there often would not be a shilling left of the money paid to the worker on Saturday; the whole lot having been cheerfully and fecklessly spent on the Sunday. Why should they save it? After all they were sure they would have plenty of money again by the following Saturday. It gradually got to the point where a young weaver-girl would not consider it an extravagance to have bought herself from her earnings: a bed, a chest, a pretty colourful dress for Sunday and a black dress for Communion days [these were considered essential adjuncts for any girl who wanted to find a husband]. Once she had secured these principal objects, she was free to indulge her vanity by buying more pretty dresses or to squander her earnings in other ways. Very few would reproach her for not putting a penny aside, since she would always find a husband and her daily earnings counted as dividend bearing capital, and indeed could have become that if she had only wanted it. In these weaver-girls' chests could be found dresses of all colours and materials, gilt necklaces and pendants as big as horse brasses etc., in which they paraded on Sundays and holidays. On the other hand, they spent very little on linen; two shirts and two pairs of stockings were all they felt they needed in that line; whether whole or full of holes was of no account; after all no one would dare to lift their skirts in church or on the streets. And they were not bothered about cleanliness; they just wanted to be dressed up and in their own way, they were very much so.[64]

'Jolly good, that's what I like to hear', riposted the rich Dorlikon farmer when Uli Brägger complained about the poor progress of his cotton business, 'If only that *Donnerslumpenzeug* [damned trash; he meant cotton yarn] was completely mucked up and nobody would buy it any more. By thunder, the country has been ruined ever since the *Donnersbauel* [damned cotton] has come into the country; it has been full of arrogant beggers, weavers and spinners.'[65] Minister Schmidlin of Wetzikon wrote on 13 December 1764: 'this year I did my very best to rid the church of Vanity with her silver, often gilt and golden, earrings and necklaces'.[66]

We are aware, when assessing the clergy's and gentry's condemnation of all needs for finery and ostentation, and the class consciousness of the town burghers, and the puritanical spirit of the age, that we should take their historical and contemporary eschatalogical experience into account as well. 'The 1760s were extraordinarily fruitful years both for wheat and for [fruit] trees and vines', wrote minister Schmidlin, 'and, on account of a good demand for cotton products, earnings were generally good, one might almost say bad, given that luxury, especially in these regions, has increased so much that morality has suffered great harm as a result. So one should not be surprised that God subsequently attenuated the mis-used surplus with shortage in the years 1770 and 1771.'[67] Salomon Schinz reports how his Fischenthal parishioners experienced the starvation year of 1817: 'the conviction seemed gradually to gain the upper hand in our region that this time of hardship had been sent by God as a scourge to improve mankind. People were frequently heard to say: let us remember this time if God lets us enjoy better days again. Many acknowledged that their foolish extravagance had increased the poverty and misery.' He hoped 'that people might restrict their luxury in dress not just because of the shortage but in the future too by thinking things over wisely'.[68] While Cousin Anneli was watching a comet she said: 'Yes, yes, ungodly arrogance, damned frills, petticoats and lovely broad ribbons; they have all brought on this sign in the sky and all the unhappiness in the world, and because the children do not have to learn the questions [of catechism] as they had to formerly. Is it not going to happen as in the days of Noah?'[69]

Let us free ourselves of the time-bound value judgements of these accounts and attempt to portray these changes in neutral terms. The country people employed in industry were obviously eager to copy town fashions and to do as the gentry did. Urban life styles became their models. Consequently, as industrialisation spread over the Zurich countryside, a new class grew up which was no longer supported by the former sense of community, and which proclaimed this fact, consciously or sub-consciously, by wearing new sorts of clothes. This formula does not, however, do justice to the historical facts. We have stressed that a significant proportion of the factory population was neither born into nor brought up among the existing communities (whether professional and social, or local and political). These people, who fell most exclusively into industrial dependency, lived on the margins of peasant life and society. So we come much closer to historical truth when we recognise the mental changes manifested in the new fashions in clothes not as the loss of an ancient sense of community, but much rather as the product of a new awareness of community. We should certainly not view the factory population's splendid clothes merely as an attempt to ape city ways; a desire to show off and throw money around. Behind all this 'state of frivolity' lay the longing for culture of a class of country-dwellers, conscious that they represented a new and original element. By dressing differently, they attempted to give formal expression to their sense of community, or, in more general terms, to the experience of being distinct from their agricultural environment. Everybody, and indeed every community, constantly needs to be able to assert themselves. The peasant did so by owning land and cattle, by his community right and his economic power. We read of farmers whose wealth amounted to 40,000–60,000 *Gulden*, but 'as regards clothes and hard work could not be distinguished from the middle-ranking members of the village community, except of course in that many of the lesser ones depended on them in various aspects'.[70] The unpropertied outworker knew nothing of this sort of self-confidence. He sought to assert himself by dressing up and preening, by ostentation and good living. The rattling coins which he earned by his work enabled him to distance himself from the farmers by his conspicuous consumption. But he could only do this when his position was strong enough to allow him to flout powerful convention. Even then he would be subjected to the mockery of the propertied. Jakob Stutz records how the rich daughters of the mill went to church in homespun and home-woven clothes 'and if some little beggar girl, with scarcely a whole shirt to her name, appeared in silk and satin and came to sit near them, many would be the fingers pointed at her, much to her shame'.[71] When they were earning good money, the outworkers vied with one another in their enthusiasm to appear in all their finery and to show their peasant environment that they had now become something different to and finer than it.

Given that the factory workers were inclined, in their search for new and suitable forms, to adopt urban clothes and manners, this demonstrates the receptive and imitative nature of popular forms of cultural expression. In any case, the reception of these forms did not occur by chance or arbitrarily. The outworkers had to enjoy an inner relationship with urban life forms to be able to adopt them as forms reflecting their class and community consciousness. The country people employed in industry were bound to urban life by their work, not only outwardly but also inwardly. The *Letter to a Burger of Canton A. about the Requirements of the Age and the Fatherland* mentions this important circumstance:

it seems to me, that people who have been removed from life in the open air while still children and locked up all day in a nasty hovel or workshop, apart from a few moments outside, compelled year in and year out to sedentary labour dedicated more to luxury than the necessities of life, must finally lose their feeling for what is simple and natural and be dominated by their tendency towards arrogance, glitter, decadence and frivolity. When several generations have been spent in this physically weakening life style, dedicated to the need for luxury, it is almost inevitable that it finally also casts the character in a weak, frivolous and decadent mould.[72]

These observations enable us to set our question of the altered diet and the altered clothes of the factory workers in a wider context. Clearly, the living standards of broad population groups had changed,[73] a change which had occurred unobtrusively and unpredictably. Far-sighted spirits of the second half of the eighteenth century had recognised how people's raised expectations from life had changed the fundamental assumptions underlying civic and social existence. The question 'What is luxury?' had become the burning issue of the age.[74] People were experiencing the Janus face of the putting-out industry.

In Chapter 1 we pointed to the fact that the Zurich textile industry rested on the emergence of a putter-out class which combined economic efficiency with firm, almost puritanical orthodoxy in the pursuit of a better life. In Chapter 5 we will see that the Protestant work ethic played a decisive part in the development of the Zurich textile industry. But in the eighteenth century a completely paradoxical situation began to emerge; the spirit of Protestantism and Puritanism, the driving force behind the process of industrialisation, stood in the way of industrialisation with its laws regulating finery and morals: *Prachts- und Sittengesetze*. The *Aufmunterungsgesellschaft* (Society for Encouraging

(Discussion)) in Basle set its prize-winning question for 1779 as follows: 'To what extent is it appropriate to set limits to the ostentation of the burghers in a small Free State, whose prosperity is founded on commerce?' It is easy to read in these words the awareness that industrialisation had placed Church and State with their moral laws before a new situation. Two essays among all the replies submitted were awarded first prize; the first was by Professor Leonhard Meister and the other by Johann Heinrich Pestalozzi.[75]

The reciprocal relationship between industrialisation and the life of the common people emerges clearly when we follow the discussion about luxury in the Basle *Aufmunterungsgesellschaft*. Both Meister and Pestalozzi and an anonymous prize-winner found themselves caught up in a truly tragic conflict, in that they experienced the discrepancy between idea and reality. They acknowledged that trade, manufacture and industry had become the 'foundation pillars of the new Free State': 'The Free State of Geneva rests mostly on the points of watch-hands; Venice, on playing cards; the Netherlands, on spices and tea-leaves; several Swiss cantons, on packs of silk and cotton.'[76] *Nationalgeist* (national character) correspondingly emerged as these founding pillars of the State grew in strength, one which could no longer be that of the shepherds and farmers:

The influence of ostentation on the direction of the national character towards industrious zeal and on the supply of trained hands necessary for maintaining the local industry – is very important – a people that has to seek its living in industry – must have a thousandfold experience of the vagaries of taste, of the circumstances, knowledge and foolishness of the purchasers – must be prepared for all sorts of changes in the manufacture of one and the same thing – must be alert to thousands of tiny savings, and maintain firm and precise order in the tiniest details of the manufacture – scrupulous attention to cleanliness and the pleasing appearance of the wares – all this must be a many-faceted and generally trained force in the national character of a people who seek their living in trade.[77]

The mental change described here by Pestalozzi did not only apply to the urban putting-out masters and craftsmen, but it applied just as much (with a few adjustments) to the countryfolk employed in industry. While the putting-out masters and merchants experienced the 'vagaries of taste' as active participants, the existence of the outworkers depended no less heavily on the whim of fashion, on market demand for coarser or finer yarn, on the thinner or thicker weft and warp required on their cloth. While the short-lived fashions required of the putting-out masters mental agility and the ability to adapt quickly, the outworkers also had to possess these skills.[78] Their involvement in the production of wares gave rise to an attitude (Pestalozzi's *Nationalgeist*) which – to employ folklorist terminology – was opposed to the traditional continuity of their previous existence. This neutral attitude was manifested in a new way of life, in refined and increased demands on life, in hitherto unheard-of needs. Leonard Meister's awareness that 'the fewer needs, the less toil and trouble, and the less inequality, and so more freedom' was of no use to him. He had to acknowledge that 'the more people's needs become refined and multiplied, the more their skill and strength develop'. He recognised that 'skill and industriousness is the father of luxury'.[79] The interplay between manufacture and the intellectual forces behind the changing needs is further illuminated by Pestalozzi:

> the son of a locksmith, who engraves garlands on gilt metal, can easily teach himself how to paint garlands on silk and move on from that to artist's work – and the seamstresses' daughter, whose attention to taste and neatness enables her to learn any skill with ease – thus does ostentation direct and form the people of the whole nation – which, with its various social classes, thereby earns its living – in the very good taste, the very intellectual attitude, the very adaptability, attention and skill, which make up the inner strength of all refined manufacture.[80]

One cannot acquire a wine taster's discernment without also acquiring a need for drinks other than water. The 'presumptuous requirements', which became 'necessities',[81] were a consequence of the new forms of employment. These needs, however, influenced manufacturing and industrial ability in their turn, 'in that the presumptuous needs became necessary, so too the diligent skill and inventiveness applied to manufacturing had to be doubled'.[82]

Pestalozzi has added to the reciprocal relationship between luxury and industry analysed by Meister a further relevant and yet new and supplementary connection 'and so ostentation made marketing the manufactured products of the industry easier – since the more refined people became – the more their skill, diligence and adaptability became characteristics integral to the national character – the more perfect and enticing their manufactured goods necessarily became, thus ensuring a constant demand for them'.[83]

What the far-sighted thinkers of the eighteenth century here recognised in its beginnings we experience today to a far greater degree: industry and economy, and with them the whole of civic and social existence, rely on the constantly changing needs of consumers. Prosperity can only endure as long as the 'dance around the standard of living' continues. Needs allow new industrial products to appear, but industrial products give rise to an even greater extent to new needs. A gigantic propaganda machine has been created to arouse these needs, which 'forces' people to buy with the help of the latest psychological insights. We are not here concerned with the business and economic aspects. We are interested in the human being as consumer and producer, and in his institutions – the State and society. Our brief glance at the present age allows us to recognise how clearly Meister and Pestalozzi had grasped this trail-blazing development. It is a process of tremendous significance, according to which man no longer leads, but is led and misled. It is a process, according to which man, with all his intellectual, spiritual and psychic needs, becomes an object. With him, all the human and organisational institutions (family, society, State), and life in general, also become the objects of economic systems. This development is commonly known by the blanket phrase 'the advance of civilisation'.

In order to avoid misunderstandings, it is perhaps necessary to mention at this point that man, society and State are the objects of economic production, manufacturing and marketing systems, in so far as managers and businessmen take the former's peculiarities into account and try to adapt these peculiarities in their own economic interest. This does not imply that we subscribe to historical materialism. We do not view the production, manufacturing and economic system as primary driving elements. Man with his mental and spiritual attitude is still the arbiter of his historical and cultural existence, even when he finds himself, as here, in a situation where he is treated partly as an object.

Let us return to the eighteenth century and pursue the discussion about luxury in the Aufmunterungs-Gesellschaft, thus enabling us to understand how in this century, which is often considered by historians as a rigid and dead period, the Zurich town and country inhabitants' attitude to life changed so much that the content and form of the institutions of Church and State were questioned. Just as people change their way of life when they establish their whole existence on a new non-agricultural base, so too the structure of society and State is changed when it rests on 'the points of watch-hands . . . on packs of silk and cotton'.

A nation that earns its living by agriculture and by dealing in coarse local produce – a nation, among which one finds many noble characters living simple lives in accordance with our old customs on their own property – a nation that has not yet been seduced beyond the bounds of moderation and restraint by the lengthy enjoyment of refined manufactured products, such a nation is in a quite different situation to a commercial state, in which the pursuit of an injurious industry has turned a thousand seductive pleasures into essential necessities through the power of habit and custom, and where the feeling for simplicity and innocence has been altogether removed from the range of domestic duties.[84]

The new attitude to luxury is an instructive illustration of how industrialisation had changed social conditions. People could no longer treat the new needs (for luxury and ostentation) with hostility, because they had become factors upholding the State. The people who acknowledged this fact found it all the harder to do so, being conscious of their responsibilities and quite incapable of approving the 'emancipation of the flesh'. They were only too aware of the 'Demon of luxury'[85] and dedicated pages to depicting the 'decadence of ostentation' as a 'principal source of the great ruin of the nation'[86] – despite all this, these educators of the people were then obliged to recognise that luxury was necessary and consequently good:

and so as ostentation formed the national character of the population for the needs of our national industry, it also preserved the fatherland and increased the number of hands needed by it as the tools of its manufacturing zeal – since it causes the population of the State to increase naturally, in relation to the sum of the earnings it casts at the people.[87]

Even the anonymous prize-winner had to admit the utility of ostentation, 'which is not in itself harmful, neither to the person who engages in it, nor to the rest of society', for the good of the people. It would be

highly unwise to forbid such ostentation, which has become a rich source of livelihood for many hard-working men and women burghers; it would be nothing other than cold-bloodedly to drive one's fellow citizens into shameful poverty and even to rage in a truly imprudent manner against one's own blood; since so easily could it happen in our Free State that the descendants of those who have participated in the present legislation, would be happy if in their needy condition, they were able to seek their livelihood in those very sources which their forefathers had so recklessly stopped.[88]

This drastic representation illustrates what we described at the beginning of the discussion about luxury as a tragic conflict, in which the Church and the authorities were caught up. The laws regulating ostentation, and the intellectual attitude of the Church and the authorities upholding them, no longer had any value since they involved 'raging against one's own blood'. Michael Bösch described this inner conflict in a speech to the 'Reformed and Moral Society' of Toggenburg:

And – the over-all earnings, which the (in this sense serviceable) cotton manufacture has brought to our country, bring in an enormous profit every year, but the immoral use which our nation makes of this advantage plunges many a patriot into embarrassment, as to whether he should desire its progress or rather its diminution, with regard to the best outcome and happiness for our fatherland.[89]

How did our three prize-winners solve the conflict between idea and reality, and what can we deduce from it for the purpose of our enquiry?

It is just as difficult 'to eradicate the abuses of wealth and all the monstrous forms of luxury', Meister acknowledges, as it is to 'kill every snake head on a Hydra'.[90]

That which their fathers, with their simple ways, found agreeable, pleasant and refreshing is being supplanted by the needs and ways of a more refined age – and it is impossible, in a small commercial state, to set limits on its principal money-earning inhabitants and, against the surge of general fashion, the similar wealth in the whole of Europe, to accept those pleasures of life which are lawful and proper to their station.[91]

Any discussion about 'limiting ostentation', according to Pestalozzi, must take into account 'that once the base of ostentation firmly established since human memory by the wealthier inhabitants has been woven into the needs, into the source of earnings and the professions, of the common inhabitants – one may not noticeably limit this firmly established base without committing an injustice against the common man'.[92] All three prize-winners employ these sorts of arguments (including the one about the function of luxury in a commercial State mentioned above) to denounce unanimously the existing laws against finery and ostentation.[93] But when it came to asking what should replace them we detect a certain amount of unmistakable embarrassment. Meister believed that luxury ought to 'be governed on the one side by skill and hard work, on the other by taste and wisdom, and so may it distribute blessings over families and the state'.[94] Pestalozzi formulated it in similar unspecific and platonic terms: 'and is it not clearly true, at least where indulgence in ostentation is concerned, that real help is to be hoped for only from the re-establishment of the wiser spirit of our constitution, earnestly concerned for the general and pure blessing of the home?'.[95]

Their embarrassment about suggesting concrete alternatives was derived on the one hand from the dilemma mentioned above, and on the other hand from the ambiguity of the existing legislation about ostentation. These laws had been devised to counter luxury not only in the meaning of the Reformation, but also with the purpose of limiting it according to a person's social station. Were these laws to be removed, then the limits set by the authorities, which had regulated the outward appearance of the different social stations, would collapse with them. Could the 'earnestly concerned spirit of our constitution', could 'wisdom and taste' really preserve the traditional clothing of each social station? The anonymous writer's solution was to allow the different stations to regulate ostentation themselves:

A truly wise and paternal government divides the whole body of citizens into as many classes as required by the different stations, trades and degrees of wealth. Each class of citizens would then decide, through its own leadership, its own laws about ostentation, since no class can dictate to another in this matter. These ordinances on ostentation would then be examined by a special state commission, and afterwards, if found to be beneficial, to be authorised by the government.[96]

His suggestion that the classes should protect themselves is enlightening because it shows how much the process of industrialisation had destroyed the social order both inwardly and outwardly. The writer was no longer able to employ the term 'Stand' (station) and had to replace it with 'bürgerliche Classe' (civic classes). These classes were distinguished according to three criteria, according 'to the different stations, trades and degrees of wealth'. However much our anonymous author wanted to divide the classes along traditional lines of thought, this was now unrealistic, since a dynamic and non-static element had been introduced along with money and wealth. If we look at the author's definition of luxury, it becomes clear how much the emphasis has shifted: luxury means 'the sort of ostentation engaged in by a person either from a desire for finery or from acquiring airs above his station and means'.[97] Whether knowingly or unknowingly his formula 'station and means' couples the old way of thinking with the burning new issue. Money has become a factor which determines class, as Meister expressed it: 'the more commercial a state becomes, the more wealth is valued, and the less nobility'.[98] We are standing at the beginning of a complete shift of emphasis, which can be exaggeratedly formulated as follows: if previously a man's station determined his degree of luxury, now his degree of luxury determines his station.[99]

We have used this contemporary discussion about luxury to try to place the food and dress of the industrially employed country people in a wider context. In his work about *The Swiss Farmer in the Age of Early Capitalism*, C.G. Schmidt demonstrates that in the eighteenth century even peasant thought was infiltrated by this spirit of the age.[100] The raised expectations of the factory population also made themselves felt in other spheres of life.[101] The discussion about luxury reveals that people's heightened needs were accompanied by an emergent desire for culture, a desire which we should see among the rural outworkers as well. We should not be misled in this by any of the complaints and admonishments by the ministers and other commentators: the outworker proclaimed by means of his new life style that he was open to the intellectual and cultural currents of the age. That he was on the receiving end of many of these currents was in accordance with his traditional way of behaviour.

The importance of the carriers and the clothiers as transmitters of urban luxury and cultural goods was paramount. These country inhabitants who had grown rich in the cotton manufacture had their own specific problems. As subjects they lacked the political and economic rights of the town burghers, but their profession and their possessions gave them many opportunities for participating in the intellectual and cultural life of the town. They tried to conceal their hybrid status by means of large town-style houses, showy expenditure, education and fine manners. They became the countryside's most important transmitters of urban life style. Salomon von Orelli characterised this section of the population with a trace of the town burgher's supercilious pride in his caste as follows (he is thinking in particular of the clothiers of Wädenswil):

The manufacturers distinguished themselves blatantly from the peasants, both in their work and in their manner of life, by their weekly, often daily traffic with the town, bringing urban fashions and habits, preferably the least tasteful of these, back to their villages; they went about dressed in the fashion of the town. Since only few of them actually grew their own food, their table was also spread differently to the peasants' tables. Their favourite food was fresh meat and they learnt to like and prepare tasty dishes in the town's taverns, which they frequented. Distinguished from the peasants by their town-burgher clothes and life style, they considered themselves truly more distinguished than them, in spite of being themselves not very much respected by them on account of this; since they, imitating the town gentlemen and strolling up and down with a bamboo cane, no less, in their hands, were nicknamed *Stekenherren* (stick gentlemen)[102] and *Langpfeifler* (long pipers) due to their using English pipes, by the peasants. When elegant folk in the towns laid their sticks aside, considering them props suitable only for helpless old men, the manufacturers also put their clean bamboos away in their coffers. When bowler hats became the fashion in town, the manufacturers adopted them too, and had to put up with their neighbours' nickname of *Rundhütler* (round hatters), casting *grober Baurenflegel* (rough peasant louts) at them in return. The show-offs among them also used words in a distinctive way; they happily appropriated

French words which they picked up somehow in town, and then frequently introduced into general currency in sadly mutilated form.[103]

This is not yet the moment to investigate the clothiers as the representatives and transmitters of cultural and intellectual goods and to correct Salomon von Orelli's class-bound assessment. Salomon Schinz bears witness to their important role as go-betweens, a source which also provides us with a clue about the distance, in terms of culture, fashion and luxury, between the lake regions and the Oberland: 'Only a few of the manufacturers themselves amassed significant wealth for themselves from their frequently abundant profits. Their pleasure lay in giving themselves airs and living well at home and on their business journeys. In this and in their fine clothes transplanted from the lake, their workers imitated them faithfully.'[104]

The clothiers and their role as go-betweens serve to move our theme on from discussing life to discussing communal life – to the social life of the country people employed in industry. The two themes are connected organically, since food, clothes and life style have to be viewed in the theatre of life. By which we mean not only the local and geographical space, but also the living space bound to patterns of the economy and of settlement, to which all human interaction is tied. Under the Ancien Régime the town and country inhabitants were divided from one another not just by the town walls; besides the various regulations about settlement there were also differences of station, and of politics and wealth, all of which stamped the rural living space and area of settlement. Thus the separate legislation ruling the countryside also determined its reception of urban life styles and the social life of those country people who worked in industry.

We introduce this section with some general reflections which relate mostly to technical aspects connected with the organisation of manufacturing work.

Spinning and weaving work, being by its nature non-agricultural, means that the celebrations and customs of the agricultural working year end by losing their meaning and importance for the industrially employed population. This affects in particular those circles owning no property or land. The agricultural working year is determined by the rhythm of nature. When nature sleeps, the farmer's work also ceases for a while, and it is only as nature stirs again that the countryman tills the fields, and his heavy tasks commence. The agricultural working year is introduced by the spring festivals; once all the provisions have been stored it ends with the harvest celebrations. We saw in Chapter 1 how much the fates of the unpropertied poor villagers were bound before industrialisation to the rhythm of this agricultural year of work and feasts. As farm-labourers, they did not only participate in the farmers' feasts and joys, but they also endured all the hardships of winter, when there was no work to do. The farmers' seasons of work and of feasting, with their respective dominant interests, were the same as the poor day-labourers'.

However, once the poor villagers' lives 'hung only from threads of cotton, which they spin or weave',[105] the farming year lost its interest and importance for them. The monotonous work of spinning or weaving, independent of the changing seasons of the year, meant that their year was no longer split up into specific parts. When people's dominant interests and rhythm of work alter, the traditional rural calendar of feasts also loses its significance. So they looked for new opportunities for interrupting their dreary everyday lives with eating, drinking, dancing and card games in company. It was the monotony and tedium of cottage industry which brought on the need for periodic relaxation and conviviality. The outward pretext for this inward need was furnished by the industrial system of payment, which occurred periodically after completion of a specific work load.

This first technical aspect of the work gives rise to a second, which must be taken into account as we consider and assess the outworkers' social life. Since industrialisation meant that many of the Oberland inhabitants no longer took part in agricultural work, the places and opportunities for meeting up, whether at work or on feast days, also changed. For instance, people no longer joined in the high-spirited procession of hay-makers, reapers and grape-pickers, whose progress to and from work was always associated with a spirit of holiday gaiety.[106] Industrialisation turned the spinning shops and places into the centres of everyday social life – gatherings which knew no fixed seasons. This non-agricultural work also altered neighbourly relations. People had less need of their neighbours' material and human assistance (the weavers more often than the spinners), and consequently far greater need of their company and conversation during the monotonous work process. Neighbourly ties became freer, loosed from material ties, but more intimate on a human and social level.

For the third technical aspect of the work, we must take another look at the system of payment in the putting-out industry. What has been said about the money economy and its influence on traditional clothing and diet also applies to social life. Food and clothes are after all important elements of social life. Salomon von Orelli wrote about the lake parishes:

The transformation of the houses and clothes was also closely bound up with a change in people's life style. For a while during the lifetime of the first earners everything to do with the daily household arrangements remained much as it had been previously, but when friends, relatives and neighbours came to visit, it was no longer good enough to give them a glass of wine or a slice of ham, with which the people in the country cottages wearing peasant dress would have felt richly entertained; the table had to groan under the weight of baked, boiled and roasted foods. People honoured their guests by treating them like ravenous gobblers.[107]

The change to their feeding habits must, as we see, be associated with their social life; life and community formed an organic whole. We will discuss the commercialised meeting places (taverns, grocers' shops) which emerged as people thought increasingly in terms of the money economy.

These remarks are somewhat previous, but their fundamental significance will be revealed. In their general and theoretical form, however, they are misleading, because they set the new non-agricultural elements in the outworkers' community far too much in the foreground. We must avoid doing this, since many customs and practices, which contemporary critics have blamed on the industrial population, belonged to the realm of peasant tradition. The outworkers still adhered not only to the new but also to the thoroughly old forms of community. We emphasised in the last chapter how the form of courtship known as *Kiltgang* was in no sense a usage (or abusage) engaged in exclusively in cottage industry circles. Industrial earnings merely provided a further section of the population with the material preconditions which allowed them to express their willingness to get married in this customary way. By basing their existence on the putting-out industry, the circle of participants was broadened, putting new life into the ancient practice, whose form and content adjusted to the altered circumstances. We can take these comments even further: the traditional practices engaged in by unmarried peasants contain social forms, which were predestined to be taken over by country people employed in industry. This applies in particular to the gatherings of unmarried boys and girls in the *Lichtstubeten* (lighted rooms).

The *Lichtstubeten* undoubtedly go back to pre-industrial times, and the institution was strongly underpinned by youth culture. The minister of Egg complained in his visitation report of 1675 of 'the oftentimes forbidden and frequently abolished *Lichtstubeten* and *Scheidweggen*, and the nightly misdoings which they give rise to: unbridled night-time wantonness and tumult by the young lads'.[108] The minister of Wyla wrote in 1699 that

the prohibited *Lichtstubeten* in suspected houses, or where there is no proper father of the household, cannot be prevented in several places, although they are the cause of the ruin of the young people, and lead to all sorts of pretentious talk inciting them to shameful deeds, and many secret sins are committed; but it is a sad shortcoming that the church elders report very little of this.[109]

Two worlds meet in this complaint: on the one hand the minister as a town burgher and representative of the ecclesiastical authorities' moral order, on the other hand the church elders, who had in their youth themselves taken part in the *Lichtstubeten* and who knew that the community of the unmarried would never allow their traditional rights to be discontinued. Also, anyone ill-advised enough to put a halt to their pre-marital practices ran the risk of having his land and property damaged.[110] Those ministers, church elders and their ilk who pursued their official duty and reported wrongdoers were subjected to a punitive raid by the youths.

The Innkeeper of Dorlikon had his windows smashed in [1688] because he would not allow card playing. In Ötelfingen [1701] nobody dares to oppose excursions to Baden on Sundays any more, for fear of the Night Boys' revenge. Indeed, the treasurer was badly caught, who was suspected of having reported the young people, on account of which his fence of 225 posts was torn down, 15 of them broken, and 8 cords of wood thrown off a wall onto the ground.

This whole complex of peasant customs and the circle practising them, the community of the unmarried, was supremly important to the rural community, with its own legal and customary moral order. The question now arises as to how these traditional forms of community were changed by the progress of industrialisation. How did the unmarried outworkers respond to this practice?

Hedwig Strehler has kept closely to the sources in her description of the *Lichtstubeten* as part of the community life of the younger generation. It leads us to ask how this traditional form of peasant conviviality was suited to the outworkers' manner of working and living. 'The greatest ruin of the young folk who rove around at night time are the prohibited *Licht-* or *Kunkelstubeten*. By this is not meant so much the rooms where people gathered together on account of their spinning work in order to save a bit of light, but all the various nightly gatherings, which are arranged for the sake of all kinds of exuberance' (visitation reports of the Zurich Lake Chapter 1697). 'In the evening, when the sun is setting, the cattle returning from the field home to the stall, and the birds in the wood are falling silent, man alone in his foolishness acts against nature and the general order' (Winterthur Chapter 1696). 'The young unmarried fellows rush around the lanes emitting horrible yells and yodels, whistling and shouting' (Regensberg Chapter 1703). 'They meet up in the *Lichtstubeten*, after sending their parents out of the house, after which they spoil and gobble up everything' (Glattfelden 1692). The minister of Egg and Oetwil (1685) has the most complaints about the *Lichtstubeten*, which are held by the unbridled youth in 'two places in his parish and daughter parish in Stäfa this winter: the first at Föllikon, by a good fifty-two persons, the other in Carmützlen, and this last on the night of the earthtremor, when this miserable company, notwithstanding being reminded by this sign of God's anger, still stayed together until ten o'clock'.[111]

Hedwig Strehler's source references reveal how much of her information came from exclusively agricultural regions. Even before industrialisation, hemp and flax spinning must have provided an excuse for taking part in *Lichtstubeten*. Indeed, the fact that gatherings of this kind were also called *Kunkelstubeten* (distaff rooms) is suggestive: this expression could scarcely have been first coined when people started spinning for the putting-out industry. It is now clear that the traditional rural institution of *Lichtstubeten* represented a form of social life, which also suited unmarried cottagers' way of working. It almost seemed as if the institution had been created for the working practices of the cottagers. The unmarried outworkers, both boys and girls, would bring their spinning wheels or spindles along and so combine work with pleasure in the company of their friends.

One might now be tempted to say that the *Licht-* and *Kunkelstubeten* became *Spinnstuben* (spinning parlours) with the advent of industrialisation. But this was not the case. *Lichtstubeten* should not be compared with spinning parlours. The participants in the *Lichtstubeten* formed a closed circle of friends. Only confirmed and unmarried persons, who had been accepted into young people's circles, were allowed to take part in them. In 1775 the governor of Grüningen prohibited on pain of a 25 *Pfund* fine 'the displeasing recruitment of young people, as soon as they have gone up to Communion for the first time, to the ranks of the night rovers, which is common in a few places'.[112]

The *Lichtstubeten* differed from the usual spinning parlours, not only because of the way their members were recruited but also by their adherence to specific meeting days. As with the *Kiltgang*, for instance, which could take place only on specific weekdays (Tuesdays, Thursday, but particularly Saturday and Sunday), and the other days were avoided,[113] so too the *Lichtstubeten* were traditionally only held on these days.

However, most of the pranks, unruliness, mischievous and shameful deeds were committed by the young people in the two nights of Saturday and Sunday . . . Then there is no end to their ramping and raging. Soon there will be no wicked business which will not have been started in the nights before or after Sunday, so that in total these are the nights when the most sins are committed [Regensberg Chapter 1704].[114]

Besides the *Licht* nights there were also the traditional feast days of the ecclesiastical year, which were celebrated with *Lichtstubeten* by the young people. In *7×7 Years*, Jakob Stutz describes the Shrove Tuesday practices during his youth in Hittnau. In the evening, he tells us, a *Lichtstubete* would be held in someone's house, and everyone would have to pay an entrance fee of a shilling. Stutz recalled the 'immoral games' which took place there with horror.[115]

Given their function as meeting places for unmarried young, the *Lichtstubeten* were certainly no schools for virtue in the sense of the ecclesiastical authorities' moral order. All the games and diversions at such gatherings, where future marriage partners met one another, were shot through with erotic significance. We have heard that people's willingness to get married increased with industrialisation. The population employed in industry made use of the ancient form of courtship of the *Kiltgang*, which by its very nature required some sort of control by the young people's circles. The need for '*Lichtstubeten* and other similar wanton gatherings at day and night time' grew with the expansion of the putting-out industry. No material ties and no parental prohibition (especially where *Rastgeben* was customary) kept the young unmarried outworkers away from such undertakings. So the *Lichtstubeten*, like the *z'Licht go*, were given a new lease of life by the possibility of living off the putting-out industry, and the young people's groups still retained their function as 'representatives of the social and festive life of the community' under the living conditions of cottage industry.[116] The practice of being forced to do the honourable thing, *zu Ehren ziehen*, is a measure of the young people's ability to enforce moral justice.[117] Unfortunately we possess no clues as to whether the industrialisation of the Zurich countryside led the unmarried outworkers to form separate groups of their own. This may well have been the case, since the putting-out workers with their earnings disposed of different means and ways of arranging their meetings and undertakings. The function of the *Lichtstubeten* as marriage bureaux meant that some form of differentiation must have been applied when selecting the participants, although the division between peasant and cottage industry groups could not have been clear cut.

We will not be mistaken in supposing that many contemporary critics, who condemned the morals and habits of the country people working in industry, muddled the *Lichtstubeten* up with the spinning parlours. This meant that industrialisation was blamed for things for which it cannot be held responsible, since the town burgher's social station and his education often prevented him from seeing conditions in the countryside clearly. We will investigate the spinning parlours later on, as the theatres of a specifically cottage industrial social life. We want first to shed a little light on the country people's traditional diversions, since they formed the raw material of country sociability and fun even after industrialisation, and cottage workers as well as countrymen took part in them. Whenever we hear of such diversions, we come across youth culture elements. The *Sabbath and Moral Ordinances for the Countryside* of 1650, for instance, sums them up for us under the rubric

all kinds of other mischief, perversion and depravity collected together: and so we find, as formerly, the bold finery and fripperies of Shrove Tuesday nights and such like, including pancake night (*Küchli holen*): Shrove Tuesday and Slaughtering Sunday carnivals; the shameless New Year, including the frequent singing in the round (*das Ring singen*) which takes place from time to time, mostly during summer, in the streets; rope skipping, which spreads out into our countryside, again, particularly on Sundays. Night-time wanderings and mischief in the lanes by young folk, lads and daughters: the *Lichtstubeten* and other similar wanton gatherings day and night, including the *Weidstubeten*; running and turmoil on Ascension Day on the Kolbenhof and Hütli mountain; unnecessary summons to go to Baden on Christmas Eve.[118]

The wood, garden, meadow and shrub *Stubeten* gave rise again and again to complaints. 'On Sundays, large crowds of young people run to the woods, the barns, the meadows and the common land to dance and jump about there. Then they go on to eat and drink excessively and to engage in other immoderate things.'[119] 'Boys with long war-tresses' come along 'dressed in all sorts of silk ribbons, feathers and coloured neckerchiefs ... but the girls' bodices are much too small, showing too much bosom, and their skirts are so scandalously short they scarcely reach down to their knees.'[120] It is a custom with them that 'on Sundays whole troupes of them move into other parishes, to visit the Sunday school indeed, but also getting involved in all sorts of mischief along the lanes and in the woods'.[121]

The law against dancing on Sundays was lifted after the Helvetic Revolution (1798), and when the marriage courts were established again in 1803 dancing was tacitly tolerated. It was only in 1815 that 'the truly ruinous dancing on Sunday is restricted to eight Sundays in the year'.[122] The young people were at the centre of every form of diversion and festivity and their enthusiasm gave rise to complaints by the authorities. They came together at weddings 'including those who were not invited' and spent 'the whole night until the morning light in rioting, yelling and shouting'.[123] It was also rumoured 'that in various places on wedding nights the bride and bridegroom are serenaded by the young people with unpleasant and wanton songs'.[124]

Complaints about cards and dice games were no less vociferous, as well as those about playing bowls on Sunday.[125] The records of the parish supervisory board for Wald of 30 June 1754 report

that the young boys, minors, play bowls for shillings and sixpences and often fester at it, and will not be dissuaded from it . . . because they tend to go on well into Whit Monday and end in blows for everything gets very out of hand, in future they are not to play for longer than till Whit Sunday and be made to observe good order and silence.[126]

On Sunday 24 April 1760 Heinrich Hess killed fourteen-year-old Caspar Lätsch, 'by throwing a fatal bowl at him', for which he was, 'with the authorities' consent', placed on 1 June 1760 beneath the pulpit and preached to about Joshua XX verses 1, 2, 3 and thereafter given a talking to in front of the honourable church elders.[127]

The rural inhabitants' party mood tended to brim over especially during local market days, which were visited from far and wide, on days of solemn church celebrations and review days. The minister of Wald remarked in his minutes of the parish supervisory board for 22 August 1752 that he had received a letter from governor Stokar of Grüningen, in which he complained about the poor summonses by the parish elders, particularly on *Kilbi* (Fair) Sunday and on the Review day. 'All elders have to admit that on *Kilbi* Sunday and at the Review things went badly, with drunkenness, blows, violence, shouts, shooting, calling the hours and drumming.'[128]

This selection from the colourful sequence of country diversions shows us that the arm of the ecclesiastical authorities' moral laws was too weak to curb the vital strength of the young folks, which, as the upholders of the festive and social life of the community, disrupted their order. The bands of young people regulated community life according to their own morals and habits. Their enthusiasm could not be contained by prohibitions. They were constantly meeting up in secret *Schlupf- Spiel- und Trinkwinkeln* (hide-outs for playing cards and drinking). Johann Kaspar Escher, governor of Kyburg (1717–23) acknowledged that the authorities' order with its puritanical strictness was itself responsible for these secret goings-on:

On account of the authorities' *Buss-Mandat* (Peace Ordinance) our country people have been forbidden all forms of public recreation, although shameful things seldom occur in public gatherings, and the *Societas Civilis et Ejus harmonia* is thereby more upheld than harmed. But since this is not understood, and public dancing, bowling and fairs and other such diversions have been completely forbidden to the young people, they seek after secret pleasures, and sit in hidey-holes to play and to engage in all sorts of wantoness in chambers, thickets and the like.[129]

In the sections about diet, clothes and luxury we learnt about the growth of the cottage workers' needs. This trend was reflected in social intercourse as well: 'The poorer the lower classes are, the more desirous they are to earn more money and live well . . . They avoid hard forms of work, and while they used to work gladly on their farms both before and after work, this time is now dedicated to idleness and good living.'[130] More and more *Winkelwirtschaften* (unlicensed pubs) emerged as earnings from the putting-out industry increased. 'The abundant earnings have rendered a large part of these people debauched and gluttonous, given over to frivolity and licentiousness. Dives, taverns and pubs are open day and night in order to restore their low spirits and keep them good humoured.'[131] There were also bath rooms heated by the bread ovens called *Brodstübli* which were eagerly patronised by the outworkers and gave constant 'rise to all sorts of indecent and grievous things'.[132]

The discussion about luxury revealed that the ecclesiastical authorities' traditional repudiation of ostentation by the common people was no longer shared by a circle of citizens conscious of their responsibility. This may also be observed in their evaluation of country pleasures, an instructive example of this being *The Sensible Village Minister* by Johann Heinrich Heidegger, a *Reading Book for Country Clergy and Farmers.*[133] Heidegger's type of sensible village minister did not try to repress the country people's diversions with zealous puritanical severity. 'I wish very much to live among merry people' he says to the school-master. He is not pleased about the way a few of the villagers leave at the end of the Sunday service to drink in the neighbouring villages' wine bars, and to spend their money on wine and games, often getting involved in quarrels and fights. So he says to the school-master, that the minister wants to make his people merry. – But I think that it is also happiness to meet the many difficulties of life with joyful courage, which sweetens many bitter hours.' The next day, the minister called the carpenter to his house 'and he set up two oaken posts with iron hooks, then four finished trestles and as many smooth-planed planks fifteen feet long, and bought two sets of skittles. The following Sunday he astonished his parish with this bowling pleasure court.' The school-master hung the pitching device in the rings and set up the game of bowls. 'Come along, dear children!' called the shepherd of souls 'have a right merry time here'. Now the playing and pitching begins, and bowls are tossed by all who want to. And so it went on every Sunday and the young lads got used to no longer going out of the village to drink wine. However, the sensible village minister went a step further and introduced 'village celebrations at certain days of the year', and allowed a *Tambourin* to come in from a neighbouring village, who played merry dances with his pipe and drum. All the folk were merry at these 'public enjoyments', but, since the minister was present, they were never 'wanton or rude'. On rainy days the minister let them all into the schoolroom. 'People generally sing psalms or religious songs from Zollikofer's collection; then the minister reads out a newspaper and explains it to the people, he also reads things to them out of books, which are useful for housekeeping or for the countryman.'

This theory of Johann Heinrich Heidegger's concerning the happiness of the common people[134] is of a local nature, but may be considered as a manifestation of a general European intellectual current. We are not discussing here how far Heidegger's picture of the sensible village minister is programmatic, or whether it is derived from real examples.[135] It is the mental historical phenomenon as such which interests us: the intellectual foundations of the existing moral order were shattered even before the Helvetic Revolution blew up the statutes in force from outside.

It would now be appropriate to continue our theme by placing alongside the traditional forms of rural sociability, to which the industrialised regions of the Zurich countryside still adhered and which they expanded still further with their money economy, other, new forms of social life which were breaking into the community. But this is not possible. We have to break off the threads and first learn about other elements of social life in the country. Unfortunately, we cannot avoid breaking the thread of continuity in our attempt to present the whole life of a section of the population which based its existence on spinning wheel and weaving loom.

The outworkers' work places must be briefly examined, in so far as they were important to the social life of the community. Spinning work should obviously be distinguished from weaving work; until the beginning of the nineteenth century the Oberland outworkers were mostly employed at spinning work. The mountainous part of the Grüningen and Kyburg districts was described by J.C. Hirzel:

Besides these different branches of agriculture, for many years now the large earnings in the factories have predominated, so that in these mountains everything is teeming with cotton spinners, and when one has laboriously climbed a steep mountain, one often finds oneself next to houses with ten to twenty cotton wheels in full movement standing outside them, being worked by a cheeky populace.[136]

Hirzel was here describing the spinning area in a hamlet typical of the scattered Oberland settlements. All the inhabitants of the hamlet who were employed in spinning work would gather together in a sociable working group, which would be joined even by those neighbours who lived far away. Depending on the time of year and the weather they would meet up in the usual and familiar places, whether in the shelter of a cottage, or on a warm and sunny hillside, or in the cool shade of a wood. Their common putting-out work created social centres for their everyday life together. It was not just the people living in hamlets and on farms who enjoyed working together; these sorts of spinning places also existed in the villages. 'Just as people in those days had spinning parlours for the winter' wrote Jakob Stutz of Hittnau 'so there were also spinning places in the open for the summer. In our little village there were two, one at the back side and one at the front, and both near a stream.'[137] Two places for spinning were typical of village life with all its quarrels. These spinning parlours and places became, alongside the taverns, the little grocers' shops and other vital services, the most important centres of life in the community. It was not only the spinners who met up at these places but peddlars, peep-show men, itinerant actors, pilgrims, messengers and travellers all preferred to rest in such entertaining and pleasant places.[138] Children would tumble all over them or eavesdrop on their elders' conversation. Little Jakob Stutz was attracted 'strongly to the spinning places just as he was to the spinning parlours'. His works provide us with the most telling portrayals of life and work in the spinning parlours and places. The tone was set by the female element, and so it was quite natural that 'mostly village tales were told and every household was picked over in every possible way'. People complained about the times, grumbled against the authorities and criticised the passers-by. Spinning parlours and places were really story-telling circles, in which the treasury of traditional tales in all its forms was exhibited and absorbed. Sagas, fairy-tales, ballads, farces, jokes and scandals, etc., were told over and over again. Stutz provides enough examples of this in his autobiographical work and in his *Gemälde aus dem Volksleben* (*Pictures from the Life of the Common People*).[139] Johann Schulthess said of the outworkers that 'their thoughtless gossip and the like has become so sweet and dear to them that any better course soon becomes unbearable to them for lack of it'.[140]

As well as gossip and story-telling, songs were frequently sung.

Even now I hear those loud songs of the psalms, religious and worldly songs, which were intoned on beautiful summer evenings, when the spinner-girls were still spinning by moonlight and the boys and girls of the little village would gather around them and, picking a leaf from the nearby peartree and holding it to their lips, would entice sweet tones from it and so join in the singing. O, how I loved to listen and how happy I felt to be there!

wrote Jakob Stutz about his youth. They sang *Schönster Abendstern* (*Most Beautiful Evening Star*); *Wie nach einer Wasserquelle, ein Hirsch schreiet mit Begier* (*Just as a Deer Cries out in his Longing for a Source of Water*); *Anneli, wo bist gester gsi* (*Anneli, Where Were You Yesterday?*); *O Strassburg, o Strassburg*; *Lustig will ih jung noh bi* (*I Want to be Merry, Young I still Am*); *Es stoht ein Hus i der Este* (*There Stands a House in the Este*), etc. They would sing through the whole repertoire of songs during their busy spinning, both merry and sad ones, but mostly religious songs and psalms.[141] We will return briefly to the repertoire of songs available to them.

To this traditional treasury of stories and songs, the ghost stories, the chivalrous idylls, folk songs and psalms was added the young spinner-folk's reserves of fun. The mood and atmosphere of the *Lichtstubeten* must have emerged fairly frequently in the spinning parlours as well, when the company there allowed it. Stutz does not conceal this aspect 'I have now told about the better part of the spinning parlours, but must also say that religious and decent worldly songs were not the only songs sung there and lovely stories were not the only ones told there. Oh, there were at times some coarse songs sung and coarse things told.'[142] The psalms were replaced by jokes and games of forfeits and all sorts of tomfoolery.

Know too, that once one of the spinners secretly span a trip-rope across the threshold, and then stood in the doorway, waiting for the other companions. As they came up with their spinning wheels, he called out to them from far off 'Hurry up and come in; there's a New Year fiddler in the parlour; we're going to dance tonight, whatever the weather. Run, run!' That made the girls and boys step to it; everyone wanted to get there first. Three of them then tripped over into the room with their spinning wheels with such a dreadful crash that the people inside were so startled they nearly fainted.[143]

The spinning places served, particularly on Review days, as outdoor parties for the unmarried young. 'The spinning places were most lively on Review days, when the soldiers came home again. O, how the young and old spinner-girls laughed when they heard the soldiers from afar, yelling, singing and shooting.' There was an 'incessant rustling and titivating' among the girls until they turned up. As they arrived, the soldiers leaped in between the spinning wheels, and 'embraced the girls, sitting down with them on their chairs and engaging in all sorts of tomfoolery, while other comrades shot their bolts in every nook and cranny'.[144]

We have been able to provide a rapid portrait of the spinning parlours and places by following Jakob Stutz's vivid description, but we must remember that he is talking about a village in which domestic weaving had already made inroads. Many of the male outworkers were obliged as weavers to stay at home, working on their own at their looms and not taking part in the merry company of the spinners. Consequently, the female sex ruled the village spinning places even more strongly than was the case with the spinning places in the mountain hamlets and farms. The extent to which food, clothes and luxury not only provided important and ever-relevant matter for talk in the spinning communities, but also became elements contributing to the cohesion of the community, has been stressed elsewhere.

The spinners' custom of getting together in groups in order to alleviate the monotony of their work with entertainment, conversation, singing and joking, gave rise to endless complaints. Whenever the darker side of industrialisation was mentioned, the outworkers' working groups would be referred to in harsh terms. 'Where people of both sexes are always together in the warmth of the parlours and in summer in the shade to perform work which demands very little of their heads or their hearts,' they pass the time in talk 'which generally turns on good living, lewdness, betrayal and theft', and whoever 'reveals the smuttiest fancies thinks himself and others a hero.'[145] It cannot be denied that the conversation and entertainment in these spinning groups could sink to a rather uninspiring level and could be loaded with erotic tension, in so far as the members of a particular group allowed it to. In such cases the spinning parlours were scarcely distinguishable from the *Lichstubeten*. However, this immoral and erotic tone was not the rule, but was restricted to specific groups and associated with particular days and times of the day. We must also remember that the farming year also provided places and opportunities at which 'coarse songs were sung and coarse things spoken and done'. So it is revealing that the unedifying stories which little Jakob Stutz listened to in the spinning parlours were played out within the context of peasant life and work:

there were really colourful stories about the life of the reapers at harvest time, when the young men and girls moved out into the countryside. Once night fell, everyone, women and men folk, had to lie down together up on the hay-stack. But little enough sleeping was done. Yea, the whole night was spent in to-ing and fro-ing like at fair time.[146]

The complaint that these cottage industry working groups were damaging the morals and manners of children carried greater weight:

they are the easier seduced, in that the factory work makes so little demand on their spiritual or physical strength that it is considered by the common people to be idleness, and such children are mostly raised in large social groups, in weaving parlours or printing shops, or in spinning places, where the more wanton members easily mislead the others with their words and example. Unfortunately, the under-age children of poor parents may also be found in such gatherings, who have to assume the burdens of adulthood early on, and acquire the taste for such things which get more and more out of control and ruin their dispositions, since they miss out on school lessons and are removed from their parents' supervision and care. This evil is spreading wherever the *Rast* system is introduced.[147]

The possibility should not be dismissed that the stages of human life, which had until then been clearly demarcated by a variety of practices, were made more indeterminate by cottage industry. The common and uniform work could be done as well by a five-year-old child as by his father, mother and grandmother, and this removed the natural divisions between people of different ages and civil status, each performing their appropriate tasks. The children most strongly affected were those whose work meant they grew up too quickly in a world to which they were not yet supposed to belong. As we have seen, manifestations of the youth culture could not always be banned from the spinning parlours, and so the children learnt various things about the lives and longings of the unmarried, before they had received the Sacrament. The narrow closed circle of the unmarried was loosened and expanded by industrial work and industrial earnings.

Our portrayal of the social and community life of the outworkers has so far been somewhat stylised. The reality was more complicated. The different ways of life in the villages, hamlets and scattered farmsteads ought to be described individually, and we will try to make up for some of this in the next chapter. One decisive factor in the life of the community, with all the customs and practices this involved, was the form of the houses and settlements, from which conservative forces emanated.

The spinning parlours and places lead us to the traditional culture and mental attitude of the outworkers. Our task would now be to learn about the institutions which transmitted this culture to the rural inhabitants under the Ancien Régime, thus influencing their intellectual attitude: the churches and schools of the Zurich countryside. Given the framework of our study, it is not possible for us to dwell on this further, and we are obliged to refer the reader to the abundant literature on the subject, full of source materials.[148] The question we want to ask is how the outworkers reacted to the Church and the authorities' institutions: to what extent was the mental attitude of the country people employed in industry altered by the advance of industrialisation? To what extent did they free themselves from their intellectual straitjacket, forced on them up till then by Church and school, and arrive on their own or with the help of enlightened popular educators at a new culture, at an intellectual attitude, which was distinguished from that of their peasant neighbours?

The quarrels about the sittings in church have shown us how the rigid institutions of the country's churches directly affected religious life in the parish. The conservative church organisation was no longer able to withstand the pressure of population in the industrial regions, especially in the Oberland, with its scattered settlements where, by the eighteenth century, the distribution of churches no longer reflected the conditions there at all. Farms and hamlets had grown so much that they were often bigger than the village in which the church stood. Other churches were indeed built, but the organisation of the parish did not adapt to the altered conditions. The old arrangement whereby villages, hamlets and farmsteads were assigned to one parish church remained standing. Conrad Nüscheler remarked on these conditions in 1786:

At first, since there were only a few churches, all the villages which did have their own church had the neighbouring villages with no church of their own, as well as all the surrounding hamlets and farmsteads, directed and ordered to attend theirs. Since that time many churches have been built; so nowadays one sees whole villages obliged to travel one or one and a half hours to go to church, although other churches lie far closer to them, yea they often have even to walk past churches only half as far away. The result is that people only seldom go to church, nor can they send their children to Sunday school.[149]

The inability of the church parishes to adapt alienated the countryfolk employed in industry. In spite of being obliged to attend church services by the authorities, they did so irregularly.[150] The admission policy of the church parishes was not designed to strengthen their community ties from within, since the material restrictions of this admission policy were directed expressly against the unpropertied outworkers.[151]

Besides these outward circumstances determining the attitude of the industrially employed country population towards church and authorities, there were also inner circumstances. The outworkers' relationship with God the 'Creator and Preserver of all things' differed from that of their peasant environment. Under the terms of popular piety, the peasant struck a bargain with God: 'I go to church for you and you preserve my harvest from hail'[152] – but this did not apply to the outworkers. The factory workers, 'among whom the feeling of dependence on God was weaker',[153] were less afraid of the avenging God of the Old Testament than were the peasants.

Among those classes who eat their bread in the sweat of their brow one finds the most feeling for religion, simplicity, loyalty and probity. The feeling of their dependence on God, who makes the seed and the crops prosper, makes them more serious, firmer in character, and at the same time brings them closer to their Creator and Preserver of all things.[154]

Church-going was an important aspect of popular peasant piety; 'their traditional outward and purposeful interpretation of everything concerning church services as offerings to God'[155] did not suffer under the dual function of the Zurich State Church under the Ancien Régime. It did little harm to the peasants' religiosity when the authorities' ordinances were not only read out from the pulpit, but the church was also used for 'the usual selling and auctioning of pigs, old cows and other meat, not to mention snails, oil-presses, bath rooms, blood-letting and shooting days and any other ridiculous and unpleasant matters'.[156]

The outworker, with his new basis of existence, who saw his former relationship with God questioned, was forcibly more critical about traditional church-going. His relationship with God and Church was de-materialised. The formalistic State Church offered him no respite from his doubts, and instead her rigid dogma provided him with many opportunities for criticism. If the outworker did not simply turn away in dull indifference from everything to do with church religion, he relapsed into a melancholy search for a personal, living God independently of church religion. His work afforded him the time for considering religious questions and doubts, and he would discuss these matters with like-minded associates during their working day together. Religious discussions and arguments were among the usual subjects of conversation in the Oberland spinning parlours and places.[157] The life style of the Oberland Separatists provided a constant source of comparison for people searching for a new form of religious life. Indeed, all sorts of different religious sects fell on fertile ground in the industrial countryside of the Oberland and flourished. People's understanding of religion, as Johann Hirzel acknowledged, tended towards mysticism, to the disadvantage of true religion, particularly in the remoter regions and through association with Separatists and fanatical women. A mysticism which merged with the general belief in ghosts and superstition in a weird hodgepodge.[158] The religious boundaries of the Oberland contributed their bit towards ensuring that people's understanding about everything to do with orthodox religion remained weak and critical.

Although the Oberland outworkers' search for religious inspiration often found refuge in beliefs which did not form part of the Church's teaching, their religious and intellectual attitude was nonetheless broadly stamped with the spirit of the Zurich State Church. The country-dweller received all his knowledge and education from the hand of the Church. The schools were subordinate to the Church and the school-master was the minister's 'loyal servant and assistant'.[159] The Protestant desire to assist the faithful in reading Holy Writ provided the chief motive underlying school instruction. Everyone had to give proof of his ability to read before he was confirmed. Heinrich Escher, minister of Pfäffikon, provides a description of the country schools under the Ancien Régime in his synodal speech of 1774:

One cannot imagine anything more dismal than the way the country schools generally look. – Imagine a heap of little, coarse and ill-bred children who assemble every day in what is generally a sad and gloomy room, in order to spend a few hours howling and shrieking. They torture themselves and are tortured in an attempt to learn a few letters, and then to put them together and read them out. Amidst many threats and blows they achieve the ability to read something, recite a few psalms and prayers, with neither understanding nor insight; by the tenth or eleventh year, or even sooner, they leave the school, their minds and hearts still quite unformed, and in most villages, they are then left without any further instruction, apart from what they enjoy in the public catechism classes, which most of them have little desire to attend, because whenever they see the teacher take up his *Zeugnuss-buch*, they remember the threats and blows they had received when learning from these books in school. It will come as no surprise to anyone that such a youth gives rise to a people who are ignorant in respect of religious instruction and in other respects ill-bred.[160]

The educational material of the country schools of Zurich in the eighteenth century consisted almost exclusively of religious books. The most generally used were the *ABC-Täfelein*, the *Namenbüchlein*, the *Fragstücklein*, the big *Lehrmeister*, the Book of Psalms and the New Testament. Towards the end of the eighteenth century new teaching aids became available, such as *Gründlicher Unterricht zum Singen der Psalmen, Chorälen und Liedern. Zum Gebrauch der Lehrenden und Lernenden in den Schulen (Thorough Instruction in Singing Psalms, Hymns and Songs. For use by Teachers and Pupils in Schools)* (Zurich 1774): *Anweisung der lieben Jugend in den Schulen zu einem christlich-sittlichen, auch äusserlich wohl anständigen und höflichen Betragen (Directions to the Beloved Youth in the Schools in Christian and Moral, as well as Outwardly Upright and Polite Behaviour*) (Zurich 1774); *Christliche Lieder der vaterländischen Jugend besonders auf der Landschaft, gewidmet von Caspar Lavater* (*Christian Songs for the Youth of the Fatherland, particularly in the Countryside, Dedicated by Caspar Lavater*) (Zurich 1774); *Biblische Geschichte zum Gebrauch der Landschulen* (*Bible Stories for Use in the Country Schools*) (Zurich 1774); *Neyliche und kurzweilige Historien für Kinder* (*Novel and Exciting Histories for Children*) (Zurich 1774); *Sittenlehrende Erzählungen für die Land-Schulen* (*Stories with a Moral Lesson for Country Schools*) (Zurich 1777), etc.

The teaching aids of the Zurich country schools, which tell us so much about cultural history, and which formed the country-dwellers' intellectual and religious awareness and education, have up till now hardly been used as source material.[161] They formed the depository of traditional knowledge and belief, and people took them for the literal truth, as they did Revelation. Religion was threatened, war, inflation and pestilence were looming, the Oberlanders warned each other, when the old teaching aids were replaced in 1811 and the *Namenbüchlein* and the Catechism were cleansed of old grammatical and printing mistakes.[162]

Besides these sacrosanct teaching aids, the Oberlanders derived their spiritual nourishment above all from the *Erbauungsbücher* (books of edification). 'A household is seldom to be found,' Heinrich Escher wrote (1774) 'at least in those regions of the country which are known to me, in which there will not be found, apart from the Bible or the New Testament, a few books for special instruction and special edification, but particularly such books as are not best designed to encourage healthy understanding and true godliness.'[163] The treasury of psalms, of religious and secular songs, as well as the manifold forms of current oral tradition with its relevance to its surroundings, all served to round off the country-dwellers' traditional education.[164]

With regard to the social aspects of community life it was necessary, as with people's intellectual attitudes and their traditional education, to refer to forms faithful to tradition. These remained important until far into the nineteenth century as the sub-structure underlying the trail-blazing innovations. It was not just their belief in tradition and community which tied the rural subjects to a life bound up with traditional practices, but Church and State also impeded the advance of progress with the leaden weight of their laws. Nonetheless, the decisive turning point in the life of the common people and in popular culture in the Zurich countryside, one which determined the way matters have turned out nowadays, must be looked for in the eighteenth century. Our piecemeal picture of life and society requires filling in here. There are two interwoven processes which started to emerge in the eighteenth century: the traditional mentality broke away from the guardianship of the Christian Church and attempted to come of age by aspiring to a secularised education focussing on the things of this world. Hand in hand with this process, life in the rural communities managed to free itself from the traditional compulsion exercised by the local community with its comprehensive functions, and it split up into groups with specialised aims and interests, with new forms of community and community ties. While this process only germinated in the eighteenth century, it achieved its full flowering in the nineteenth century: the century of popular education and national unification. We will attempt to show just how closely these changes in traditional life were connected with industrialisation in the following pages.

Various disconnected threads in the narrative must now be resumed. We recognised the emergence of a desire for culture in the outworkers' need for luxury. The altered material needs of the country people employed in industry were supported by a corresponding mental attitude. The outworker's manner of life proclaimed his open attitude to intellectual and cultural trends. His material needs were accompanied by intellectual needs.

Johann Heinrich Pestalozzi saw the altered intellectual and material culture in the industrial regions of the Zurich countryside clearly:

For ages the Zurich burgher's education was far ahead of the countryman's, who soon found that in every clergyman educated in this town there dwelt a man, to whom innocence would cling like a child to his father. But these circumstances are no longer present and we should not close our eyes to the fact that the level of culture in the factory regions has brought the countryman in many ways closer to the burgher and even to the pastor. And nor should we conceal the fact that knowledge and culture are steadily dwindling in the towns: they have chained themselves to wealth in every branch of life as a result of the refinement of luxury . . . Wealth, Enlightenment, luxury and vanity have so changed conditions in the factory regions, that the educational institutions and legal dispositions, and the restrictions on trades, with which the old pastor-folk used to keep these regions quiet, are now absolutely inadequate for the present-day needs of this country . . . we can no longer live in the simplicity of this country's old makeshift manner of government.[165]

The process of which Pestalozzi is speaking had advanced furthest in the industrialised lakeside parishes. Their position near to the city, their involvement in transport activities and the presence of old-established vineyards favoured their development. We want briefly to pursue these changes, not only because the new intellectual attitude and way of life appeared most strongly here, but also because the ground has been prepared for us quite exceptionally well by Diethelm Fretz in his work *Die Entstehung der Lesegesellschaft Wädenswil* (*The Rise of the Wädenswil Reading Society*).

Two groups, distinguished from one another by their education and social station, must be named as transmitters of the new popular culture. The first was made up of an enlightened circle of town clergymen and burghers who wanted to make available to the countryman the fruits of knowledge born on a rationale and intellectual stream of thought in the Ascetische or the Öconomische Gesellschaft (Ascetic and Economic Societies). In its insights and efforts, this group was far ahead of the established order. In many respects it pointed the way for the second transmitter group, which we have already met. It was the rising social class of the clothiers, of whom Pestalozzi says that their respectability (*Ehrenfestigkeit*), their culture, industry and their economic and manufacturing strength surpassed those of the ordinary artisan burghers in the town.[166] While the enlightened town burghers saw their efforts as part of a mission to bring culture to the people, this was not the case with the clothiers. The latter were concerned with the questions arising from their involvement in the putting-out industry and which they tried to solve within the framework of community life in their villages.[167] Out of the old local communities there developed new social and educational circles; a progression which we will follow by taking the Wädenswil Reading Society as our example. The development of this educational institution may be seen as typical, though the educational institute as such is in many ways unique.

The first moves towards improving the education of the rural inhabitants beyond the level of the parish schools came about following the authorities' recommendation that group singing be introduced. Since the middle of the seventeenth century, the authorities had recommended 'night schools' to the country pastors 'and they were established all over the country by the end of the eighteenth century'.[168] They took place after school, between seven and nine in the evening, when school boys and girls and both single and married music lovers practised singing psalms (mostly on Saturdays and Sundays). It is obvious that the youth bands used these night schools for their own purposes, and, in spite of the school-masters' and church elders' vigilance, *ordinari allerhand Inkonvenzien*[169] (usually every form of disturbance) occurred. These Singing Schools could become 'the spores of modern work in the sphere of mental culture',[170] as long as the preconditions and requirements necessary for such a development were present. The example of the Wädenswil Singing School illustrates such a process in great detail. 'About forty years ago' (*c.* 1750), wrote Salomon von Orelli, 'the young people of both sexes would gather together in Wädenschwyl to practice singing psalms'.[171] In this *Singschule*, as it was called, people started off by singing from the usual collection of psalms and songs in Bachofen, Schmidlin, etc. But it would not stop there; 'In those big parishes it was easy to find someone who could accompany their simple vocal music with the 'cello or the violin . . . In order to gain entry to the Singing School, and because they were attracted by the novelty, many young people learnt the music, who would otherwise never have thought of so doing.'

The Singing Schools were given a further impetus, but in quite a different direction, when they were joined by the *Feldmusikanten* (military bands).

In order to be able to practise in something other than marches, the *Feldmusikanten* were brought into the Singing School . . . They made good progress; the psalms and holy songs now became too easy and they asked in the towns about the sort of music popular there; they managed to get some and tried it out until they got it right. At which point the humble name of 'Singing School' was scorned and its members accorded themselves the respectable title of 'Music Society', and when they heard that the townsfolk did not go to the 'Music Society' but to the concert, then the gentlemen and womenfolk of Wädenschwyl went to the concert every Sunday evening, to which they very politely invited the governors or other town worthies who might be visiting the place.

The first phase of development was over: the old Singing School had become a Music Society, taking its example from the town and keeping in step with the times. The former representatives of social life, the young people, were no longer the only participants in this process. The demands made on the members had become much too specialised for that. A new class of member, with refined aspirations, took over the leadership and determined the level of entertainment (we will get to know them later on).

A major milestone in the history of the Wädenswil Music Society, which grew out of the old Singing School, was the inauguration of their newly built church in 1767. The Wädenswil music-making circle was unable to find anything in the canon of contemporary music whose contents provided an adequate reflection of their 'unique undertaking and their self-conscious, exaggerated sense of celebration'.[172] So they set about creating their own celebration cantata. Johann Jakob Nägeli, the parish curate, wrote the book, and it was set to music by an unknown composer.[173] The composer arranged for the following instruments: two oboes, two trumpets, two violins, two violas, one bassoon, one contra-bass and two French horns. They were not satisfied with that, but borrowed 'an organ, a piano and many other instruments besides' from a town Music Society. They also brought in supplementary musicians from outside. The celebration was a great success. Guests from Zurich, Winterthur, Schaffhausen, etc., took part in it. On the Monday after the inauguration ceremony (24 August 1767) the celebration cantata had to be repeated. New performances were planned, but were prevented from the Zurich end, demanding the return of their instruments. Fretz interpreted the obstruction of these culturally first-rate concerts as

the indication of the Sovereign's concern to prevent each and every town practice from being transmitted ready-made to the countryside, because it had not grown up genetically from the natural needs of land and people, but as a ferment, and was much more likely to give rise only to unhealthy feverish mental states, instead of providing true recreation.[174]

However, as we saw, the Wädenswil Music Society and its celebration cantata did grow up 'genetically from the natural needs of land and people'. But not all the town burghers were able or willing to admit this. They did not acknowledge the intellectual maturity of the rural population.

The inauguration celebrations of the Wädenswil church must have stimulated its neighbouring lakeside parishes. A Music Society was formed in Stäfa, without any claim to having ever been a Singing School, as Salomon von Orelli reports. Their concerts were attended by town visitors as well. Salomon von Orelli reported on their activities that the Music Society in Stäfa aroused even greater respect than that of Wädenschwyl on account of its outside audience. It preened itself somewhat about this, but in a short time it also achieved the advantage of greater skill than the former and turned more to foreign compositions. I still remember, at the beginning of the seventies on the occasion of an inspection by the Highways Commission, how they were invited to an Opera Seria, which however was not given in honour of the committee members, but for a couple of young persons who were travelling abroad; a big barn was turned into a theatre and the serious opera acquired by various means the features of an opera buffa, but the music was performed pretty well, the experts said, and the musicians copied the bravado and affectations of the travelling virtuosos in a masterly manner.[175]

The celebration cantata for the inauguration of the Wädenswil church and the prevention of further performances by town intrigues shed a different light on the intellectual and cultural situation of the Zurich subjects. It was patently obvious that the urge for 'new-fangled modes of expression in life and culture'[176] was growing stronger. The town was the centre from which they all radiated, but the urban forms could not simply be taken over; the country was far too dominated by the urban authorities and the country inhabitant was divided from the town burgher by too many restrictions of a social, economic and political nature. Nevertheless – industrialisation was driving the process on. Obviously the rural inhabitants tried to master their agonising intellectual immaturity. They bestirred themselves to set up social and educational institutions from within their own community, in order to share in the spirit of the age through them. We must recognise that this development was spurred on by real desires. Mental and cultural needs grew out of the altered basic conditions of rural life and community. Urban forms of life and society not only could, but had to furnish their examples because the industrially employed population was connected to them both inwardly and outwardly. It is important to understand these problems within the context in which the industrialised regions of the Zurich countryside found themselves: the urge towards intellectual maturity, towards new forms of education and social life more appropriate to their living conditions, involved the rural inhabitants in a search for new forms of community and new community bonds. New wine requires new skins. The authorities limited themselves to issuing dispensations and prohibitions. It was only the 'popular educators and benefactors' (enlightened town burghers) who assisted the country subjects in their efforts with advice and actions.

In this situation we are all the more concerned with the driving forces, which grew up within the rural population itself. Diethelm Fretz has given these forces names and individualities. They were those persons

who, as mediators between the town textile master, the traders in raw products and finished fabrics, and the manufacturing countryside, directed the new local manufacture in every respect and led a whole train of persons behind them, whose services assisted the busy clothiers and carriers and their clients as they came and went. They made up the circle of innkeepers, messengers, grocers, bakers, milkmen, etc. . . . . The clothiers and their circle, the clan of the *Fabrikanten* with all their new-fangled ways, which bound them from behind to the textile workers, and from in front to the town, the only market for textiles, incorporated the strengths which were chiefly instrumental in determining the new Wädenswil's form of existence.[177]

We have already heard Pestalozzi's assessment of the rising social class of the clothiers. He recognised their awkward position and promoted 'purposeful male and female educational institutions, in accordance with the wealth and industry of the country', since it was beyond doubt that 'the manufacturer requires a different school to that of the beggar child, who weaves for him'. 'Moral Societies' should also be founded, to cater for the many aspirations of the Zurich subjects.[178]

The clothiers, carriers, provisioners, etc.,

both in regard to the acquisition and also to the application of the school learning permitted them, did not belong to the common run of the village population . . . Unlike the majority of the village population they disposed of a means of obtaining information and transmitting thoughts which was applied in the first place to imparting professional instructions, but which otherwise rendered these people generally adept at picking up and evaluating ideas from their reading.[179]

The normal education of a town burgher was barred to the clothiers and there were no educational institutions in the country (apart from the parish schools). So they had no option but to broaden their horizons and satisfy their thirst for knowledge through self-education. In 1769, Jakob Breitinger (a professor at the Carolinum) was already surprised and displeased to find 'that in some parishes along the Zurich Lake people are to be found busily learning French', which was, in his opinion, only 'so as to be able to read Voltaire and similar writings'.[180]

The clothiers' hunger for education and books cannot be explained merely in terms of their particular educational situation. The passion for reading was an eighteenth-century phenomenon, which resulted in book shops, lending libraries and reading circles being established. In Zurich, Heinrich Köchli was the first to found a reading library in 1740.[181] The increased need to read gripped the countryside, where industrialisation was creating the necessary intellectual and material preconditions for it. The clothiers, who were used to reading, were the first to be gripped by the intellectual fashion of the age. They got hold of the reading material either directly through the town lending libraries and reading circles or indirectly through the mediation of town burghers based in the villages. They discussed their newly won knowledge eagerly in the evening societies. The Wädenswil *Fabrikanten* turned the tavern 'Krone' into the centre of their social life. This inn provided the setting for a conversation and discussion circle.

Evening gatherings of this nature must be seen as the countryside's educational institutions. They arose at the same time as the music societies, which were carried on the same wave of longing for culture. The circles overlapped, and were responsible for all cultural aspirations in the parish, including theatrical productions. Salomon von Orelli wrote: 'the fine arts and the Enlightenment were already so widespread in Wädenswil that the young people themselves acted out comedies on a stage set up for the purpose'.[182] The actual initiator of these performances was Kaspar Billeter, who subsequently became famous through the Stäfa rising. Proudly he stresses in his autobiography that 'in Wädenswil, I repeatedly introduced theatrical entertainments into country celebrations, and days given over to general enjoyment, instead of the smutty, tasteless and thoughtless pleasures of the carnival'.[183] This attitude to the old practices of the unmarried young people is typical of the Krone circle and the Music Society, with their passion for education and their new ways of celebrating. The 'smutty carnival pleasures' no longer matched their educational level and ideal and had to be replaced by plays of cultural value, like those in the town festivals. In spite of all this, the new wealth of culture was still tied to the old feast days and so became anchored in ancient custom.

Neither the conversation circle nor the Music Society constituted a firm organisation with fixed statutes. They bore all the features of a local society with far-reaching, albeit not all-embracing, functions. Nevertheless the spirit upholding them was new and no longer committed to the old festive traditions of the community. New forms of community and new community bonds were about to emerge. The Music Society, which grew out of the old Singing School, and the conversation circle in the tavern at the Krone were the seeds of the present-day Club.

The decisive step was the foundation of a local Reading Society. When we follow the birth and existence of the Wädenswil Reading Society, we see that something fundamentally new was taking place in the social life of the local community. This is not to dismiss the fact that the Wädenswil Reading Society developed according to its own laws nor to stretch our interpretation of this example too far. When a rural Club is formed, its shape is always determined by local forces of an economic, social and intellectual nature. But in spite of this restriction, we must clearly recognise the overall features in the emergence of the Wädenswil Reading Society. From the conditions in Wädenswil one may deduce fundamentally important information about the new form of rural community life, the Club. The formation of the Wädenswil Reading Society is not a freakish manifestation but basically connected with the altered conditions of existence in the industrialised regions of the Zurich countryside.

The first minutes of the society, headed 'Projected Plan for Setting up a Reading Society in Wädenswil' record the thoughts which motivated the founders of the association:

Everyone is aware that there are so many friends of reading to be found among us and that their number increases all the time; also the usefulness of reading books is becoming more and more evident to unprejudiced minds. This consideration led a few good friends to think that if it were possible to set up a society of book lovers, one would be able to satisfy one's passion for reading, desire for knowledge, inclination towards these noble pleasures, call it what you will, cheaply, or maybe even more cheaply, than when one reads from the lending libraries of Zurich, and one would enjoy the further advantage of getting the books straight from the presses, since one either does not get them at all from the lending library, or only after a long delay.[184]

This introduction constitutes a splendid document about the educational situation in which the clothiers, carriers and outworkers found themselves. It shows how the Reading Society was founded in response to a real need for education, and how much the clothiers emulated a secularised educational ideal, eager for new and the very newest reading material. Heinrich Zschokke's motto: 'Education for the people is freedom for the people' (*Volksbildung ist Volksbefreiung*), which the workers' associations and the educational societies of the nineteenth century took up and carried on with ardent fervour, is hinted at in these first minutes of the Wädenswil Reading Society, even though the words were formulated by a different intellectual and spiritual mood, and belonged to different mental and historical circumstances.

An important motive for founding the Society (according to the minutes) was the desire to be able to choose and procure one's reading matter oneself, independently of the town lending libraries. Diethelm Fretz's comprehensive book list provides information about the selection. Since every member had the statutory right to place orders for buying books, works such as Ludwig Kaiser's *Arnold von Winkelried oder die Schlacht bei Sempach* (*Arnold von Winkelried or the Battle of Sempach*), Friedrich Knuppel's *Bildung, Erziehung, Volkswohlseyn, Patriotismus* (*Culture, Education, the Common Weal, Patriotism*), were procured alongside another category of book such as *Friedrich mit der gebissenen Wange* (*Friedrich with the Bitten Cheek*) or *Taschenbuch fur lustige Leute* (*Pocket Book for Merry People*). The female element in society made itself felt by its choice of specifically ladies' magazines, such as the Leipzig *Frauenzimmer-Almanach zum Nuzen und Vergnügen* (*Women's Almanach for Use and Pleasure*), or *Die Einsiedlerin aus den Alpen* (*The Hermit Girl of the Alps*), as well as the monthly *Amalien's Erholungs-Stunden. Deutschland's Töchtern geweiht* (*Amalia's Hours of Recreation. Dedicated to the Daughters of Germany*). Another tendency within the Society chose political reading matter: *Der Nachtbote aus Frankreich* (*The Night Messenger from France*), *Leben und Schandtaten des Herzogs von Orléans* (*The Life and Misdeeds of the Duc d'Orléans*) were procured, for instance, and francophile literature was also circulated.[185] Revolutionary ideas fell on fertile soil among the clothiers' educational circles.[186]

Alongside these intellectual and cultural motives leading to the constitution of the Reading Society (and which were also expressed individually in the selection of the books), the founders were also, according to the minutes, led by clear economic considerations. A Reading Society would allow one to 'satisfy . . . one's passion for reading and desire for knowledge more cheaply'. This argument demonstrates the spirit of economy with which the clothiers, schooled in their manufacturing business, were imbued. Extracts from the statutes of the Reading Society will show what an important factor the money economy was in this joint enterprise, and how a money-economy mentality can result in new community ties. The story of how these statutes arose is interesting in itself. The initiators and authors of the 'projected plan' established thirteen 'laws' as the basis of their Society. The constitutional session took place on 10 October 1790. All eighteen members (among whom a widow and five unmarried daughters) approved the thirteen laws and added four additional articles to them. These statutes, while fine in theory, had to be amended as soon as they were put into practice. Already on 7 April 1791 a further three 'new laws were made' (according to the minutes). This gave rise to opposition. 'In order to avoid eventual reproaches and recriminations in the Society' (according to the minutes), a committee was elected with powers of arbitration. Solutions were drafted. The Society statutes were rewritten in 1792 on the Feast of St Berchtold, ending with the revealing sentence: 'and finally the laws recorded above shall remain absolutely as they are for at least a year and nothing in them be changed, nor new laws made'. When the allotted period expired on St Berchtold's day in 1793, four more articles were immediately brought into being.

This brief but eventful summary of the history of the statutes demonstrates fairly substantially how rational and artificial the new forms of community and the new community ties were. While the Reading Society certainly grew organically out of the old local community, it was no longer anchored in it. Community life was no longer based on customary and familiar neighbour-hood relations and community ties. People wanted another sort of social assurance. The members who paid to take part in an organisation fixed in the statute book wanted to know that their rights and duties were precisely defined down to the last detail. They were passionate practitioners of a formalism characteristic of the new emergent community relations. Anyone familiar with the life of nineteenth-century associations knows how greatly the statutes were valued and knows too that arguments about the statutes often formed the only vital aspect of the associations.

Some of the details of the legal arrangements for the Wädenswil Reading Society will illustrate how purposefully and rationally both form and content of the new Society were conceived and how material the Society bonds were, or, rather, could be.[187] The history of the statutes as well as the statutes themselves document the new concept which came into being along with the Wädenswil Reading Society. The members formed an exclusive society, whose statutes reveal that a money-economy mentality with a clear rational purpose had replaced the traditional sense of community rooted in custom.[188] One might argue here that a legal arrangement always appears rational and artificial and its living reality only becomes apparent when put into practice and applied. This circumstance must certainly be taken into account where the Wädenswil Reading Society is concerned. Social life within the Society was governed by personal ties between individual members independent of all statutory prescriptions. Yet the arguments about the statutes show that in this society feelings of community and personal ties, and so on, no longer offered any security, and that it was only the written laws which guaranteed that the new community functioned properly. One might be tempted at this point to say that the Wädenswil Reading Society, as manifested in its organisation and activity, should not be viewed as something fundamentally new in village community life. Form and content develop out of the Society's purpose (the independent purchase of reading matter). So the materialistic community bonds were a consequence of the capital investment necessary for carrying out the appointed task. In short, the purpose of the Reading Society could be said to be a unique phenomenon, which did not reflect an altered life of the common people.

These objections are invalidated by the example of Maschwanden. In 1797 Pastor Brennwald wrote about his parish community as follows:[189]

In my village the menfolk especially seem to be rather more cultivated than the author found them to be in his parish of Cappel [meaning Meyer, who had addressed the assembly prior to Brennwald]. Not only do several newspapers come into the village, but consequently other books are also read, especially historical ones. Fäsi's *Geographie*, Stumpf's *Chronik*, Bluntschli's *Memorabilia Tigurina* are not at all unknown here. If anyone has such a book, he is happy to share it, or else it is read out in company. *Abel's Death*, which came here fortuitously, has done the rounds through quite a few houses. – Clever guys too – and some who love to discuss all matters rather too eagerly can be met here.

In Maschwanden, then, people's desire for reading matter and culture was still embedded in the old neighbourhood relations. It was not restricted, as in the Wädenswil Reading Society, to an exclusive circle of members, and they did not have any rules. The local community in Maschwanden was so vital that they were able to solve their reading and education problem within its framework. Nor indeed was it the object of the association to establish new forms of community and new community ties. They developed out of the altered conditions of existence and the altered life style which were not as widespread in Maschwanden as in Wädenswil. Pastor Brennwald writes very instructively about this:

Where luxury in clothes is concerned, I have never seen so little as I have among the female sex in this region . . . The women preserve their mothers' and grandmothers' clothes carefully and they all wear the same clothes. The reason for this is that they seldom go out of their region, and never go to Zurich or in any other town, and it seldom occurs to any of their daughters to become a town maid, which is in any case of great benefit to their morals. Most of the women in our region have never seen Zurich in all their born days, unless it be on their wedding day. When, as seldom happens, someone is brought here from the lake of Zurich or elsewhere by marriage and brings her fine clothes, her long skirts etc. with her, she is mocked at, and if she is rich, called a *Schleike* (a troublemaker), but if she is poor, a *Haatsche* (a wanton)! Even more remarkable is the men's extravagance in clothing. Many of them are cotton merchants, horse and cattle merchants, pig merchants, or dealers in fruit, cider or brandy . . . I have here various men whom one would take for real gentlemen, but whose wives and mothers still go around in the age-old national costume.

We realise from this description of obligatory village custom why Masch-wanden did not need a reading and educational institution; the local village community with its comprehensive functions was still intact. We see too, how the need to read, together with an urban, gentlemanly life style, was brought into the village by the clothiers and their hangers-on.

The urban form of Society, the Club, only developed when the conditions of existence in the industrialised countryside had produced a class of population which felt that its social requirements were no longer fulfilled by the old local community, and believed that the urban forms of association, with their joint enterprises, were better suited to their circumstances. We have tried to follow this development of village community life by taking the Wädenswil Reading Society as our example. It was far in advance of those of the Oberland industrial countryside.[190] But, despite their backwardness, the same process was also at work in these regions. For instance, following a musical perform-ance to celebrate the Reformation in 1819, Music Societies were formed in Wald and Laupen in 1823, which Hübli and Hittenberg also joined in 1827. In the year 1827 the 'Rule of a Singing Society for Friends of Singing, both Children and Adults of Both Sexes, for the Better Use and Application of their Hours of Recreation, and especially as a Means of Encouraging Morality in the School District of Laupen' was established. The foreword to the statutes of this Society reads:

In earlier times, around fifty years ago [*c*. 1770–80], the singing in our region is supposed to have been raised to an exceptional level. Regular gatherings were held to practice the singing. Anyone who could attended them. Besides the usual night schools, where the Lobwasser Psalms were sung in choir, other practice sessions for contrapun-tal songs accompanied by instruments were set up.[191]

We see how the development in Wald resembled that in Wädenswil down to the last detail: the night school branched out into a more demanding singing circle, which drew in instrumental music. A particularly festive occasion (the celebration of the Reformation in 1819), requiring a larger organisation, provided the necessary stimulus for the foundation of singing societies along the lines of a Club. The local community was no longer able to satisfy the heightened demands made on its social life; rather its tasks were taken over by specialised organisations. Comprehensive functions were foreign to it. Any-thing which did not fall within its domain would be taken over by a new association, founded for this purpose. So the Club mentality gave birth to more and more new societies. Village life lost its centre and was compartmentalised into a varied Club life. In 1875, fifty years after the foundation of the singing societies of Wald and Laupen, we read in the *Volksblatt vom Bachtel* (*People's Paper of Bachtel*) the following notice about the society-orientated life in the Wald Parish:

In the midst of all occasions and festivities of this and that nature, it might indeed be not uninteresting to see for once a list of the different Clubs and Societies which contribute their due part to them. There are no less than thirty-one of them, namely: three male choirs, two mixed choirs, two Women's Clubs, two Reading Societies, two military shooting Clubs, three Music Societies, one Rescue Corps, one women's choir, a Society for the improvement of stock breeding, a Society for every Wednesday, Thursday, Friday and Sunday, and a Club for workers, alms, dramatics, industry, *Grütli*, for church singing, supporting the military, acrobatics, for the people and for the protection of animals.[192]

The collapse of village life becomes clearly visible in this gallery of associations (nowadays the number of Clubs listed by Heinrich Krebser would be five times greater still). Like the village, the individual villager's social life involved him in a variety of Clubs 'Anyone in the manufacturing villages [of the Oberland] who does not belong to at least a dozen Clubs is considered shy', wrote Peterhans-Bianzano pointedly.[193]

We have tried to use the example of the conditions in Wädenswil to show how the old framework of agrarian forms of sociability and community were burst asunder by the effect of the putting-out industry. The heightened demands on life and social life, accompanied by a correspondingly intellectual attitude, and driven by a corresponding urge to acquire culture and education, no longer found the necessary space to unfold in the old local community; in other words the old local community could no longer satisfy these demands. The Club with its particular purpose stepped into its place and brought new forms of society and community bonds. That the life of the common people had altered is manifested by the founding of the Societies.

It has already been mentioned that the example of Wädenswil acquired general significance, although we are aware that it is in the nature of the Club to owe its existence and individuality to the many local peculiarities. We will deal with the founding and life of the Clubs in the Oberland more thoroughly in the planned second part of this enquiry. The appearance of the Club in its finished state, regarding both legal formalities and content, belongs to the nineteenth century, with its particular historical and intellectual circumstances. But its seeds and first stirrings developed, as we have seen, from the situation in the later eighteenth century. The driving and shaping forces were the altered basic conditions of human life and community.

We mentioned at the beginning of the last section that the new forms of community and community ties developed hand in hand with a secularised educational ideal which concentrated on the things of this world. The example of the Wädenswil Society has shown us with exceptional clarity how both processes merged. Everywhere in the industrialised regions of the Zurich countryside there was a lively move towards intellectual maturity, announcing the century of the education and enlightenment of the common people. It was the fate of these educational efforts that revolutionary philosophy (French books and newspapers) found its way to them.[194] In the Wädenswil Reading Society this led to an inner crisis and to rifts. For instance, a revolutionary song of the Reading Society on the Pfäffikon Lake went as follows:[195]

> Die sind verbannt, die mit Verleumders Ränken,
> Der Menschen Recht, Freiheit und Gleichheit kränken,
> Wer nicht fürs allgemeine Beste spricht,
> Taugt zu uns nicht.
>
> They are banned, who with slanderers' wiles
> Insult the people's rights, freedom and equality,
> He who does not speak out for the best for all
> Does not deserve to be among us.

The philosophy of the French Revolution was shot through with patriotic ideas and with the canons of the old tradition of freedom.[196] The clothiers and their circle held this banner aloft. They did not find their adherents among the farmers and in agricultural regions, but among the outworkers and in the industrial regions. Annemarie Custer's dissertation makes this quite clear in her chapter on 'Revolutionary and Loyal Sentiments towards the Authorities among the Common People'. Apart from the lakeside parishes, where most of the leaders lived, the district of Knonau belonged 'to the troubled regions'. The district of Grüningen and the mountainous part of the Kyburg district counted 'among the most revolutionary parts of the country' – all markedly industrial regions.[197]

The revolutionary traits in the character of the outworkers and clothiers cannot surprise us. We have seen how, through their work, they participated more consciously in the events of the age and had a more critical attitude to the institutions of Church and State. They felt the anguish of their intellectual, economical and political tutelage more strongly than did the traditional farmers, holding firmly to their long-established ways. When, as in the industrial territory of Zurich, these character traits of the outworkers combined with the temperament of the northern Alps shepherd folk, the result was tension and revolution. This is to merely hint at the importance of the contribution of the industrially employed population in preparing the way for the great upheaval at the end of the eighteenth century. We must refrain from going into this more closely, since this would require a separate presentation of the historical and intellectual preconditions (in the local Zurich and the European context) in order to do justice to the changes in the political, social and economic structure, which led to the great revolution.

We have attempted in this chapter to understand and present the life and society of the early industrial countryside. Let us briefly recapitulate, in order to remind ourselves of the connections once again: we have learnt about the changes to diet and clothing, as well as the generally heightened needs and the raised standard of living. The significance of this new life style for people's sense of self-confidence and self-awareness has been extrapolated: the new life style contributed to the ability of the industrially employed population to disengage itself from its rural environment and to experience itself as an independent entity. This gave rise to a specifically outworker mentality, which Richard Weiss characterised in the following words:

Here, in this border zone between the Alps and the Lowlands, there arose from the fusion between small farmers and early industrial workers a type of person which has been eternalised in literature by Ulrich Brägger's self-portrait *The Poor Man from the Toggenburg*: 'A worker-farmer, although close to nature, but not peasant-like, not dull and securely tied to his own land, but mentally agile and agitated by the changing events of life and by the fluctuations between times of prosperity, with his carefree enjoyment of life, and times of crises, with the most bitter poverty; living in constant uncertainty, which drives one man inwards, brooding on sectarian matters, in poetic fantasising or in dumb resignation, but allows another to break out in political revolt or in successful business enterprises and sometimes in moral depravity.'[198]

The creation and existence of this type of mentality will be looked at from various points of view in the following chapter.

The outworker life style has led us to the new assessment of luxury and the standard of living under the influence of the putting-out industry. We moved from here to social life, attention being paid first to its traditional forms. We saw that the industrially employed population was still thoroughly committed to these traditional forms of sociability, which had grown out of a rural and farming world, with the appropriate bonds of society. In any case new elements were already appearing among the outworkers. On the one hand putting-out work brought new rhythms, opportunities and theatres for social life; on the other hand the basis of existence in the putting-out industry offered other possibilities for shaping social life.

The intellectual attitude behind these traditional forms of community life and sociability has been sketched in a few strokes. We showed how the traditional education of a rural and farming world was trapped in the fetters of tutelage by the ecclesiastical authorities. However, the traditional forms of social life with their appropriate community bonds were shattered by the influence of the putting-out industry, at the same time as were the fetters of an intellectual tutelage by Church and State. We tried to demonstrate this in the last section.

All this scarcely adds up to living unity. We are aware that only fragments can be retrieved from the many-coloured weft of life. To extend this metaphor: we are further aware that *Ziesen* (thin patches) and *Nester* (tangles) have winkled their way into our fabric. We will try to repair them in the following pages.

We will close this chapter with the verse inscribed on the house of an Appenzell outworker, who thus acknowledged that his existence was based on the putting-out industry. His house motto also leads on to the next chapter, which concentrates on the home.[199]

> Dann ein Mode chum der andern wicht
> Das zeigt dass unser Gmüet is licht,
> Und wankelbar in alle Schand
> Vil Nüerung in allem Land.

> Then one fashion to another changes
> Which shows that our hearts are fickle
> And irresolute in all shame
> There is much innovation in the whole country.

4 ❖ The impact of industrialisation on the house and the rural economy

The changes to settlement and housing and to the rural economy under the influence of domestic work in the putting-out industry have endowed the picture of the Oberland cultural territory with its characteristic traits, which it has retained until today. The problems we want to deal with separately in this chapter have already been outlined above many times and in very different connections. It can only be a matter of a piecemeal presentation of the complex material, most of which has still to be researched locally. We must limit ourselves to recording a few dominant traits, which necessarily involves a degree of stylisation,[1] beginning with a few remarks of a fundamental and general nature, to remind ourselves about matters discussed earlier on.

Let us begin by remembering that industrialisation and the possibilities for existing created by it should not be held solely responsible for the type of changes and the way they occurred. They simply present one component, the other being assembled from those forces which we identified in Chapter 1 as factors impeding industrialisation. They are the traditional forms of land right and land use, which were preserved by the restrictions of a rigid economic order and were upheld by the traditionalistic spirit of an ancient peasant economic mentality.

In a purely agricultural enterprise the house (and the outbuildings) and the land belonging to it (including the actual use of the land) are mutually dependent. The number of people who live and work on the farm is also included in this dependency relationship. Economic order, inheritance rights, customs and practices together form defences which safeguard this equilibrium. We have seen that in the arable zones of the Zurich Unterland the defences were strong enough to prevent the putting-out industry from getting through and gaining a foothold there. But the cottage industry and putting-out work spread through the regions around the Lake, in the Knonau district and in the Oberland, with several different consequences for the traditional ways of settlement, building, living and for peasant agriculture. It is important to mention here that the consequences varied from region to region, because the local legal, economic and traditional defences all varied.

Generally speaking, it can be stated that industrialisation released the

111

home from its dependence on the land. In the first instance this meant that more people were able to live in such houses and dwellings as already existed, which affected both traditional ways of living and the ground-plans of houses and dwellings. In the second instance new settlements could be founded with the help of industrial earnings, which were partly or wholly independent of nature, that is, of land use. There was a strong need in the industrial regions of the Zurich countryside both for new settlements and for filling in and extending existing houses and dwellings, resulting from the rise in people's willingness to marry, from natural population growth, changes to the structure of the family and to family cohesion – in short, from the emergence of the life style and community life we have learnt to associate with the industrial regions.

Even in places where the economic order permitted new settlement, the old settlements would be filled in and extended first. However, on methodological grounds, we want to concentrate first solely on the construction of new dwelling places. So we will not as yet consider changes to the lay-out of existing dwellings or changes to the inner subdivisions of existing houses (which would be more consequential in historical terms), but concentrate on the new settlements.

The need to found new homes was opposed by the limitations imposed by the economic order in its local and regional variations. Two legal instruments in particular served to impede and prevent new settlements and any sort of building at all. The first was the prohibition of *Hinausbauen*, building outside the precincts of the village.[2] The second legal instrument was the material restriction on villagers' rights to the commonalty and to membership in the village community, both of which were tied to the house. We learn about both legal instruments in a report to the Economic Commission of 1808 about Embrach, which says

On account of the right and laws of the village community no citizen may build outside the village, partly on account of the wood, partly for safeguarding the properties, plants and fruits, that none may bring anything home surreptitiously. Neither may anyone build another house in the village, unless he demolishes an old house already belonging to him, so that the number of citizens does not increase too strongly and result in a shortage of timber and firewood, because there is no private wood there and they all have to chop their own from the common wood.[3]

This example shows us how these prohibitions derived their sense and effectiveness from the ground rights and the use of land in a three-field system (with common lands and open-field farming, etc.). The greater the importance of these two legal instruments for the survival of a rural community, the more that community would ensure they were maintained and the more rigorously they were applied. We will see further on how this led to characteristic forms of living and building in certain industrial regions. We will also see how the prohibitions could not only be by-passed but also removed as a result of the pressure of the industrial population.

In the Oberland the preconditions for prohibiting building outside the village and for imposing a material restriction on village rights were mainly lacking.[4] In the 1808 report quoted above we read, for instance, that 'On the mountain at Turbenthal nearly everyone has a house of his own on his land and there is no communal right preventing building outside the village on one's own property in this region.'[5]

Consequently the need to found new settlements could be implemented fully in these regions. In the event a wave of new settlements ran parallel to the development of cottage industry, representing an important stage in opening up the Oberland. We may call it the cottage industry phase of an inner colonisation of the Oberland, and can follow its progress with the help of Hans Bernhard's research into the economic and settlement geography of the Töss valley.

In 1634 there were 260 settlements in the Töss valley (villages, hamlets and farmsteads). In the period between 1634 and 1800, 219 new independent places of residence were added to that number.[6] The upper Töss valley took by far the larger share of this new settlement. There were, for instance, ninety new places in the parish of Fischental, thirty-six in Sternenberg and thirty-nine in Bauma, whereas there was not a single new settlement in the parishes of Seen, Töss and Veltheim, and only one in each of the parishes of Neftenbach, Pfungen, Dättlikon, Rorbas and Freienstein.[7] When we compare the number of new settlements in relation to their altitude (see table), a clear picture emerges.[8] These figures are fairly conclusive: the bulk of cottage industry settlement was limited mainly to the hilly and mountainous zones. Previously uninhabited and thinly settled regions could be opened up due to the putting-out industry and its earning possibilities. The new dwellings depended less, or indeed not at all, on the nature of the countryside. Of primary importance to

Altitude (m. above sea level)	New Settlements (between 1634 and 1800)
300– 400	1
400– 500	6
500– 600	10
600– 700	39
700– 800	77
800– 900	47
900–1,000	19
1,000–1,100	6
1,100–1,200	4

the survival of these dwelling places were the earnings from putting-out work (spinning) whereas agricultural produce, in so far as any farming was done, was of only secondary importance. The ground did duty by offering space for building dwellings. The settler was looking for living space in the most restricted meaning of the word, i.e. the possibility of settling down, and he did not demand of the land that it feed him as well.[9] The new settlements were founded mostly in the side valleys of the Töss valley.

Here the settler has wormed his way up to the highest sections of the valleys, and into the gullies of the Nagelfluh mountains, where there is often scarcely enough space available for laying out a dwelling and a small vegetable garden. The steep escarpments, covered with nothing but timber, prevent agriculture and there is no valley soil capable of being ploughed.

The mountain settlements were 'founded by the settlers, with almost complete disregard for the natural conditions, on cliffs, on the highest terraces and even in the peaks region of the Nagelfluh mountain territory'.[10]

Bernhard's work contains a map (Appendix 6), which shows the changes in the settlement pattern between 1634 and 1800. Bernhard's results for the Töss valley apply to the whole of the Oberland. The secondary, typical cottage industrial phase of an inner colonisation is identified by its characteristic form of settlement (single farms, which can expand into hamlets); by their settlement locations (side valleys, slopes and heights); and by the characteristic forms of housing (which will be discussed later on). The extent to which the wave of settlement was due to putting-out work for cottage industry is demonstrated not only by its rise and expansion, but also by its demise; such dwelling places were laid waste in the nineteenth and twentieth centuries. The cottage industrial settlement in the Töss valley shared the fate of cottage industry, which was unleashed by a new phase in the opening up of the Oberland: that of factory industry, with its particular settlement forms and locations and types of housing. The factory industry phase stamped the cultural territory of the Oberland with yet another set of features.

At this stage, we shall refer to the people behind this cottage industry phase of settlement only by mentioning a correlation between the population growth and industrialisation. It will lead us on to enquire about alterations to existing houses. We have taken three parishes from the upper Töss valley and three parishes in the arable country (with a few vineyards) of the lower Töss valley and compared them.

Between 1634 and 1771 the population growth was as shown in the first table.[11] In the second table we have contrasted the number of people employed in weaving and in spinning in the year 1787.[12] The comparison shows the industrialised parishes clearly in the lead. Concerning the comparatively thin population in the agricultural regions Johann Caspar Hirzel asked whether the Plague had snatched all the people away – supplying the answer himself:

| | No. of inhabitants | |
	1634	1771
Upper parishes		
1. Fischental	466	1,789
2. Sternenberg	152	805
3. Bauma	453	2,487
Lower parishes		
1. Wülflingen	709	940
2. Neftenbach	748	1,095
3. Pfungen	243	324

	No. of weavers	No. of spinners
Upper parishes		
1. Fischental	5	1,522
2. Sternenberg	3	488
3. Bauma	73	1,229
Lower parishes		
1. Wülflingen	—	81
2. Neftenbach	—	33
3. Pfungen	—	18

Yes, one of the fiercest plagues, but one which creeps in surreptitiously . . . since these people live only from their farms and are always concerned lest they be reduced to poverty and destitution should the number of mouths increase. For this reason a father will allow only the oldest son to marry, and the others go into military service, or stay at home as servants and die unmarried. In this way they prevent increase which means that the slightest onset of disease, or the occasional infertile marriage, lead to the region being depopulated.[13]

We have already studied this problem.

The heightened need for living space in the industrialised regions is adequately documented by these figures. It was evidenced not only by the new settlements but also by the enlargements made to existing dwellings. Farm-steads grew into hamlets and hamlets expanded in size and population to become as big as villages. It is difficult to grasp and present this process because the necessary local research has yet to be done. With the help of land registers, farm inventories and other archival material one should be able to establish the number of newly built houses in individual villages. In any case, the population growth in individual settlements provides us with some indications. In the parish of Bauma, for instance, there was only one place of residence in 1634 with more than fifty inhabitants. By 1800, however, there were fourteen places of over fifty inhabitants. Thirty-four people lived in the hamlet of Mühlebach (parish of Fischental) in 1634; by 1771 there were one hundred and twelve. The population of Esch (parish of Fischental) changed from two in 1634 to forty in 1771. Bauma grew in this period from eighteen inhabitants to one hundred and forty-one, and so on.[14] The valley settlements were the first to show a large growth in the population, since there was generally not enough room for such development in the mountain and lateral valley settlements. There were, however, exceptions: the farms of Hinterstrahlegg and Vorderstrahlegg (1045m. above sea level) housed twenty-seven inhabitants between them in 1634. In 1771 they had grown into a fine hamlet with eighty-two inhabitants.

What has been said about the new settlements also applies to the enlarged dwelling places. This process occurred independently of the way the land was farmed, being based in most cases only on earnings from putting-out work. The process of enlarging dwelling places shaped the cultural territory of the Oberland as effectively as did the new settlements. It was this building and settlement activity which created the preconditions for the subsequent factory industry, which found in these enlarged hamlets and villages the settled population it required in order to provide a sufficient pool of labour for its factories. However, many of the places which had expanded dramatically during the cottage industry period and whose geographical location was not suitable for introducing a factory industry were condemned with the demise of cottage industry to lose their inhabitants and to die. The three examples shown in the table from the parish of Sternenberg illustrate this process.[15]

			No. of inhabitants				
	1634	1670	1721	1771	1850	1870	1888
Buchwald	3	6	15	26	16	10	—
Matt	13	27	29	56	59	47	29
Tiefenmoos	—	4	10	28	60	33	21

The new settlements and enlargements to existing dwelling places arising from cottage industry were accompanied in the Oberland by new forms of housing typical to cottage industry. The outworker made new demands on his house, whereas the old demands made by farming lost their significance. With industrial earnings he and his family acquired economic self-sufficiency. The material ties to his family group (in terms of the living space and economic area) were loosened and no longer possessed the fateful significance they held under farming conditions. He thereby acquired the possibility of founding his own household. We saw in Chapter 2 how the organisational structure of the outworker family encouraged it to split up into separate units, each with its own area and property. Tied up with this process were the changes to inheritance law, also mentioned above. Starting from these formal and organisational motives, cottage industry communities were moving in the direction of single family homes. This developed into the form of house typical to cottage industry, the *Fläder* or *Flarz* houses.

The *Flarz* house in the Oberland region of hamlet and farmstead settlements must be distinguished from that of the village settlements, where the lack of space and the economic restrictions led to particular forms of their own. The Oberland *Flarz* consists (generally) of a row of attached houses often with room only for a kitchen, living room and bedroom. These chain-like agglomerations of dwellings, with their flat *Tätsch* roofs, appear to have grown organically, in the sense of a primitive subdivision of cells. In fact this comparison is more than just a metaphor: the Oberland *Flarz* is a clan house. The organic growth of the *Flarz* chains represents the growth and subdivision of the kinship group. Just as the farming family group split up with the advent of cottage industry into economically self-sufficient and spiritually isolated units, so too did the communal peasant household break up into separate single family cottages. Studying the land registers shows that the inhabitants of a *Flarz* chain were originally closely related to one another. The parents' house would be joined by the houses of their children and grandchildren . Old houses were often torn down and two attached houses built in their place, to which new single and double houses could then be added. This development was accompanied by dividing up the farmland, changing the way the land was used, splitting up the farm buildings or by giving the existing farm building a new function. The farmland would often be worked by no more than one household, the rest contenting themselves with a cottage garden, a goat and other small animals.

The Oberland *Flarz* developed from outworker family relationships and conditions of inheritance. Their form of housing was appropriate to their economic and family circumstances. The *Flarz* form provided the outworker with a separate dwelling, a single family house which was legally his, and, most importantly for his political status, a rooting point, a bond with his homeland. This is why he clung to this property 'with back and stomach', however indebted he might be. In the Oberland region of hamlets and farmsteads, however, it was not the restrictions on the number of people entitled to village rights which was responsible for the chain-shaped constructions. It was the conditions of land ownership, economic and financial considerations, the assistance and company of neighbours during putting-out work, and other factors, such as facilitating the transport and distribution of the raw materials and finished goods through the road-less woodlands, which contributed to the development of the chain-shaped *Flarz* houses in the Oberland. The *Flarz* forms in the villages may also have served as examples for the farmsteads region. The lack of freedom of movement under the Ancien Régime contributed towards forcing the outworker kinship groups to build and live within a narrow area. The extended family did not, however, form a working and consuming unit. In this, as with its family structure, it was completely unlike a peasant extended family (as for instance in the arable regions of south-east Europe or in the *mezzadria* regions of Italy). Earnings from the putting-out industry allowed the property to be split up. This meant that the extended family as a working and consuming unit was broken up into individual and economically self-sufficient households, which were now only loosely tied to one another. Towards the end of the eighteenth century, the crises and poverty of the period caused some of the links in the chains of *Flarz* houses to fall into outsiders' hands. The increased freedom of movement after 1789 hastened this process, and the communal housing of kinship groups disintegrated.

Apart from the *Flarz* house, a further type of house grew up alongside the putting-out industry. Unlike the *Flarz* house, it remained more strongly associated with farming. It was the preferred form of house in the new settlements in the mountain sites and lateral valleys. The dwelling consisted of kitchen, living room (with a row of windows for the cottage industry, as with the *Flarz* houses) and one or two bedrooms. The barn and byre were built cross-wise onto the house. They were generally timber constructions. The roof was pitched steeply and covered with shingles. This type of house originated from different economic and social conditions to those of the *Flarz* houses. The economic precondition was a symbiosis between putting-out work and agriculture. It was the outward order and the inner dynamism of the Oberland small farm economy which enabled this symbiosis to take place, which was mostly connected with a shift to grasslands and stock farming. This sort of farming was adapted to a dual economic base. The social conditions had to match these economic preconditions.

There was no room here for the extended family. The limited farmland on which the family members depended along with their industrial earnings could not support any sharing or subdivision. The form of house and the farmstead tended to compel its inmates to continue living under peasant conditions, although cottage industry obliged them to adopt new forms. The dual economic base involved a particular intellectual and spiritual mentality: industrial employment gave rise to an entrepreneurial spirit (as well as the material resources for farm improvements and alterations). Both the farmstead and the peasant economic mentality preserved the traditional way of life and the structure of the family (self-sufficient farming, inheritance rights, etc.).

A report which appeared in the *Volksblatt vom Bachtel* in 1944 contains information about this sort of cottage industry smallholding. Our informant, who was born in 1876, wrote that

It was in the year 1848 when my parents moved from Fägswil-Rüti to Obereggwald . . . Many a one of the younger generation will tell themselves that there aren't any houses at all on the Aberegg. But stop; just there, where today the two byres are standing, there stood then houses with barns built against them . . . A small living room, kitchen and two bedrooms had to suffice for the six of us. The stove which heated the living room was unique. It was a clay oven and whenever it was heated, it did not just give out warmth, but also spread the unique clay smell around . . . The nearest neighbouring house was the Rutschwende. A chimney had never been built in this house. The smoke just seeped through the whole house. This was also still the case in a dwelling, called the Cloister, in Raad. – Many young people probably don't know either that earlier on there were also two houses in Hessen; Vorderhessen and Hinterhessen. But they too were demolished, just like the ones in Oberegg and Rutschwende. The meagre yields which the smaller and remoter homes produced made it impossible to consider building such houses again . . . In my mind's eye I can still see the women walking back from the spring with a copper pot full of water on their heads. In the living room, there was generally a corner with two benches and a table. Instead of a sofa most places had a 'stove bench'. There were a few more stools around the table. The rest of the space would then be filled with two or three hand looms.[16]

In the eighteenth century these places were mostly still spinning and not yet weaving. Any extension or partition of these cottage industry smallholdings would depend on the size of the inhabitants' property, their earnings from cottage industry and their social standing in the parish.

The most developed form of this type of house (and of the dual economic base it rested on) was to be found in an industrial region outside the Zurich territory. This was the Reformed part of the Appenzell country, where in the eighteenth century a fruitful partnership between agriculture (mainly grazing) and cottage industry was achieved. Both forms of production had attained a high level of specialisation and the travellers' accounts ring with praises for the prosperity of this region, manifested by the many new houses. Ebel wrote:

There is something special about the appearance of this village [Gais] and one sees at once that here live neither simple cowherds and peasants, nor burghers and artisans. These former herdsmen owe their prosperity to the industry, which has spread widely over the whole of Reformed Appenzell . . . Their industriousness is extraordinary and for the last three hundred years it has so increased their wealth that . . . almost the whole village now consists of beautiful new houses, real palaces of wood compared with the huts of most of the inhabitants of Innerrhoden.[17]

The form of this typical Appenzell cottage industry house is similar to the Zurich type of house described above. Like them, the byre and barn stood cross-wise against the house, the windows were set in a row, the roof was pitched steeply and covered with nailed shingles. Often the whole house would be covered with shingles, which were then developed as a wall decoration. These houses also had a loom shop, where fine yarn would be woven into cloth. From the technical point of view the Appenzell textile industry was superior to that of Zurich (at least partly). The Appenzell house was a richly decorated building, witnessing to the prosperity and taste of its inhabitants. Industrialised Toggenburg enjoyed the same sort of economy and form of buildings. The blooming industrial regions of Appenzell and Toggenburg had a strong influence on the neighbouring Oberland of Zurich, given that it possessed similar geographical and economic (sometimes also legal) preconditions. 'The new houses in Fischenthal imitate the Toggenburg manner of building', reported J. C. Hirzel.[18] They even copied their loom shops as well as their refined weaving technique. However, only a few farmhouses in the Zurich Oberland were as richly decorated and as fine as those of Appenzell and Toggenburg, since this required adequate farmland, which was mostly lacking in wooded country.[19] We will discuss the correlation between cottage industry and the rural economy further on.

Leaving the hamlets and farmsteads of the Oberland, let us now take a look at the villages of the industrial regions. This form of settlement also produced a *Flarz* house, whose development was unmistakably influenced by parish rights and the economic order. We have already mentioned that the restrictions on rights were loosened under the pressure of population in the industrialised regions. The number of rights was doubled by decision of the village community (as in Hinwil and Wetzikon), or else divided into half, third or quarter rights. Such measures created the legal preconditions for building desperately needed dwellings. This was the decisive criterion and not the attempts to allow more families a share in the commonage and in the parish rights and duties. As we know, village rights were tied to the houses, so subdividing them meant that new houses could be added to the old ones. This gave rise to the *Flarz* house form, whereby two, three, four or more houses were joined together, according to the number of shares in a village right. Legally, such houses counted as only one house and the individual parts as a half, a third or a quarter of that house. Lack of space in the villages often made it difficult to line the part-houses up gable-end to gable-end. This led to agglomerations of part-houses, crowded in at right angles as well as in rows, producing all sorts of subdivisions, additions and rebuilding. The extensions could include the farm buildings as well. The barns and byres could be assimilated into the *Flarz* construction and turned into dwellings and part-houses. There is, for example, a five-part *Flarz* in Unterhittnau; in 1750 Johannes Boller bought two farmhouses, apparently built against one another, on the site where the *Flarz* later stood. Each farmhouse possessed a full village right. Between 1750 and 1789 four part-houses were created in this building. A shed was turned ino a part-house, and an old building knocked down and replaced by a double house. When the inheritance was divided in 1789 between Johannes Boller's four sons, each one got a part-house and half a village right. One son (Heinrich) had already died. His three sons (Johannes Boller's grandchildren) assumed his inheritance, divided the house and the half right again and added a further dwelling between the lower barn and the byre.[20]

This example is typical of the villages in the border zone between the Oberland and the Unterland. The old arable economic order with its restrictions on settlement and building still existed, although the putting-out industry had gained a foothold in these zones. This economic order directly affected building and consequently the new form of house. Therefore, these *Flarz* forms have to be designated as rights-possessing houses. This example also shed light on the situation of the owners of such houses in this construction period. As in the Oberland, families employed in industry were seeking a separate space for themselves and a share of the property. Individual families were chained together by their village right which was tied to their house. This gave rise to communal housing within the family group, whereby the individual parts of the family lived separately in part-houses. Their share of the right ensured that they were rooted in the village community, and consequently in their homeland. Such a family group would be kept together in one place less through inner need than through outward compulsion. Each family was economically separate and engaged in its particular form of livelihood. Property and usage were subdivided down to the last detail. Heinrich Boller (Johannes Boller's grandson) had, for instance, been given the right by his brothers Johannes and Jakob to stack pinelogs and timber in front of their farmhouses. The part-families could extend and shape their houses according to each one's economic success in industry and agriculture (if they still did any). The various parts of the *Flarz* houses thus acquired idiosyncratic features.

The economic order had even greater influence on the construction and form of the houses in places where parish rights were not bound to the house but to the *Rauch* (hearth; literally smoke). The chimney, stove or oven carried the rights, which meant that in many villages, houses could be built so long as they had no chimney, oven or stove.[21] This practice of making smoke carry rights and duties went back to medieval conditions of tenure. In the seventeenth and eighteenth centuries people resorted to these ancient legal forms in order to protect the common woods and to prevent the village community from being overrun with strangers. This prohibition too was by-passed under the pressure of population and the housing shortage. People built *Flarz* houses so designed that the smoke from their individual stoves would issue from a communal chimney. If there was no chimney, it would collect in a communal attic shared by all the cottages. People also got around the regulations by building a communal kitchen to be shared by several separate part-houses. It is clear that these building restrictions and the ways of circumventing them resulted in strange forms of building, types of houses and subdivisions of the living rooms, which must in many respects have affected the inhabitants' lives and life together. One example must suffice, of a house in Opfikon:

This was originally divided equally into three. But the kitchen, just like the entrance hall, ran through the whole house, and no part was partitioned off from another. The three living rooms were represented by three stoves in the kitchen. Each part of the kitchen had its own staircase leading upstairs, and even today there are no walls dividing the three sleeping quarters from one another.[22]

The village right and economic order became extremely irksome straitjackets in those villages where the rights were not tied to the smoke but to the stove and the living room. This regulation was particularly prevalent (in its local variations) in the parishes of the Knonau district. The village community of Knonau issued a petition on 8 February 1683 demanding, for instance, that half rights should not be divided up any further and that 'a half right should have no more than one oven and one living room'.[23] The *Einzug* (the entry fee payable on becoming a member of the commune with commonage and voting rights) was relatively small in these villages and so such regulations must have resulted in very unhealthy living conditions in the industrial regions, with their strong natural population growth. The sources describe conditions which are scarcely imaginable today.

One often sees three to four households, related in the second or third or even more distant degrees, squeezed together in one living room. The discomfort they experience leads to many grievances, which often give rise to dangerous in-fighting, and since young and old often sleep together in one room, the opportunity for dangerous outbreaks of precocious lust is present.

The 'general custom' in the Knonau district 'of living in the unmarried state until forced into marriage through their inability to avoid pregnancy any longer' is attributed by the author to these living conditions.[24] J. C. Nüscheler describes these truly pitiable conditions even more tellingly. We quote him rather extensively because we will deal with the cottage industrial living conditions at greater length further on.

This [the prohibition on building by limiting the number of ovens, stoves or living rooms] produces the unpleasant consequence that in most villages nearly every house has two or three living rooms with three to four households in each of them. In the other houses four married couples are to be found living in one room, and a very small one at that. Imagine a house with only two living rooms next to one another, with only one stove or griddle to cook on, and then consider whether it would really be possible to give way in a friendly manner to one another all the time etc. ... Although I did straightaway find these people to be much more tolerant than I ever thought I would find them. Now imagine further a fairly small living room, its stove close to the door, with four or five windows opposite, and two little folding tables in both corners. There are two more little tables set against the wall opposite the windows, so that each married couple has their own. Then add a further two or three children for each married couple, as I have seen with my own eyes. What a racket, what a noise must ensue!

His account continues with a description of domestic life in this sort of living room. The various households could not eat together at the same time, but they had to have their meals in shifts. Each time grace was said, it would be disrupted by profane talk by the non-participating households, etc. Nüscheler admits

It grieves me, it must be said openly, that on these occasions I saw many people debase themselves lower than animals and that I saw some people in these families who longed desperately to be able to live for once in their lives on their own in a corner, however small, with their children, so as to be able to perform their duty adequately as parents and Christians. It must be understood that a cottage with two living rooms cannot have eight bedrooms. So two or more married couples with all their children must sleep in one bedroom. How they are able to carry out their marital obligations in the presence of these, I simply do not know.[25]

Driven by such need, individual parishes were obliged to grant 'quarter ovens'. These provided the legal preconditions for building new dwellings. The example of Maschwanden illustrates the controversies within the parishes. On 11 November 1787 governor Holzhalb reported to Zurich that four parishioners had come to him and complained about their restricted living conditions. The villagers had asked the governor urgently to allow them to erect quarter ovens. Their lack of space would be alleviated by this 'good deed' since new 'living rooms' could then be built. This would then produce 'less argument and grievance' and they would be freed from 'many inconveniences'. But the bailiff argued against errecting quarter ovens by saying that such a permission could only be granted if the entry fee was levied at the same time.[26]

The quarter ovens originally entitled their owners to build new living space only. We cannot overlook the fact that the four part-ovens had to be connected, or at least share a common chimney stack. This stipulation necessarily led once more to *Flarz* houses being built. But even this restriction had to be dropped in individual parishes. The events leading up to this are vividly illustrated in the quarrel over a building site in Mettmenstetten-Dachelsen. A writ of 4 July 1788 complained about two members of the village community who were in possession of only a quarter of a parish right and who intended to errect a new house on their land. The writ added that only the possessor of a whole or a half right was allowed to build a new house, and that the possessor of a quarter right was only entitled to add new buildings to an old house. Even this right was 'a special favour'. The writ appealed against granting permission to build. But the two villagers managed to establish that they could not add any more buildings to their house because their neighbours would not concede them any land for building. Consequently they asked for permission to build, since it was, 'on account of their two numerous households, extremely inconvenient and for many moral reasons very oppressive to live for long time in a room owned in common with another numerous household'. These afflictions secured the two villagers' permission

that each of them may build a new house separate from the old dwelling, but with the clear and express condition that not more than one living room with a quarter oven six *Schuhe* (feet) long, four *Schuhe* wide on the outside and three on the inside, shall be erected within, and that they, like all other owners of a quarter right who in future may wish to build new dwellings will be forbidden by the highest authorities from erecting more than one living room with an oven of the prescribed shape in it, and that the acting Overseers of the village community should be given the duty of carefully checking all these new dwelling houses throughout the year, to see whether the high authorities' instructions have been carried out precisely and dutifully.

A little later on this alteration to the parish right was written into the draft for a new entry charter.[27]

We pointed out at the beginning that two completely different components were at work in these changes to settlement, building and home life: to wit, industrialisation and the ancient economic and parish order of the countryside. Light has hitherto been shed almost exclusively on the latter. We started out in those regions which had no or insufficient legal grounds for acquiring influence over new settlement and building. We then moved on to study the different possibilities for limiting building. There are so many variations of these old rural regulations and their changes in the seventeenth and eighteenth centuries that we have been able to list only a few of them. Our last example (Mettmenstetten-Dachelsen) demonstrated with exemplary clarity how the ancient rural regulations could affect building and living down to the last detail (the size of the oven). It further illustrated how these regulations could be softened by cottage industry. Our methodical approach is justified by the way it has revealed the inter-dependence of the forms of settlement, building and home life. We know that the process of industrialisation was also caught up in this dependence.

We have until now only discussed the influence of industrialisation in so far as the process of industrialisation with its economic and social repercussions awoke the need for new space for living and settlement. A closer look at the influence of industrialisation shows man as the upholder of industrialisation at the centre of our investigation. Having come via settlement and building to his home life, let us now retrace our steps and begin with the outworker's life and his need for a home.

The outworker's demands on his dwelling, especially on his living room, were different to the farmer's. The nature of his work heightened the importance of the actual living room, whereas the significance of the agricultural outbuildings was either lost or altered. The weaver was tied all year round to his work place in his house, whereas the spinner could perform his task in the open, depending on the weather, but he too spent a large proportion of his working time in his house. They both needed room for their tools and for carrying out their work undisturbed. This meant that the outworker's need for living space was greater and more urgent than the farmer's. The purely technical side of putting-out work thus contributed to the shortage of living space. The fact that before 1800 weaving was carried out almost exclusively in villages (whereas people in the Oberland hamlets and farmsteads took on spinning) was closely associated with the organisation of the putting-out system and to technical problems of transport. This circumstance led to an even greater lack of space in villages which were already crowded due to the restrictions on building. Unlike in the Appenzell and Toggenburg industrial regions, weaving in the Zurich countryside was done far less in cellars specifically built for weaving than in living rooms. It was only towards the end of the century when there was a greater demand for fine muslins, which required a damp woof, that weaving cellars were built into new and old houses. This feature of the Zurich textile industry served to reduce the available space even further. Two or three looms often stood side by side in the same living room.

Lack of space was a problem not only in the villages but also in the hamlets and farmsteads, which were not subject to building restrictions. Poverty and crushing debts prevented new dwellings from being built. People retrenched as much as their circumstances permitted. In many places, the living room was divided up. But all this changed with the first flowering of the textile industry. The good earnings encouraged many people to undertake the risk of building a new house with the help of a mortgage 'since the interest on the borrowed capital was soon earned'.[28] Far too many trusted to the false glitter of those golden years. Their houses and properties were almost without exception loaded with debts.

When their living rooms were turned into workshops and people were forced to spend more of their lives in them, the need for housing increased. People tried to work in a clean, attractive and pleasant environment. They built more and more smoke-free kitchens, they panelled their living rooms and bedrooms and attached great importance to installing stoves with effective flues; windows were enlarged and, where necessary, the eaves were shortened to allow more light to enter the working area. Alterations like these were in line with the technical requirements of the work. But the weaver's or spinner's involvement with fine cloth did not only demand tidiness, light and cleanliness from him, it also developed in him an aesthetic feeling for improving his environment. The cultural life of cottage industry was thus the product of the interaction between the technical demands of their work and the outworkers' way of life and life style. We have already met the need for ornament, finery and luxury among the industrial population, a need which they also experienced with regard to their houses and homes; everything from the building materials to the interior decoration is evidence of a creative urge directed at ostentation. C. Meiners commented about this in 1788, writing that

all the villages and hamlets which have many factory workers living in them are distinguished from the rest by the newness, the beauty and the solidity of their houses. Instead of living like their fathers or grandfathers in dirty wooden, straw-thatched huts, the manufacturing peasants live in stone houses, covered with tiles. Diligent and thrifty workers vie for honour in the beauty, cleanliness and brightness of their dwellings, and in the extension and perfect cultivation of their patch of land.[29]

The need for decoration and ostentation in cottage industrial circles must be seen in a thoroughly positive light and its significance in terms of popular culture and the life of the common people recognised. Contemporary commentators, fired by puritanical zeal, generally condemned it as a 'tendency towards finery and luxury'. Here too (as with fashion in clothes) the urban life style set the standard. J. Ebel wrote that the parish of Fischental was 'made up of scattered dwellings along all the mountain slopes . . . and from time to time one sees houses, whose outward appearance and inner furnishings are completely urban'.[30] The rural clothiers, who had attained money and influence, were important transmitters of the new, urban life style. Since

many of these manufacturers had grown from being well-off to being rich people . . . many more larger and more expensive houses were built than previously; when the industry first started, they aimed only at comfort and more room, because that was what they lacked, but now the chief aim of these new buildings is eye-catching splendour, following which previously unknown and expensive household goods were also procured.[31]

Another source tells us about the clothiers; 'The wealthy and their children built beautiful palaces and furnished them in the most expensive manner, so that they challenged the primacy of the richest houses in the capital.'[32] This was how the refined life style and the pretentious, intimate home requirements of the Rococo age penetrated beyond the society of town burghers into the countryside, to the clothiers and from them seeped down to the outworker circles. This life style was especially prevalent among those economically viable households and families which combined factory earnings with agriculture, stock farming or vineyards. Possession of hard cash enabled the outworker to equip his home with new furniture, and the growth in people's willingness to marry and in the number of youthful weddings necessarily led to the purchase of new household equipment. This could no longer be inherited all of a piece, as in the peasant family group, but was divided up and had to be made up with new pieces.

These are, to be sure, the bright sides of cottage industry life, and they are offset by its dark sides, which were also derived from the work itself. The contractual and quantitative production and payment system of putting-out work could easily result in household matters being neglected. 'The poverty or avarice of the workers or their families often puts earning money above everything else. The cleanliness of the households, the orderliness of their lives . . . suffers mightily from this.'[33] Light and shade are mingled in this report by the minister of Männedorf:

People do say that this occupation [domestic weaving], has on the one hand a beneficial influence on the cultural life of those who engage in it: the fine material, the lovely colours, the pretty patterns, the cleanliness with which the stuff has to be handled, have a softening effect on their dispositions and are averse to roughness. It is true that the weaver-women's feeling for taste and fashion is often markedly developed . . . But where cleanliness in other matters unrelated to this work is concerned, it is only to be found there where a mother's tidying hand rules the house, while the daughters are employed at the loom, but were one to take a look there where a young wife dedicates or has to dedicate herself to this work, without any household help, the picture changes at once. Whereas her loom is scrubbed and cleaned, as required by the work, in the kitchen the crockery is not washed, in the bedroom the beds remain unmade until they have to be used again . . . and so on through the hundred details, which together make up a household.[34]

There is no way that one can talk about a *Wohnkultur* in those overcrowded dwellings which Nüscheler's report describes for us. Even the most necessary household goods were in the way. Nevertheless, there is evidence here too of a tendency towards a greater desire to raise the standard of domestic life.

Where building is concerned, it must be mentioned that the cottage worker with his earnings had a greater choice of building materials than the peasant, whose efforts towards self-sufficiency obliged him to use local materials. He could replace old local materials such as shingles and straw with tiles, and the use of stones for building spread from the lake districts to the Oberland too. The use of non-local materials was also a consequence of the increased building activity resulting from industrialisation. The industrial regions soon ran out of timber for building (this applied less to the Oberland). In many parishes the subdivision of parish rights had resulted in over-exploitation of the forests. This meant that the members of a parish were no longer willing to allow every holder of a part-right the timber for building a new part-house. So wood-saving timber-frame constructions, filled in with stone or mud and wattles, became the favourite building method. Less valuable timber, such as the rapid-growth pinewoods, could be used for the little row houses of the *Flarz* type. Timber was further devalued as a building material when building with stone became the fashion and was regarded more highly. The town burghers' baroque houses made their influence felt.

Let us end this chapter with a brief survey of the reciprocal relationship between cottage industry and agriculture. This brings us back to the problem of the form of economy and settlement. We have already studied elsewhere the mental and spiritual, as well as the economic and legal, preconditions necessary for a fruitful symbiosis between agriculture and cottage industry. Wherever we have encountered synchronised relations between agriculture and cottage industry we have found a rational and intensive use of the soil, and economic farming methods. In any case, agriculture had to adjust to the new conditions and the possibility of adjusting had to be present. The earnings from cottage industry were directly associated with this sort of agricultural changeover. Having cash in hand meant that better stock could be acquired, improvements introduced, and that straw, manure, clover and sanfoin seed could be purchased. The outhouses could be enlarged to allow more cattle to be stalled. Meadows could be drained and orchards laid out, and qualitative improvements were implemented in other areas. In the *Philosophical Tradesman* Johann Caspar Hirzel compares the industrial earnings of the Zurich out-worker with a magnet, which 'draws everything to itself from the furthest regions', in order to improve and to intensify his farm. The author makes a farmer's daughter and outworker reply to his question whether she and her companions owed their property to the 'cotton manufacture' by saying 'What else? Without this [cotton manufacture] we would be working for a pittance. But, praise be to God, our earnings are good and we can cultivate our land with honour.'[35]

The tendency was towards changing over to a labour-saving form of land use: 'In the manufacturing parishes many arable fields are turned over to pasture, or else grain harvests are replaced with clover harvests, because these involve less expense, trouble and loss of time than working corn fields does.'[36] C. Meiners, who established this, wrote extensively about the efforts to improve and intensify agriculture with the help of industrial earnings.[37] J. C. Hirzel, who described the agriculture of the Oberland, sings its praises: 'Here one sees the greatest factory earnings united with constantly expanding agriculture and clearance of hitherto unexploited lands, evidence for which is found in the many houses one encounters in this region.'[38] The minister of Schönenberg acknowledged in 1857 that silk weaving was 'very beneficial' to his parish.

This is already shown in relation to agriculture, whereby earnings acquired through weaving have made it possible for significant numbers of farms to be improved, whereas without these earnings many places cannot spend so much on their landed assets; many small farms have experienced yields greater than those of bigger farms in the past, as a result of the improvements. These improvements could, however, only have been undertaken when the necessary means were acquired by weaving.[39]

At this point, it is important to mention the causal relationship. These farming improvements cannot be seen simply as a result of industrialisation, even though they could only be carried out with the help of industrial earnings (and were spurred on by the cottage work). They were to a far greater extent the product of the reciprocal relationship between industrialisation and the traditional order. We have seen that putting-out work was able to gain a foothold in the Zurich countryside in places where the economic and communal order allowed it to (or was unable to prevent it) – that is, in regions possessing the legal preconditions for altering their farming methods. This was, for instance, the case in regions around the Lake, as well as in those parts of the Grüningen district and the county of Kyburg, where a system of individual land use (*Egartenwirtschaft*) was practised. The alterations mentioned earlier could be carried out there, where people were allowed to build houses on outlying land. There was no open-field system to oppose new ways of using the soil; old farming land could be put to better use and new land could be cleared. In the arable regions farmed according to the three-field rotation system, attempts to alter and intensify farming methods and produce came up against a rigid order. Open-field farming, building prohibitions and communal grazing on fallow land and stubble – in short, a whole series of regulations prevented the introduction of stall-fed cattle, intensive fertilisation of meadows and fields, improving meadowland and planting orchards, and so on. As a result, the regions with strict three-field rotation and open-field systems, despite the fertility of their soil, ended up producing less than those industrial regions whose system of agriculture allowed farms to be changed over and a free hand in the use of the soil. J.C. Hirzel, to whom these connections were obvious, drew a detailed comparison, backed up by statistics, between the counties of Wädenswil and Regensberg. The result was 'that in Wädenschweil, the seat of the strongest factory workers, the state of agriculture is at least as perfect as in those regions of the country with such special advantages that the inhabitants devote themselves entirely to agriculture and, compared with these, it feeds four times as many inhabitants'.[40] Hirzel has listed a few of the important preconditions which favoured agriculture in the industrialised regions:[41]

1. Where houses are scattered.
2. Where there is still plenty of land left over for clearing.
3. Where one is in contact with regions, which provide the necessary cash for improving the properties.
4. Where stock farming provides the chief form of income from the properties.
5. Where sufficient materials for fuel and building are present or easily procured.

Basing himself on Hirzel's research and filling it in with his own observations, C. Meiners sums up: 'Without opposition, then, the factory work in most of the regions of the Zurich territory has promoted not only population growth but also the embellishment and enlargement of the villages, the improvement of the stock and the land, and in many places has changed the harsh, stony land into the most fertile, easy and rich soil.'[42] It was possible for a healthy and adaptable agriculture to develop hand in hand with industrialisation (especially around the town and in the lakeside districts) making intensive use of the soil along the lines of market gardening.

The situation was, however, quite different in the industrial regions which still clung firmly to an old agrarian economic order, although this order no longer reflected the social and economic conditions (otherwise cottage industry would never have been able to infiltrate it). The zones of contact and conflict were where cottage work and agriculture were as yet unable to reach a compromise and symbiosis. This affected above all the Knonau district and the more level, arable regions of the Grüningen district, where we encounter the constant complaint that agriculture was being neglected in favour of putting-out work. We have already emphasised that the reasons for neglecting the arable land are to a great extent to be sought for in the rigid communal order. It was difficult to combine putting-out work with farming in regions where the open-field system determined all field work down to the last detail and set compulsory dates for ploughing, sowing, harvesting and hay-making for everyone. It was difficult to make alterations and adjustments within this rigid framework. This meant that people 'preferred to work sitting down to wearisome work in the fields'. The prohibitions on building were very closely bound up with this economic order. They contributed towards the decline in these places of agriculture in connection with cottage industry. J.C. Hirzel recognised that the industry was disadvantageous to agriculture in places 'where the houses stand close by one another and form whole villages' and 'where limits to the houses according to the number of rights rule'.[43] The subdivision of parish rights did not help. On the contrary, splitting up the land and distributing the outhouses made running the farm even less economically viable, as long as people were unable to change over to a labour-saving and intensive use of the land. Many households were no longer able to make full use of their share of a right in the commonage. There is no doubt that the rich farmers were responsible for these conditions, with their economic mentality and their village and parish policies. In many places they thwarted all attempts to divide up the common lands and to remove the unwieldy open-field system. J.C. Hirzel informs us that this gave rise to an 'aversion to agriculture' among the cottagers and day-labourers, and the farms were 'managed more and more negligently'.[44] Strong forces were at play, which wanted to remove the straitjacket of the traditional economic and parish order and which strove to have the common lands divided up. The population engaged in industry played a trail-blazing role here, but the opposition was great and only a few common lands were divided up before the Helvetic Revolution took place. The purely agrarian regions where cottage industry had scarcely infiltrated shook off their three-field economy very late. In many places it was only world trade and the ensuing fall in prices which managed to crack the system. Specialised and intensive farming belonged to the future. The cottage industry must be seen as the forerunner of such a specialised and intensive agriculture.

The gamut of physiocratic ideas was absorbed very early on by the population engaged in industry, and their factory earnings also helped towards putting them into action. The cottage industry transformed the traditional rural economic and living space, thereby rendering traditional institutions of a legal and economic nature obsolete.

So it was not only cottage industrial settlement, building and life styles which changed the face of the Zurich cultural landscape. Agriculture too, as it developed in connection with cottage industry, changed the fields and common land and reshaped the countryside. The travel accounts of the age witness eloquently to this. Our aim in this chapter has been to grasp the changes brought about by the interrelation between industry and the existing order – in other words, to expose at least a few threads of this densely woven fabric.

5 ✤ Work in the putting-out industry and its effect on the life of the common people

In the previous chapters we attempted to identify and interpret the changes to the life of the common people and to popular culture under the influence of the putting-out industry. In this chapter we tackle the question of how the nature of work in the putting-out industry can be related to these changes.

We must begin by setting a limit: many aspects of fundamental importance to the nature of work in the putting-out industry will not be discussed in this part of our investigation. They are reserved for Part two, where they will be set against and compared to factory work. What is more, we have not provided technical descriptions of the work processes and have included only as much information about the organisation and structure of the Zurich putting-out industry as is required for our line of enquiry.

Let us begin with a fundamental precondition for work in the putting-out industry in the seventeenth and eighteenth centuries – the Protestant work ethic.

In the 'Description of the Poor in the Whole Countryside of Zurich' ('Beschreybung der Armen uff der ganzen Landschaft Zürich'),[1] each petitioner's entitlement to alms was vouched for with this endlessly recurring phrase 'Can indeed pray and spin' (*Kann wohl bätten und spinnen*) – a formula which summarises the ecclesiastical authorities' ethos of a righteous life.

Max Weber has demonstrated the connections between the spirit of Protestantism and Puritanism and the capitalist economic system. In the same way, the rise and development of the Zurich putting-out industry cannot be understood without reference to these religious historical and sociological aspects, quite apart from the influence of Protestant religious refugees on the manufacturing life of Zurich. It was not only among the Calvinist entrepreneurial types, but among the Zurich putting-out masters too (Protestants cast in Zwingli's mould), that was combined 'a virtuoso capitalist business sense with the most intensive forms of a piety which penetrated and regulated the whole life of these same people and groups of people'.[2] Research into economic history will establish how the development of the Zurich putting-out industry can be linked with Zwingli's teaching and its dogmatic hardening and interpretation in the sixteenth and seventeenth centuries. The

131

testimonials by leading Zurich putting-out masters would provide particularly important source material, by showing how religious thinking was intimately interrelated with the economic mentality. Folklore is concerned with the popular reception of the old Protestant spirit and its manifestation in the life of the common people and in popular culture.

In his *Auslegung und Begründung der Schlussreden oder Artikel* (*Exegesis and Reasoning on the Final Address or Article*) of 14 July 1523 Zwingli elevated work to a clear moral precept. This made him a co-founder of a Protestant work ethic:

Secondly, it follows that all who punish people for not keeping holidays, do wrong (I mean this only concerning those holidays which are celebrated merely in idleness); for the Christian person is also master over the holiday. Yea, it would be far better, if on most holidays, after hearing God's word and celebrating the Last Supper, people went back to their work . . . Keeping a holiday in our present manner by eating and drinking, card playing and useless gossiping is, when seen in the clear light of day, more sinful than godly. Then I read nowhere that idleness is a Divine Service. I know well that it would be more pleasing to God if on Sunday, after having accomplished the Divine Service correctly, one were to mow, cut, make hay or carry out other necessary work, instead of giving way to slovenly idleness. For the man who has Faith is greater than the Sabbath.[3]

It is not difficult to recognise how the spirit of the Zurich 'Sabbath and Moral Mandates' was based on these interpretations of Zwingli's, although a later church ordinance pays strict attention to ensuring that no work be done on Sunday. The Protestant work ethic developed as an integral part of the Protestant conduct of life. This was dominated by a deeply serious moral and religious attitude. The Protestant work ethic distinguished itself by 'driving a person to work, not only when he is hungry, but making him obey an inner compulsion, which harnesses his strength far more effectively than can mere outward necessity'.[4] The ethnic was by and large defined negatively by the concept of the sinfulness of idleness; idleness being a 'very harmful thing', which keeps a person away 'from his orderly work and profession'.[5]

Collecting all the source material in the sermons, ordinances and above all in the teaching material for the country schools, documenting the authorities' concern that their subjects led moral lives, and the trouble they took to cultivate a Protestant work ethic would in itself constitute a thesis. The word 'cultivate' is no exaggeration. Popular attitudes to such an important area of human life, as work undoubtedly represents, can only be changed over a lengthy process. The work ethic had first to be implanted in the breast of the common people: 'Christianity and desire for work, implant them early in your breast!'[6] Games and idleness were sins for children too. From their earliest years they were 'kept diligently at work' and 'bred to spin',[7] for 'Idleness is the root of all vice.'[8] The attitude of early capitalism to child labour can only be understood and assessed from the point of view of Church and religion. When the Stutz family sat at their hand work through the long nights, the oldest sisters warping, and Jakob spinning with his younger siblings, their mother would gladly tell them about her childhood days,

how they had to spin till they were nearly dead and yet got no crust of bread in their mouths all week . . . She would then go on to draw further comparisons, about how our life set against her childhood days was heaven-like. We have food, clothes and a bed, which thousands would gladly have as well, and so we should be glad and pray and work willingly. He who prays not is not blessed, and an idle person is the devil's headrest. But we should not think that we will get to heaven on roses, no, the way there is rough and narrow and overgrown with thorns.[9]

Thus were the puritanical rules of life implanted, straight from his mother's lips, in little Jakobli as he sat at his spinning wheel. These rules also culminate in the formula 'work and pray'. The extent to which the opinion that idle folk were the devil's headrest had been received into the country people's traditional way of thinking is illustrated by another of Jakob Stutz's stories. He describes the life and troubles of the Hittnau spinning work place and reports the following incident:

I remember a joke, which was carried out here once by a Sternenberg chappie. He was little old Heiri Wirth, who dealt in toys, screws, ladles and such-like, and who had just come down from the mountains with his heavy pack and wanted to rest a little in this place. A woman, at that time a wealthy farmer's wife, used to sit among the spinners almost every day, idle and resting her head on her hands. Heiri knew that this woman simply did not like working and, being a diligent man, he was all the more annoyed by this idle woman . . . He looked benevolently at the diligent spinners and praised them, while collecting a handful of little twigs and shavings on the ground and casting dispraising looks at the idle woman; then he handed her the twigs with a stone with a scornful smile, saying 'Look, woman, there you have something to play with. Knock up a little house!' This elicited such ringing laughter that the woman rushed home and did not let herself be seen idling in the spinning work place again for a while.[10]

Work belonged to the Christian way of life, to righteousness, and among country people engaged in industry it became a customary obligation which no one could avoid. A shabby spinner, who visited the tavern almost every day, is reported to have spoken of himself as follows in the Hittnau spinning work place: 'He had undertaken not to be thrifty and work any longer, since he only had to hand his earnings over to the damned *Stecklimannen* [i.e. the clothiers]. No, on his oath, he would be thrifty no more.' But he was corrected sharply: 'And I tell you, you must be thrifty and labour; the authorities can force you to.'[11]

Such examples show how the old Protestant spirit of work was embedded in the common people's consciousness. This is a mental historical process of outstanding importance. It affected the life of the common people not only in the economic sector, but it also determined its whole shape and feel. It is undoubtedly one of the most enduring processes. Even after the old Protestant conduct of life was weakened by the advance of industrialisation, by new ways of life and a new feeling about life which threatened the foundations of everyday Christian beliefs, the spirit of work still made itself felt. That such a secularised form of the Protestant work ethic was possible is attributable not least to Protestant teaching itself. The reception by the common people of this largely untraditional teaching entailed the acute danger of a secularised work ethic actually becoming a substitute religion. Let us cite only one reference showing how work and the secularised work ethic retained an element of religious dedication. The *Grütli-kalender* for 1925 contains a quotation from Robert Seidel's text: *Arbeitsschule, Arbeitsprinzip und Arbeitsmethode* (*School of Work, Principle of Work and Method of Work*, 2nd edition, 1885). This quotation, entitled 'Work', reads like a psalm, a song of praise or a prayer:

Work! with which Thou straightenest the crooked, comfort the sorrowing, lead those who have strayed onto the path of virtue; Work! Thou solace of the weak, salvation of the poor and joy of the strong; Work! Thou salve for the fallen, staff for the stumblers and tonic for the good; Work! Thou reflection of the Highest Power, Thou who raiseth us to the likeness of God, Work! to which Thou hast raised all mankind and hast led it out of Barbarity – Thou wilt apply thy powerful strength for training and education even to the malleable material of the growing generation, and a lovelier and better youth will blossom through Thee, to its own joy and blessing and that of the world.[12]

The intensive popular reception of the Protestant work ethic and its endurance is one of the most astounding phenomena of the modern age. 'Working as a result of an inner compulsion' can certainly not be attributed to the mental and spiritual attitude of time-less and primitive man and is surely no general human characteristic (being active, yes, but not 'working in the sweat of your brow'). This is sufficiently evidenced by the attitude of past and present cultures towards work. The Protestant work ethic was as unnatural as possible. That it could nonetheless become popular can be attributed to the values which it created. We know these values: Zurich owed its industry, 'Foster-mother to our country', as it was called in a report of 1833,[13] to its Protestant and puritanical spirit of work. Max Weber was not alone in recognising this link. Already 150 years before him, Councillor Schmidt wrote in his *New History of the Germans* the following surprising sentence, coming as it did from an eighteenth-century Catholic: 'In one area, however, the morals of the Protestants, especially in Germany, have taken a turn, which one would never have guessed at initially; to wit, in the appearance of a certain thrift, sobriety and industriousness, which can almost be viewed as something different in their character.'[14] J.C. Hirzel, who took up this quotation in his speech, unfolded an imaginary view before his audience, illustrating how these 'morals of the Protestants' manifested themselves in the life of the common people and in popular culture. He advised them to climb a mountain, from which both Catholic and Protestant regions could be viewed, as for instance from the Rossweid or the Vögelinsegg. From up there one could see 'the great difference between the countries of the Reformed and the Catholics'. In the Protestant regions one finds all sorts of signs of activity, diligence, and reflection; the country is richer in people and more lively; the farms are better worked; the houses are uniformly more solidly and tastefully built, if one disregards the few monasteries and dwellings of families who have risen through military service. On the Vögelins-Egg in Appenzell Ausser Rhoden one has a viewing point similar to the one I described on the Rossweid. On the one side one can see into the Thurgau, on the western shore of the Bodensee, whose population and agricultural methods are similar to those of the Zurich Lake region. On the other side is the Appenzell Alpine region, which is not by nature better than the region of the canton of Schwyz along the Biber. But here everything is alive, the whole area is divided up by fences into smaller or larger plots of land, mostly, however, of moderate size, with a well-built house standing on each plot; and every year one discovers new houses on newly cleared land, right up to the mountain peaks. A great difference springs to the eye when one leaves Appenzell Ausser Rhoden and enters the Inner Rhoden, or leaves Uznerland for Toggenburg, or leaves the Mark for Glarnerland. But just as we notice this difference writ small within the Swiss Confederation, so too is it obvious when we direct our gaze onto the larger economies of Europe, England, Holland and the Protestant states of Germany, which are models of the most perfect culture, both of diligence and skill in trade and manufacture. In France too industry blooms nowhere more splendidly than among the Huguenots, who still run most of the factories. And in the sea ports of the other Catholic states trade is in the hands of Protestants, whereby the Principle we have adopted is confirmed the more, in that the free use of an enlightened common sense, hard work, thrift and good morals increase both wealth and population.[15]

Hirzel's description could be countered with the argument that the author's judgement was not objective, that as a Protestant he was engaging in a polemic against people of different faiths. But this was not the case. Hirzel quotes the 'Commentary' to a New Year greetings from Köllin the Catholic magistrate of Zug, printed in a *New Year Gift to the Youth of Zug* in 1785 and 1786. Köllin wrote:

See how happy hardworking inhabitants make a country. If you want to see a living picture, you have only to cast a glance on neighbouring states. Whence their happiness, their wealth and their power? Go into their nurseries and see how the tiniest children are already made to do some work, any sort of work, simply to prevent them from acquiring a tendency to idleness. Go into their schools, go into their art and work rooms! Go into their places of trade! See how busy they are, how diligent, how indefatigably willing to work! Now whence do their riches, their status and power come? When all are diligent worker-bees, must not the hive be rich in honey?'[16]

It is obvious to us as well as J. C. Hirzel that magistrate Köllin was thinking about the industrial regions of the Zurich countryside. The open-minded Catholic took the Protestant work ethic as his model. It was Köllin who included these two verses, which we have already quoted, in his New Year greetings: 'Christianity and love of work, implant them early in your breast!'

We must end these few remarks of a general nature with a backwards glance; they appear to contradict the foregoing chapter in which we saw that in the industrial regions of the Zurich countryside, the 'common sense and thrift' of a Protestant conduct of life had to give way to heightened demands on life.

J.C. Hirzel himself acknowledged that there 'where factory earnings have for many years been highest' there was also found the most 'inclination to finery and extravagance in food and drink'.[17] How can this contradiction be solved?

We must recall the connections we established in our discussion about luxury: the Puritan and Protestant spirit formed the driving force behind industrialisation. But as industrialisation advanced the old spirit of Protestantism had to change, because the new industrial conditions of existence gave rise to new needs among the population. The expansion and development of the industry depended on these increased needs. The strict laws governing ostentation and morals – manifestations of a Puritan spirit – restricted industrialisation. This gave rise to a similar paradoxical situation as that seen in our discussion about luxury, but viewed from a different angle: Protestant religious teaching aroused the spirit of work, but the results of this work destroyed the dogma which created it, and changed the feeling about life from which it all started.

These introductory thoughts of a general nature bring us to the questions discussed in this chapter.[18] The folklorist approach puts man and his attitude to work and working at the centre of our enquiry. What did the industrial system of production with its economic rationalisation mean in terms of the life of the outworker? Industrial labour forced a majority of people into similar employment. Once they had slipped into industrial dependence, these people were at the mercy of the industrial system of production. Every sales stoppage, every fashion change, every new method of work directly affected their lives, but by and large they put up with this passively. Even when these people were familiar with weaving and spinning from working on their peasant holdings, working for the putting-out industry demanded a completely new approach to work. The outworker's attitude to life was moulded by this, and although its emergence was too involved to allow us to gain a true insight into it, we will try to sketch its rough outlines in the following pages. Arnold Niederer has perceived the whole extent of the problem:

Rationally and purposefully organised work has, ever since the manufacturing period, developed increasingly into work in general. Countless people, bound by their origins mainly to spheres of life determined by tradition, have been turned by means of this necessary and unavoidable development into useful components of the rational, mechanised and modern economic apparatus. They have thereby undergone a change in their mental make-up, the significance of which can scarcely be exaggerated.[19]

Let us first cast a glance at the old-style peasant economy (where cottage industry had not yet managed to set foot), thereby allowing us to evaluate, in an indirect and clearly negative manner, the new industrial methods of work and attitude to work. In the ancient peasant economy both processes and methods of work were handed down and established by tradition and depended to a great extent on natural factors.[20] The peasantry was directed not by its own rational and purposeful deliberations, but by the example of its fathers and forefathers alone.[21] The peasant clung doggedly to his ancient customs. In the eighteenth century, the economists of urban Zurich learnt about the peasant's mentality and his faith in tradition. 'His prejudices opposed everything lying beyond the ken of his antiquated way of thinking and by obstinacy, inflexibility and reluctant behaviour he often rendered the best arrangements powerless and useless', as Inspector von Birch reported in 1787. The peasant countered the efforts at economic reform with the argument: 'You are right, but I will stick to what I know and have often done before.'[22] Just as the old peasant methods of work and attitude to work were not determined by rational and purposeful thought, so too was the peasant's economic thinking devoid of economic rationalism. There was little or no space in the circle of peasant life and economy for competition, individual effort and social advancement, especially not where three-field farming with its open-field system determined the methods of work and the use of the soil down to the last detail. The parishioner cared more about his dignity, power and status as a farmer than about the economic viability of his farm.[23] 'There are such [farmers] who would forfeit an inheritance of some hundred *Gulden*, rather than apologise or produce even one kind of respectful gesture', reported minister Irminger of Henggart in 1783.[24] It is clear that the putting-out industry was able to secure only limited influence where this attitude to work and this economic mentality were prevalent. Both the material and the mental preconditions worked against it: the demand for work was satisfied and the old-fashioned farmers were not aware of the concept of rational and purposeful work for the sake of gain. Nor did the religious concept of work, which forced people to work that they might not be idle, have much chance of being realised in the ancient peasant economy and way of farming.

This characterisation of the peasant way of thinking applies mainly to the arable farmers on the level zones of the Zurich countryside, which were characterised by their three-field farming system. The scattered settlements of the Oberland, marked by the predominance of individual property and land use, required an individual economic mentality and attitude to work, which came much closer to the economic rationalism of the putting-out industry. In Chapters 1 and 4 we searched extensively for the social, economic and legal factors responsible for this. The material and mental preconditions for purposeful and rational work in the service of the putting-out industry were incomparably better in the Oberland farmlands than in the arable farmlands of the Unterland.

Let us cast a further glance at those classes of the population whose lives were bound earliest and most exclusively to the putting-out industry. We learnt about them in the 'Description of the Poor in the Whole Countryside of Zurich'. They were the smallholders, the day-labourers, and charcoal-burners, the whittlers of scoops, the basket-weavers, the widows and orphans, the unmarried daughters and the elderly, in short the whole army of people who subsisted painfully on the margins of the peasant community. These people were predestined by their mental and material conditions to become wage-labourers in the service of the Zurich putting-out industry. Working for the sake of gain was taken for granted. They were familiar with the rational equation: here the work, there the wage. They were aware that their labour was their only economic asset. As day-labourers and seasonal workers they were used to doing temporary work and to not receiving any share in the produce of their labour. Their relationship with work was consequently characterised by the absence of bonds and involvement. The land they worked, whether their own or another's, gave them no security, but forced many of them into a life of wandering. Before industrialisation there was no question of these classes of the population having enough work. We have learnt about the work vacuum. The Protestant motto for a righteous life 'pray and work' must have echoed mockingly for the poor countrymen of that age: it is easy to preach about praying, but where in their homeland could they find work and bread? It was only the exogenous putting-out industry which gave them the chance of earning a living in their own country and they reached out eagerly towards the industrial sources of earnings, and built themselves a new existence in their homeland with them.

Now, regarding the popular reception of the Protestant work ethic, we must consider that a new work ethic could only be received into popular conscious-ness and remain there uncontested when there was an adequate supply of work. The work supply had, furthermore, to be by nature appropriate to the work ethic. We must further remember how the economic mentality of the propertied sector drove the economically weaker sector into industrial dependence. This has been extensively discussed in an earlier chapter. J.C. Hirzel describes how the rich peasants of the Greifen Lake region oppressed the smallholders and did not want to share out the common land. He added: 'This oppression aroused in the smallholders inertia, stupidity and recalcitrance towards agriculture, which was in consequence practised increasingly less effectively in these regions and the opportunity provided for a harmful preference for spinning to be indulged.'[25]

These sketchy observations have cast indirect light on work in the putting-out industry and on the outworkers' attitude to their employment. Let us now take a look at these specific topics.

Both spinning and weaving were parts of a process of production whose organisation and management rested in the hands of the urban putting-out masters. Under the Ancien Régime the social and political status of the outworker, as a subject, meant that he could not be more than a tiny cog in the production machine. The raw material of his work was grown in countries whose names he hardly knew, and a proportion of the finished goods was also sent out to distant nations. What did the outworker know about the cotton harvest in Cyprus or Macedonia? How was he able to explain why the raw material ran out and why sales suddenly stagnated? And then what of 'the spirit of fashion, which lays down the law to the tradesman so fitfully and capriciously'? A Zurich putting-out master of the eighteenth century compared it 'with the Wind, which no man knows whence it cometh and whither it goeth'.[26] All these factors eluded the outworker's understanding to a great extent, although they had an immediate effect on his work. The spinner was given a specific quantity of wool by the carrier or the clothiers, which he turned into more or less fine yarn via several processes. He received an appropriate wage for this. The carrier would bring the yarn to town to the manufacturer from whom he got the raw material or else he could hand the spun yarn straight over to be woven and would deliver only the finished rough cloth to the town manufacturer. The uniform spinning work dragged on monotonously. It fitted in with none of the holidays or seasons, and the amount of work done was assessed in purely quantitative, rational and contractual terms, measured by mass, in *Pfund* or *Schneller*.[27] That was how people calculated their daily and weekly earnings; they made a level-headed and quantitiative estimate of the matter in hand and set themselves a certain amount of work, the *Rast*. The only thing that mattered was the amount achieved. In Jakob Stutz's *Gemälde aus dem Volksleben* (*Pictures from the Life of the Common People*) the following song is sung by children as they spin:

> There was once a pious little spinner
> She spun every day eight *Schneller* in number
> Eight *Schneller* in number, like silk so fine,
> They shone like silver and jewels.
> She had the prayerbook always on her lap
> And prayed by her spinning wheel without a break.
> The blessing of her work was great.
> She did not fall short of the *Rast* even once.[28]

The *Rast* and the *Schneller*, purely quantitative and contractual ways of measuring work, are called the blessings of work in the song. We cannot measure how far Stutz as a domestic spinner and weaver was aware of this purposeful and contractual attitude to work. After this song, Stutz makes the grandmother urge the children on with their work:

> So spin, children, spin and take care!
> Now make your wheels hum, now!
> Drawing the threads out long as the bobbin,
> And do not make me any lumps in it.
> Now we earn a *Batzen* for each *Schneller*,
> But who knows how long this will go on.
> So spin, children, spin and take care!
> When you have fulfilled the *Rast*, the rest belongs to you.
> And so you will earn a *Schilling* for yourselves.
> So spin, children, spin as much as you can,
> Spend your time and hours together wherever you can.
> You are still young. Oh, were I still like you.
> How my spindle would hum day and night!

Their grandmother introduces her materialistic exhortation to work, with its references to *Schneller*, *Rast*, *Batzen*, *Schilling*, money, time and hours with the following explanation:

> Yes, truly children, if you spin so well,
> And make the yarn so fine and clean
> And pray early and late, so will you come at last
> Into Heaven, in Heaven above.

This example illustrates how the religious concept of work had fused with the outworker's rational and purposeful attitude to work. With spinning (and partly so with weaving) the work ethic had to degenerate into worship of quantitative achievement, because cottage work provided countryfolk engaged in industry with few opportunities to excel qualitatively in their work. There were indeed different qualities of yarn.[29] Skilful daughters distinguished themselves by spinning *Brief* or *Löthli* yarn. This was a fine yarn spun by hand onto the spindle, and far better paid than the rougher spinning-wheel yarn. So a degree of choice was possible with spinning. Goethe noticed this in a Zurich spinning community and wrote about it:

> This employment [spinning *Brief* yarn], which is pursued only by steady and thoughtful persons, gives the spinner a gentler appearance than working on the wheel does; the latter suits a tall, slim figure best, thus making a calm and tender form appear to great advantage. I noticed several such different characters engaged in different work in one room and ended up not knowing whether to devote my attention to the work or to the workers.

Goethe's report mentions a fine instance of the pride the spinners took in the quantity they produced. One of the girls working at a spinning wheel bet Goethe that she could spin between 8,000 and 9,000 ells a day at her wheel. At this a quiet and shy *Brief* yarn spinner spoke up and assured him that she could spin 120 *Schneller* a pound (wheel-spun yarn produced only 20 to 30 *Schneller* a pound). This spinner had just filled a *Schneller* and 'was able to demonstrate how the practised spinner's employment was invested with innocent self-esteem'.[30] In spite of the possibility of choice, hand spinning was governed just as much by the principle of quantity as was spinning with the wheel. With *Brief* yarn, too, pay was reckoned according to the number of *Schneller*. The actual product aroused far less satisfaction than did the pay it amounted to. The joy of creation was mainly a joy of making money. Reckoning in *Schneller*, *Schilling* or time characterises the attitude of the countryfolk employed in industry to their putting-out work.[31]

Such an attitude to work gave rise to various consequences. People began competing with one another over the daily number of *Schneller* stipulated. Time is money – this frenzy began to take effect. The whole course of the day was arranged accordingly. The housekeeping could only be done when the *Rast* work was finished. The smallest children, who could not yet earn money, were packed off to school so that they 'were taken out from under their mothers' feet'.[32] Older daughters were initiated into almost none of 'the most essential household concerns'.[33] There were many women workers, as minister Jakob Oeri reported in 1784 about Wil, who 'were not capable even of darning some worn-out clothes or of washing'.[34] The minister of Männedorf wrote in 1857 about the silk hand-loom weavers 'What's more, this uninterrupted employment at the loom is linked to another disadvantage, which only becomes apparent when the weaver-girl wants to set up her own household: she knows nothing about cooking, nothing about darning, she is unused to keeping the rooms clean, in short, she can't do anything except earn money at her loom.'[35] Miss Hermine Kunz (Hiltisberg, parish of Wald, born 1878) tells about her grandmother:

Grandmother had done nothing all her life except spin. She did nothing about the housekeeping. We children found it very funny whenever she helped with the washing, when she had finished a cloth. She always wove white silk, wide, she was very precise; her daily *Rast* was 9 ells. She started at five on the dot and worked until nine in the evening. After about three weeks, she would have finished a cloth for which she would get around 30–2 *Franks*.[36]

Conditions were similar for the new generation of outworkers. They were incapable of any other work and in times of no work, they were able only with difficulty to opt for physically exhausting field and day-labouring work. 'Unwilling and at the same time unable to do unfamiliar work, many could be used for almost nothing, especially not for fairly strenuous physical work.'[37] 'Too little accustomed to endurance and exertion, mostly knowing only one factory work, grown up in parlours or loom shops, many had neither strength nor skill left for farmwork, especially when they had to tackle hard labour; many were also too indolent to learn new work [when sales stagnated and production stopped].'[38] Pestalozzi also described this phenomenon. His words ring with concern and horror: 'The mechanics of a miserable factory knack appeared to thousands and thousands of people to be enough to ensure the happiness of their children and their country forever.'[30]

The industrial system of production was undoubtedly responsible for this situation, which allotted rational and purposeful work to an army of wage workers, who were trained and recruited for this work alone. Thus was achieved the process whereby 'people are divided up into sub-functions, characteristic of many modern production processes'. Economic rationalism is unable to take much account of people's physiological and psychological natures when these do not serve its purposes. As a logical consequence of this principle, 'human individualities and eccentricities, seen from the point of view of production, [were stamped] as mere sources of error.'[40] People who had slipped into industrial dependence had to adapt, thereby decisively influencing their lives and communities. We are poised in front of the central question of our folklorist enquiry: how did the industrial method of working, the principle of quantitative production and, in overall terms, the structure and organisation of the Zurich putting-out industry affect the character and life of the common people?

Let us start with a detail which reveals the connections. The outworkers 'have a bad reputation on account of their untrustworthiness at work'.[41] Wherever cottage industry is discussed, such complaints are to be found. Outworkers had many opportunities to make some unlawful profits: the workers embezzled the raw material, yarn or cloth, they sold or pawned the delivered wares, they padded out their quota by some sort of cheating, and so on. Jakob Stutz tells us about his parents' experiences in the clothiers business:

When my mother was acting as a carrier for the spinners and weavers, who came along almost every hour, she experienced not just a lot of trouble but also much anger and irritation. Very few of them were satisfied with their wages and most of them were cheats and thieves. The *Schneller* were either moistened so as to weigh more, or else they were not the right length and breadth. There were just a few Separatists, who in the true sense of the word worked faithfully and honestly and did not pinch even a *Heller*'s worth from what was entrusted them.[42]

These abuses were so deeply entrenched that none of the measures taken by the authorities had any effect. It was pointed out in the minutes of 24 September 1716 'that, regardless of all chastisement, untrustworthiness is constantly increasing and will soon be beyond endurance'.[43] The Factory Ordinance of 16 August 1717 stated

And because in the past various forms of untrustworthiness have been practised by the workers, so, seventhly, shall it be incumbent on the manufacturers [in order to put a halt to such criminal undertakings] to make the names and surnames of workers who can be satisfactorily convicted known to other manufacturers through a person specially appointed to this end. It shall then be forbidden to employ such untrustworthy workers.[44]

In spite of all decrees and prohibitions Johann Schulthess felt that

the extent to which each place is corrupted depends on how long it has been penetrated by factory work. I have only to think of a village well known to me since my childhood, where only sixty years ago a few dozen of its inhabitants had to stand in front of the church door holding strands of wool as a penance for stealing, to calculate how far their descendants will have progressed in the evil, about which the deceased Antistes Wirz has given evidence in this hall, that in his time it had already become so common that whole villages were infected with it, and it had struck root so deeply that they no longer considered it a sin, but in their hearts even blessed themselves![45]

Fifty years later the minister of Männedorf announced similar conditions in the silk hand-loom trade and explained why these abuses were not disappearing from cottage industry:

A very bad moral evil accompanying silk weaving is disloyalty to the employer, the more so that the workers do not consider it to be disloyalty and refer to it among themselves under the technical term of humbugging. On the whole manufacturers do not set great store by this, knowing how much can be embezzled on average and setting their pay accordingly; for their part the workers also know that the manufacturers make up for their loss through lower pay and they make up for it by humbugging.[46]

A 'Report on a Few Industrial Conditions in the Canton of Zurich' (31 May 1833) pointed out that 'a special reason for encouraging the introduction of mechanical weaving is the widespread system of cheating which has penetrated our hand-loom industry'.[47]

It is clearly apparent from these witnesses that the outworkers' customary cheating and stealing had developed out of the system of production and pay in the putting-out industry and must be understood as being really a form of self-help. It was obvious that this deceitful behaviour, sanctified by custom, formed the character of the common people. Of course it was only a detail, but when we look more closely at the question as to how this evil practice arose, we see how it grew up out of the organisation and structure of the putting-out industry. We recognise further that the same features of the system of production which led to customary stealing and cheating were to have far weightier consequences for the way of life in the cottage industry, although these were not immediately obvious. We can gather from the minister of Männedorf's account what a great latitude existed or could exist in the cottage industry system of payment. These conditions were deeply rooted in the nature of the textile industry. There was a market demand for all sorts of yarn and cloth. Fashions changed in rapid succession and with them the marketable articles. Further, this branch of manufacture, which depended on world trade very early on, was extremely sensitive to crises. This applied as much to the supply of the raw materials as to the sale of the finished goods. Given these facts, it was difficult to find a stable rate of pay, valid over a long period, within the system of production of the putting-out industry. This applied especially to the period before the Helvetic Revolution and its particular political, social and economic conditions. Under the Ancien Régime the putting-out industry encompassed people with completely different political and economic rights. The clothiers were to a great extent able to determine the spinners' and weavers' wages, but as subjects they were bound through their profession to the urban putting-out masters. They secured commissions from them at a specific manufacturing price, and were obliged to procure the raw material in the city and to deliver the finished goods there too.[48] The clothier was only a variant of the country undertaker in the production system of the putting-out industry. Yarn carriers, cloth carriers, loom menders and others, with a greater or lesser degree of independence, completed the picture. It is easy to appreciate that the human and social structure of the production system of the putting-out industry under the Ancien Régime possessed very little ability to bolster itself against fluctuations in demand and supply. The army of wage workers suffered most from these. The putting-out master tried to offset his manufacturing risks onto the clothiers and carriers, who, not being economically self-sufficient, passed them on to the outworkers. This economic mentality was obvious, as was the attitude of the outworkers, who tried to keep out of harm's way by lawful and unlawful means. Their weapon was embezzlement. They were forced to use this weapon all the more because pressure on wages was not the only thing they were powerless to oppose. Their earnings were also reduced by bad raw materials, incorrect bills, insufficient equipment and similar injustices. It could even happen that a weaver would be punished for his honesty by the carrier; if he returned superfluous yarn, he would have the pay for his piece of cloth reduced. Given this practice, he would require the honesty of a Separatist not to substract the superfluous yarn.[49]

The conditions under the Ancien Régime described above have been impressively documented in the factory mandates and decrees. The town authorities were constantly trying to achieve set rates of pay and to protect the outworkers from unjust exploitation. In 1662 a specific institution was founded, the Commercial Directorium (Kaufmännisches Direktorium), to supervise and manage the factories. A Commission for the Protection of the Workers was called into being in 1717: it met every week and anyone could complain to it about injustices they had suffered.[50] However, the wording of the mandate provides sufficient evidence of how ineffective the authorities' decrees were in practice. We have chosen a few examples from the compilation of 'Zurich Factory Legislation'.[51] They provide a lively picture of conditions in the putting-out industry. For instance, on 3 July 1675 the council ratified a pay arrangement set up by the Commercial Directorium for the 'Silk combers, silk spinners and silk winders'. The Directorium justified its regulations as follows: 'To prevent the unfair and unChristian start of various of those tradesmen, who some time ago sorely oppressed the poor working people by reducing their little wages.'[52] We read in the introduction to the Factory Ordinance drawn up by the authorities on 16 August 1717 that, for instance, 'Further, because in some of these factories their wage has not been fixed but in others their pay is not proportionate to their work' the council finds it necessary to establish firm regulations. The rates of pay in the different *Fabriken*, that is, in the different branches of the textile industry, 'must be fixed'. Let us pick out a few places. With spinning in the 'woollen factories', it must be 'left to each manufacturer to act conscientiously in fixing fair wages, because it would not be expedient to set a particular wage on account of the constant changes. The opinion was that the manufacturer, before handing the wares over to the spinner, should indicate the price he has stipulated they be spun for.' A specific minimum wage was established. Regarding the cotton spinners, it was also acknowledged that 'In respect of the differing quality of the cotton the wages cannot be assessed so precisely, but the following order should be obediently observed and obeyed' (then follow the rates of pay).[53]

These examples show how uncontrollable was the system of pay in the putting-out industry and the extent to which the outworkers were delivered into the power of the manufacturers. They could indeed call for checks by the authorities, but who could force the manufacturer to deliver further work to those outworkers who complained to the Commission about him? In regions near the town, the spinner or weaver might be able to find another employer easily, but this was not the case in the remote valleys of the Oberland. And how easy it was for an accused person to take his revenge. The cotton weavers' wages, for instance, were accompanied by the following stipulation: 'It is understood with all these weavers' wages that, just as with the silk factories, the manufacturer shall procure the equipment for the worker and also keep it in good condition.' This loan system enabled the manufacturer to keep a tight rein on a mutinous weaver; he would give him faulty equipment or he would fail to sent the loom-mender along for the necessary repairs, and the weaver would suffer a considerable drop in his wages.

The factory mandates also illustrate how the clothiers and carriers were responsible for these conditions. The decree of 1717 went as follows:[54]

Secondly, because we have been aware for some time that remarkable irregularities, which are very disadvantageous to the poor workers, have occurred on behalf of the carriers, so it is our earnest desire and opinion, in order to prevent all forms of abuse, that as many carriers as possible be dismissed and that no carrier be appointed closer than three or four hours' distance from the town.

Following this a scale of pay was established according to the carriers' hours of travel, which probably proved difficult to enforce in practice. The carriers were also referred to again:

What is more, the ministers should keep diligent watch on the doings of the carriers. These last should bring the name of the spinner on a paper sheet or leaf along with each little package of yarn. The manufacturer would then write the amount paid each spinner on it, and enter the spinner's name in his note-book at the same time.

Many carriers and clothiers tried to pay their outworkers in less valuable tokens, instead of ready money. If they were also bakers or grocers, they would force payment in kind on them as well. In an attempt to regulate this abuse, the Factory Ordinance of 1717 stipulated: 'the carriers should also not be bakers or grocers, but they should pay their workforce their due wages in ready, undepreciated and current money, but not in goods or foodstuffs'.

The carriers' and the clothiers' large responsibility for these fluctuating and uncertain conditions of pay is adequately illustrated in these sources. We are aware of how much the countryfolk employed in industry were dependent on these links in the chain of production. A methodical approach makes it clear that the human and technical structure of the putting-out system cannot be considered in isolation, but must constantly be set alongside the political, social and economic conditions of the age. This applies not only to Zurich in general, but also more specifically to the different industrial regions of Zurich. Local forces and influences often proved so strong that they shaped the human and technical structure of the industry according to their individual features. Johann Heinrich Pestalozzi wrote:

Historically it is true that Zurich manufactured muslins twenty or so years before Appenzell. But as a result of the freedom of trade, the Appenzellers overtook Zurich in the art of its manufacture and likewise in its income by twenty years. This too is true: the common workers in this region have not been reduced by the manufacture to the same degree of poverty as the spinners and weavers of the Zurich area have been.[55]

District captain Beyel reported in 1787

that the cotton manufacture proceeded satisfactorily so long as the merchants in the town held the business wholly in their hands, but ever since they appointed these clothiers and their like and allowed the manufacture to pass through them and bought cloth from them, everything fell into confusion. When the merchants, for instance, got enough commissions they pressed their clothiers for the wares, and they then raised the weaving and spinning pay above average and when the commissions did not come in for a while, then the price they paid the clothiers fell again and so would the wages. As a result the trade was rendered uncertain and irregular and had a very harmful influence both in the town and in the countryside, both on the moral and on the economic condition of its inhabitants. There were strong divisions in this trade, with the burghers mostly becoming merchants and the manufacturing side coming into the hands of the country people.[56]

Beyel's formulas and values are of his age. Let us recall the attitude of the countryfolk employed in industry to marriage and the family, to the land, to their food and clothes, to luxury, to social life, etc. Let us further recall the outworker's lack of thrift. All these attributes now appear in a much clearer light. We see that the outworker's life was tied to an economic system incapable of providing him with any security. It was conceived along rational and expedient lines and had to obey the laws which had determined its existence. The outworker, who had built up his life wholly or partially on an industrial basis, had to submit to these laws. And submit he did. His attitude to work concentrated necessarily on gain. He met his daily needs through the 'medium of money, which is indifferent to quality'[57] and so was obliged to think in terms of a money economy. In short, his life and social life adapted to the new conditions, and the outworker's thought processes were subjected to the influence of economic rationalism. But – and this is now decisive – the outworker adapted as a traditional person to his new basis of existence. Whatever it was that led him to work in the putting-out industry (it could be any one of an infinite number of reasons), he was still caught up in the common people's belief in tradition. The connection with the previous chapters is thereby established, in which the altered forms of life were considered from the point of view of work in the putting-out industry.

One would now be justified in asking whether this does not contradict all our previous statements, in which we stressed the more open and dynamic mental attitude of the country population employed in industry, and tried to demonstrate its manifestation in popular culture. It would in any case be a contradiction, were one to muddle up belief in tradition with traditional property. The traditional property, both of a material and spiritual kind, pertaining to the outworkers had undoubtedly changed and was distinguishable in many ways from that of the peasants. The outworkers' traditional property had, by its very nature, to be appropriate to an industrial basis of existence, that is to say, stamped with the money economy and the whole dynamism of this economic system. But the common people retained their faith in tradition. This phenomenon[58] is most clearly shown in the attitude of the outworkers to their basis of existence: all the fluctuations in pay, all the stagnations in sales and all the elements of uncertainty in the putting-out industry were unable to shatter their trust in the 'mechanics of a miserable factory knack'. While the outworker no longer said: my father and grandfather did not manure their meadows and 'yet they were no fools but sensible people. How should I improve on what they did?',[59] he did, however, cling with equal stubbornness to factual experience: my parents or neighbours also span or wove, they too owned no land and saved just as little as I do. They had fat and lean years just as we do, but the putting-out industry always fed them. However rational the outworker's attitude to his work might be, however much he had learnt about flexibility with regard to his work, his attitude to his 'dynamic and technical existence' remained irrational and traditional.[60] The mountain peasant took avalanches and landslides in his stride as the normal occurrences of a lifetime and the arable farmer reckoned with damage from hail and frost. Stagnations in sales and fluctuations in wages were part of the outworker's life. The difference between them was only that the outworker's existence was not based on the soil, but on earning ready money. Natural phenomena did not directly threaten the outworker's basis of existence. Instead he was at the mercy of the elements of uncertainty in the industrial system of production, and money as a medium reacts sensitively. To him, these elements of uncertainty were just as irrational and obscure as hailstorms were to the peasants.[61] It was just as hard to convince the peasants of the utility of taking out insurance for their cattle or against hail as it was to explain the sense of a savings or medical care scheme to outworkers and factory hands. When Jakob Stutz was admiring a rich clothier's new house in Weisslingen with his mother, he discovered his first *Strohlableiter* (lightning conductor). 'Look!', said his mother, 'the gentleman has had these rods stuck on his house so that the lightning will not strike there. But that is called tempting God and it is a great sin.'[62] Was there any reason why the outworker would not employ similar arguments based on popular belief to bolster his reluctance to save?

We must now relate this brief and fragmentary commentary to our enquiry. How did the nature of his industrial basis of existence affect the outworker, born as he was into a sphere of life determined by tradition?

The outworker bound himself with his basis of existence to a new dynamism. Because he clung to this with his traditional mentality, it was able to become the basis of a compulsory norm. This led to a new relation to life, to a new attitude to life. The outworker's attitude towards his human and material environment is illustrated by an account by a pastor of Grüningen:

In our parish the dominant employment is silk weaving, whereas cotton weaving employs only a very small number, perhaps a twentieth of the weavers. The experience of a sequence of years has shown that these earnings are not in themselves enough to provide a family with a secure livelihood, or to produce even some kind of firm prosperity. Where such prosperity begins to blossom, it already has its main roots in a well-managed farm and a well-established household. It is apparent that the usual earnings are quite inadequate for establishing an outer or inner basis, because they are too liable to all the various fluctuations which destroy not only the outer appointments and manners of life, but even the characters of the workers, so long as they lack another means of support. The fluctuations affect them ever more lastingly and deeply, because they often result in the worker being overloaded with work, and then having to be idle again. He becomes the slave of his work, instead of its master . . . So while these earnings are a very welcome supplementary economic support for individuals and whole households who already have an outward (and especially an inner) form of support – and the employers will always prefer to employ these workers, as being the most reliable – whereas all the other workers, who are not seeking to establish their prosperity on a lasting basis, but only to enjoy it, driven from one desire to another, gradually sink into poverty and destitution, finally to become charges on the parish as soon as work and earnings cease.[63]

As described in this account, people's basis of existence was founded on the putting-out industry. Cottage industrial earnings fluctuated so greatly that they could not guarantee any constant standard of living. Families with no farm to provide a reserve or to cushion them felt the full force of the fluctuations in earnings. Their outward standard of living and their inner attitude to life was subjected to these dynamics. Because the outworker, as a traditional person, permeated these unsteady and fluctuating conditions of existence with his wholly irrational, traditionalist mentality, he imbued them with a customary solidity and sanction. This gave rise to an appropriate attitude to life. The putting-out industry, with its own laws and dynamics, led the outworkers into a new world. They had to find their inner balance, as well as assert and establish themselves in a technical and dynamic world; always a lengthy process. They were not supported by their ancient peasant traditions and inheritance, they needed a new material culture and an attitude to life more suited to their basis of existence. We learnt about the industrial ways of life in the previous chapters. Now the nature of work in the putting-out industry sheds some light on the life of the countryfolk employed in industry.

We have consciously avoided the term 'protelarianisation' in our characterisation of the cottage industrial attitude to life, since it can scarcely be used in an academic sense any more, having been over-mortgaged with political and other meanings. Even when we use the term 'proletarianisation' without any emphasis, that is, understanding it as a form of mental and spiritual behaviour, a relation to life, the danger of misrepresentation would still be present. But it is important to recognise among the outworkers of the seventeenth and eighteenth centuries, the forms of existence and the attitude to life outlined above. It was then that these first came into being, and not just with the advent of the machine age or of Liberalism.

The bonds of the old peasant communities did not apply to the industrial basis of existence any more (in so far as the outworker had ever been rooted in a peasant sphere of life). But there was no danger that the outworker would not achieve new communal bonds, because as a traditional person he possessed a strong need for community. Once we have recognised this, our line of enquiry in this chapter produces the following question: how do the outworkers achieve an awareness of their own community from their employment and their work?

The peasantry and its work experienced, following the new awareness of nature, a considerable rise in esteem and transfiguration. This intellectual fashion was a purely urban phenomenon and was limited only to a select circle.[64] The non-peasant countryfolk employed in industry did not share this high regard for peasant life at all. 'Agriculture, these props of morality and of a solid prosperity, began to be despised by the ignorant and uneducated mass of common people.'[65] Jakob Stutz tells us about the sale of his parental farm:

That autumn the aforesaid auction really did take place, and more than half the farm was sold and even very cheaply, because, as far as I remember, manufacture was doing well. Therefore people preferred sitting at their looms to sweating in the fields. Many said that they would not accept the biggest farm as a gift, or, should it come to them floating on the stream, they would just let it pass by and would certainly not pull it to the bank. Now an average *Galli* [short for calico, a coarse cotton cloth] weaver was able to earn a weekly 5–6 *Gulden*, while sitting in the dry and living well, whereas the farmer had to work in wind and rain and not get anything from it. Thus did they esteem the peasantry in those days of rich earnings, whom the factory people considered with scorn and mockery.[66]

In the *Pictures from the Life of the Common People*[67] the young spinner-girl Babel says to farmer Hans:

> There can no better person be than me.
> When it is cold, I sit in the warm room,
> When the sun shines, I am in the cool shade:
> When it is raining I am sitting dry under the roof.
> Look you, if I could certainly have
> The richest farmer, I surely would not take him.

Not satisfied with this, she tells the other outworkers: 'Let's sing a song for Hans'. Babel and the other spinners sing:

> When the farmers go to the plough
> We can spare our shoes:
> We are all right!

> When the farmers mow and sweat
> We can sit in the shade:
> We are all right!
>
> When the farmers painfully stoop,
> We go about with upright backs;
> We are all right!
>
> When the farmers get up early,
> We can turn over in bed;
> We are all right!

It is clear from the industrialised countryfolk's attitude to the peasantry that they enjoyed a high degree of self-awareness. Wherever this self-awareness declared itself, it fed on the same nourishment. They mocked the peasant on account of his harsh toil, subject to unkind nature, and they proudly rattled the coins in their pockets, earned through manufacturing. Clearly, the outworkers' self-awareness was determined essentially by their work, a form of employment where the pay meant everything to them and the work itself but little. They were proud that they did not have to earn their bread in the sweat of their brows. 'They laugh at the peasants and their sweat, since they know how to feed themselves more comfortably', came a report from Mettmenstetten in 1789.[68] The pastor of Wildberg wrote the following about the Oberland outworkers:

Spinning and weaving are the preferred means of livelihood of these mountainfolk. One may frequently find parents, grandparents and grandchildren together in a room at the spinning wheel and loom; sometimes in the warm sun, sometimes in the cool shade, as it pleases them, grown sons and daughters gather together, swinging their spinning wheels in mischievous fun, either arrogantly mocking the peasants who bear the burden and heat of the day, or looking down on them with pity.[69]

This sort of teasing about professions and social position are evidence not only of a self-awareness, but they also constitute a 'negative expression of the communal spirit'.[70] Their scorn and mockery helped the outworkers to experience themselves as something separate and better. They did not consider that the farmer laughs in times of no earnings, when the harvest has been brought in and the barn has been filled.

This type of self- and community awareness on the part of the outworkers grew with the expansion of the putting-out industry. We will scarcely be mistaken in assuming that they attained their decisive development in the first flowering of the Zurich textile industry during and after the Seven Years War. In 'this period, which they call the Golden Age',[71] we are told in a diary kept by a Toggenburg inhabitant that 'every lad earned 2 to 3 *Florin* a week and spent about a third of this pay on food; and even the smallest children . . . earned 15 *Kreuzer* a day'.[72] It is clear that these periods of rich earnings gave a powerful boost to the outworkers' self-esteem. The suddenly swollen flow of money made it possible for them to document their profitable profession worthily.

They distanced themselves from the peasantry by means of new cultural and material goods, appropriate to their basis of existence and their feeling about life. But the peasants, who had no share in the golden blessings of those years, underwent a mental and spiritual crisis. The peasants' awareness of their social standing was swamped by the flood of industrial earnings and many a one said to himself in these periods of prosperity 'Mir bured jetzt bim Webstuehl zue' ('I'm going to farm with the loom now').[73]

In spite of all this, the outworkers' pride and self-esteem were granted no stability; they too fluctuated. How quickly the fat years gave way to lean, how quickly potatoes replaced expensive veal and Sunday finery had to be traded in for flour! The peasant's pride was more stable. He owned house and land, he was rooted in economic strength and even years of poor harvest could not break him. Likewise the peasant community was far more strongly based on material ties, on pasture and common rights. The outworkers' communal bonds lacked this material stay; they fluctuated somewhat. While sharing the same employment did bind them together, this employment in turn also set them against one another. In periods of stagnation, every fellow worker was obliged to view his mates as competitors, stealing his bread from him. For this reason, crises were likely to forge a common destiny for the outworkers, while simultaneously developing a negative community awareness. We will return to these questions in the next chapter.

Although the outworkers, by mocking the peasantry, felt themselves to be something special, their awareness of their profession and social standing should not be exaggerated. We know how fluid was the transition from peasantry to putting-out industrial workforce. We should not assume that a 'class consciousness' existed (in the sense of a 'class conflict' of the nineteenth century). Such ways of thinking were as foreign as possible to the outworkers. Anyone who knows the history of the Swiss worker movement, knows that the impulse to form a 'class conscious' political federation came neither from the outworkers nor from the factory workers; nor were they even affected by its first stirrings. The artisans were the driving force behind the 'social question'. The International Association of Workers was able to lean in part on the intellectual foundation laid by the pioneers of a Swiss worker movement, and to impregnate and bolster it with its new ideas. These ideas were never able to establish a foothold in the old domestic and manufacturing industries of Zurich. Every union leader in the textile industry knows on how stony a soil his efforts at agitation will fall in the Oberland.[74] The outworkers under the Ancien Régime were subject to the town authorities, just as the peasants were. The scorn they felt for them arose from their delight in a booming trade. It was dissipated in sociable working groups, in circles of like-minded persons and constituted no more than the usual local and professional teasing. The feeling of being different, which was manifested in this scorn, scarcely extended beyond the narrowest local sphere of life. The strands of cotton which the outworkers span or wove bound them together (within the limits of their mental horizons) and separated them from the peasantry. But they did not possess that inner unity, which could be described by the modern term 'solidarity'. Not even the disturbances over the introduction of machine spinning nor the Uster burning (when power looms were introduced) covered that term. These movements were carried and driven by a quite different intellectual and spiritual mood of the common people.

The outworkers were bound together by strands of cotton, but the technical processing of these strands divided them again. *Brief* yarn spinners were proud of their fine yarn, which was more desirable and expensive than the wheel yarn. The muslin weaver felt he was better than the weaver who just had rough wares lying on his loom. The multi-colour and fine weavers looked down on the *Galli* weaver, as did the silk weavers. Salomeli regarded his work with pleasure, but Lise's is 'ungodly cloth, nothing but overshot, undershot, lumps, broken threads, holes, in short, slattern's cloth'.[75] A spinner or weaver who had delivered fine work for years would be sadly grieved when forced by his 'stupid sight' to resort to rough work.[76] While all this serves to emphasise the distinctions and differences between the branches of work in the putting-out industry, the binding elements inherent to this division of labour must also be mentioned. A family of outworkers could form its own production group, in which every member of the family, according to age and ability, took part. Old men and tiny children prepared and spooled the wool. The grandmother and the somewhat bigger children span. The reports of the Ascetic Society stated: 'if the children are not tall enough to sit at their work, they they must do it standing up'[77] – 'one sees six-year-old children standing at the cotton wheels and spinning'.[78] Young daughters, boys, fathers and mothers wove. Thus were the rooms filled with workers and their implements. Since the work was divided rationally between the various processes, everyone could watch them right up to when the rough cloth was made. We met such a working group with the Stutz family. Before Uli Brägger became a yarn dealer, he span and learnt how to weave. He described this period: 'In my own little house I set up a loom, taught myself how to weave and gradually taught it to my brothers, so that finally they could all earn their bread by it. The sisters for their part well understood how to spin *Löthli* yarn.'[79] By means of this division of labour children grew organically into the monotonous working method. It is no dramatic exaggeration to say that the outworker child learnt the rhythm of his work in the cradle: his cradle stood near the loom and was tied to it by a string, allowing the weaver to rock her child quiet while treadling the loom.[80] Physical and mental work were quite separate in outwork. Jakob Stutz, for instance, composed his poems while he wove.[81] It is well known that the spinners and weavers were 'inclined to reflection and speculation'.[82] However, this schizophrenia was allayed by the practice of working in a social group, in which the monotonous mechanisms of the domestic work were forgotten in singing, joking and erotic games.[83]

As we mentioned at the start, work in the cottage industry must be contrasted with work in factories. The comparison between domestic and factory work will be drawn in Part two of our enquiry, the foundations for which, in so far as they concern domestic work, have been laid in this chapter.

People's attitude to work, their work techniques and community, and their spatial environment, have a direct effect on the life of the common people and on popular culture. Included in this are the human and material ties which were forged with the advent of industrial labour. These ties helped to ensure industrial existence and gave the new conditions of life an anchorage bound up in community and tradition. New norms of behaviour grew out of these ties, since they were distinguished from the traditional and mainly rural ties and safeguards.

The human and material bonds to which the outworker's life was linked as soon as he built his existence on processing cotton, were true bonds in a folklorist sense, since they were borne by community and tradition. This is shown nowhere more sharply than in times of crisis: the times of crisis reveal that the outworker was fettered to his basis of existence by his mental adherence to community and tradition. This may read like a paradox, but a customary way of safeguarding existence can also grow on a foundation which guarantees no security, but only fluctuating insecurity. We will pursue these problems in the following chapter.

In this chapter we started off with the Protestant work ethic. The opportunities for earning one's living in the putting-out industry provided the preconditions for a popular reception of the Protestant work ethic. But this new work ethic could only be implanted in the people's breasts when the putting-out industry provided the work. The subsequent fate of this work ethic based on religion was determined when it combined with the opportunities for work and gain in the putting-out industry. Once the Protestant work ethic had eloped with early industrial wage labour, the fundamentals of religion were destroyed, religious motives were secularised and moral values were given material content. In this and the previous chapter we mentioned how this led to the construction of new norms and forms of life. In the next chapter we will attempt to see the connections and to lay the emphasis from another point of view. Work ethic and industrial wage labour must be understood in the light of a new assessment of poverty, one influenced by the particular historical period and mentality, determining on the one hand the 'social and political climate' of early industrial living conditions, and on the other hand the outworkers' traditional mental attitude to their basis of existence.

6 ♣ The outworkers' attitude to poverty and crises

In this chapter we will attempt to darken the picture we have drawn of the outworkers' living conditions. The method employed up to now has obliged us to deduce the changes to their forms of life from how the life of the common people appeared during times of prosperity. This was dictated by our line of enquiry and method of research, since the times of prosperity provided the outworkers with not just the material, but also the spiritual preconditions, the zest for life, which enabled them to set themselves apart from their former, mainly peasant, environment in an independent life style. At the same time, periods of higher prices, of crisis, work stoppages and terrible poverty were no less effective in forming the outworkers' conditions of existence. When we attempt in the following pages to fill in our picture with these gloomy tones, we will get little help from an 'objective' observation of the prevailing conditions. For instance, we neither can nor want to calculate the 'standard of living' by relating wage rates to the 'cost of living index'. This does not appear to be a useful exercise in a folklorist enquiry, because such methods pay too little attention to chronological and mental historical aspects. We must try to understand the economic and social conditions of the industrialised population from the spirit of the age and we may not judge them with our modern socio-political values.[1] This may seem an obvious proviso. It is, however, difficult to put into effect, because we are scarcely aware of how accustomed we are to thinking in different categories, precisely in the social and socio-political sphere. It is as if we were using a different system of measurement. For this reason it is appropriate to begin by examining the question of how the Ancien Régime responded to poverty, crises, price rises and lack of earnings. With its institutions and the spirit which supported and directed them, did it have a 'social' policy in today's meaning of the word?

Let us start with a few remarks about Poor Relief: After the Reformation the care of the poor became a moral obligation of the State's since the secularisation of the monasteries and religious foundations had robbed the needy of their most important charitable institutions. The appropriated church properties were used to open a fund for the poor and to create a state Alms Office. The internal organisation and operations of this and other institutions do not concern us here.[2] But in any case, the state institutions were not sufficient to meet the need. It was for this reason that already by the seventeenth century the rural church parishes (along with the communes) were ordered to participate in the Poor Relief by distributing produce at harvest time and the resources of the Poor Fund. Subsequently the care of the poor devolved increasingly on to the Church and communes.

Of far greater importance for our enquiry is the spirit which maintained these institutions and which directed Protestant Zurich's policy towards the poor under the Ancien Régime. C.G. Schmidt saw this clearly: 'Protestant religious instruction gradually evolved principles for the care of the poor, which differed considerably from the charity of the Middle Ages'.[3] The weekly bread dole, one of the most important forms of state relief for the needy, demonstrates the attitude of the ecclesiastical and lay authorities towards poverty and almsgiving; bread was distributed to the poor countryfolk entitled to draw Relief every Sunday or Tuesday after the morning service in the presence of the whole parish. Each person was summoned by name and had to accept his ration in person by the baptismal font. He was not allowed to send someone else, unless he was ill. The recipients were reminded during distribution of the dole that they had lost their active rights as citizens by joining the Poor of the Parish. Since 'by all this we want [to ensure] that none of those belonging to town and country, who receive the usual alms, should not be summoned to the commune assembly, therein to vote, but shall be excluded from it'.[4] This shows us that poverty, which had been raised to new and powerful heights in the late Middle Ages, was now no longer the crowning virtue. People had forgotten that Christ himself came to us in poverty. Receipt of alms, and with it the right to exist, was only granted to those who earned it by righteous deeds. Only those who prayed and worked, or who at least wanted to work, were entitled to the bread dole, to shoes, woollen cloth or alms in money. It was incumbent on the pastors and those in authority – church elders, bailiffs, etc. – to distinguish the work-shy poor from those willing to work. The Alms Ordinance instructed them to keep idle people at work, earning their bit of bread honestly, by exhorting and punishing them. It is easy to see that the ecclesiastical and lay authorities' attitude to poverty was very closely associated with the development of a Protestant work ethic. The spiritual roots were the same as those we have already met in the concept of the religious basis of work (working so as not to fall into sinful idleness). This religious basis devalued poverty. On the other hand, in an age when the doctrine of dual predestination had been pronounced dogma (1665), wealth, business ability and success were seen as the outward signs of membership of God's elect, when wealth was coupled with old Protestant piety.

A similar devaluation applied to begging, whose features emerge much more sharply here. It is known how Holy Writ transformed the beggar prototype into 'a focal point of religious and social life, in which all the rays of charitable love are gathered'.[5] In the baroque age, within the Jesuits' spiritual sphere, the beggar was wonderfully transfigured by the legend of St Alexius, which won deep-seated popular support. The attitude of the ecclesiastical and lay authorities in the Protestant states was quite different (partly too in Catholic areas where begging had become an abuse). Mandates 'against the shameless and open street begging' were constantly renewed during the seventeenth and eighteenth centuries. In 1590 Samuel Hochholzer, 'Burgher and servant of the word of God in Zurich' compiled a 'kurzen und einfalten Bericht vonn dem unverschämten Bättel' (brief and simple account of the shameless beggary) in which he compared beggars with a 'raging forest stream, which covers and obstructs the good fields with rubbish and renders them infertile'. He asserts 'that begging is the root of all ungodliness and that one should remove this evil with power and severity, providing the poor householders instead with the necessary sustenance, that they may never be forcibly driven to beg'.[6] People tried to control the evil by means of harsh prohibitions and police measures. Beggars were threatened with corporal punishment, with hard labour and the stocks, and people even wanted them taken away to serve in foreign armies or the Venetian galleys. The parishes were to carry out beggar hunts at their own expense and to set up village watches, 'that thereby our land is freed of all useless beggar kind and that each and everyone may enjoy the blessing of the Most High in better peace and security'.[7] (These beggar hunts took place in Catholic areas too.)

They employed every available means to uproot the popular belief that giving alms to beggars could cancel out one's sins. This was no true alms-giving, they explained to the people, but only fake holiness. They refused to accept almsgiving as a part of good works. Every one who 'threw something out to the beggars' was to be punished with a 'compulsory fine' of 20 *Pfund*.[8] They also tried wholly to 'cross out' giving shelter to beggars. In order to justify such police measures against the poor, they not only referred to the Old and New Testaments and the Church Fathers, but also called on the 'wise heathen Plato'. Furthermore, 'Chrysostom, an old church teacher' said: 'We do not support lazy and idle people but we exhort them to work'; and the 'wise man Syrach' has written: 'My child, have no truck with begging: it is better to die than to beg.' People substantiated their regulations about alms with remarkable feats of exegesis, as the following quotation shows:

Then first spoke Almighty God himself to his old Jewish people in the fifth book of Moses, Chapter 15: that no poor man shall be among you; by which should not be understood the righteous worthy poor, but such poor as engage in open street begging and relapse into idleness, and that such people should not be among us; and although it has been mentioned by kind-hearted natures that beggars were also found and recorded in the time of Christ, it should nonetheless be known that in those days the Jewish police and government was no longer in the best shape but had deteriorated, and consequently no order could be maintained in anything, including the charitable institutions.[9]

All this merely hints at the religious basis to the state Poor Relief. The new attitude towards poverty (and so towards begging and almsgiving) gave rise to moral and ethical values which formed the social outlook of the age and were responsible for the 'social' policy of the Ancien Régime. By dividing the poor into those entitled and those not entitled to receive alms, the Church and State denied a section of their indigent population the right to exist, and they absolved themselves of responsibility for them. Entitlement to Relief was made to depend on willingness to work. Work was 'the first condition, under which the grown person is entitled to live and all beggars deserved to be punished for their own improvement, since 'every other kind of charity towards them is a moral, religious and political crime'.[10] Poverty and work were very closely linked. The Protestant work ethic, allied with the attitude of the ecclesiastical and lay authorities towards poverty, resulted in a human type which seemed to have been specifically created to support the process of industrialisation – a creature who used to be called *homo oeconomicus* on account of his attitude to life and work.[11] It is scarcely necessary to refer these questions to Max Weber's and R.H. Tawney's seminal works, which expose the global significance of these connections.[12] Both writers maintain that the religious attitude cannot be considered as a catalyst which transforms other material, without itself being transformed. The religious attitude itself is influenced far more by the 'entirety of social and especially economic cultural conditions'. Both writers also expressly refuse 'to substitute a one-sided materialistic interpretation of culture and history with an equally one-sided spiritualistic and causal interpretation'.[13]

Let us briefly indicate the direction in which the problems lie: poverty became a moral and educational factor, since it helped to guide people away from sinful idleness towards work. On top of this came the attitude of the ecclesiastical and lay authorities, manifest in countless mandates about morals: good earnings increased arrogance, luxury, gluttony, gambling and dancing. People were enticed away from the path of temperance and piety. This ethic supplemented those economic ideas and theories which saw poverty and the spectre of famine as essential goads driving men to work. They stood for the point of view that people only work so long as they are obliged to meet their essential needs. For this reason wages must be kept to a subsistence minimum.[14] In 1816, for instance, David Bürkli wrote in the *Zürcher Freitagszeitung* (*Friday Newspaper*) with axiomatic self-assurance, simply mentioning it in passing, that 'the mother of industrious work is necessity'.[15] Thus did the interests of the ecclesiastical and lay authorities and the commercial and economic interests of the age converge.

The Ancien Régime did not want to support the idle poor; but neither was it able adequately to support those willing to work and to protect them from poverty. Willingness to work only guaranteed people's entitlement to Relief. Thus was barred the way to a social policy which could have set up preventive measures to avert poverty. The Ancien Régime's social policy adhered to the policy of Poor Relief, whether positively, with charitable institutions, or negatively, with police measures against the poor. Poor Relief was pursued all the more firmly because poverty was considered an unavoidable condition: 'Poverty is an infirmity inseparable from the present imperfection of all human institutions and especially of civic society.'[16]

The Ancien Régime provided the outworker with no safeguards against crises, work stoppages and price rises. It undertook no measures to guarantee those willing to work a subsistence in times of need. The few attempts by the authorities to ensure the outworkers a minimum wage remained completely ineffective in practice. The State did, at any rate, allow foodstuffs to be released during price rises and crises and ordered provincial governors to release a bit of land for indigent, landless outworkers to cultivate. Emergency employment was also permitted by the government, for instance in 1771, but only in a very limited way. In the same way, after the terrible experiences of 1771, the parishes were directed to lay in grain supplies, but even this directive met with scant success.[17] It was above all by means of prohibitions and threats that they tried to overcome indigence. The beggars' weddings were prevented, brandy bars were watched, and they made endless attempts at extirpating the evil of begging. This also applied to the second half of the eighteenth century, when the ideas of the Enlightenment were being increasingly adopted by the leading circles of town citizens. People were now really concerned about poverty and sought for ways and means of mitigating it. The problem was discussed in the various societies, essays competitions were introduced and official enquiries were set up. Ideas about natural law entered the discussion about re-structuring their Poor Relief policy, involving a new approach to the problem of the right to existence.[18] These philanthropists sought with paternal concern for a new way of providing for the poor. But even their efforts were firmly embedded in the Poor Relief policy. Suggestions were made about building poor houses and orphanages. Parishes were urged to summon meetings at which the starving children of poor parents were to be distributed among the propertied parishioners, that they might be 'cared for and kept, snatched from beggardom, clothed, schooled and accustomed to work and to a moral manner of living'. People pointed to the parish of Wald, where at one such meeting 'of sixty children, who were so presented, not one was left behind'. Commissions were 'set up specially to regulate lack of earnings'.[19] Opportunities for giving unemployed outworkers new employment or for redeploying them in agricultural work were sought for.

The first attempts at a social policy appeared, although the mental foundations for this sort of thing developed only slowly. Traditional perceptions and moral concepts kept on obstructing any insight into the social and economic situation of the population engaged in industry. In 1857 the minister of Bäretswil could still write, for instance, that 'the sources of impoverishment' are to be sought in pleasure-seeking, slovenliness and in the disproportion between the number of taverns and the means of the populace. Subsequently he had to admit that 'the constant fall in the value of money is often markedly disproportionate to earnings'. Food, clothes, house rent and other needs of life had risen by a third, but not wages, 'which was very soon felt among people of the lower stations, who have to work just to feed themselves'.[20] People often came perilously close to the self-righteous attitude of: 'help yourself, and God will help you', which helped morally to underpin the unrestrained competitiveness of early capitalism. Minister Hottinger, for instance, who described the misery and hardship of the Oberland population in 1817 most movingly, called on the outworkers (albeit with paternal solicitude): 'You have seen the workings of Divine guidance. Through the schools of hardship and scarcity it leads you to true salvation. Your destiny lies in your hands, and, as you yourselves prepare it, so will it be . . . But you must learn to do without and to exert yourselves.'[21] Such texts document the moral climate, in which the judgements about poverty, crises and need were made.

'Patriots' conscious of their responsibility followed the development of the industry in the second half of the eighteenth century with concern. By 1787 around a third of the whole population of the state of Zurich was involved in cotton manufacture.[22] The majority of these people had no security against crises. People were aware that cotton, the 'foster-mother' of the State, had become indispensable. Johann Heinrich Pestalozzi warns urgently that 'we simply cannot calculate the inevitable consequences were 20,000 spinners and weavers to be without work in our country for only fourteen days'.[23] The putting-out industry's sensitivity to crises became more and more apparent. People recognised how little the course of development could be anticipated and predetermined. The repercussions of market stagnation and lack of earnings widened steadily as industrialisation advanced. C. Meiners summarised these patriots' fears: 'The life of a third of our subjects, they say, is anyway uncertain, and dependent on various chances, which can neither be controlled nor avoided, since it is simultaneously in the hands of fickle fashion, or of envious and lucky competitors, or of autocratic monarchs.'[24] Such fears were only too justified. We will provide figures later on showing how large was the percentage of the rural population which sank into hopeless poverty and hardship in times of price rises and crises.

Despite these terrible experiences and urgent warnings the authorities lacked the power and ability, and often enough the insight and will as well, to take effective preventive measures. Johann Heinrich Pestalozzi spoke harsh words about the mental attitudes and the state of the institutions under the administration of the Ancien Régime.[25] In so far as the urban economic order represented the interests of the town burghers, it prevented the rural population from achieving any independent safeguards, created out of the social and economic conditions in the countryside, against failed harvests, crises and price rises. The rural subjects found that their hands were, to a great extent, tied. This applied not just to the outworkers, the clothiers, the carriers, the loom menders and others, not just to the people employed in the putting-out industry, but the rural craftsmen and farmers were also restricted in what they could or might do by countless regulations and prohibitions. In 1795, for instance, Salomon Graaf of Rystal (parish of Elgg), who could find no work and tried to support his family by selling dried fruit, had to pay the governor of Kyburg a fine of 6 *Pfund* and the plaintiff 6 *Pfund* as well. It was stressed at the time that the guilty man had not been fined a greater sum, because he was poor. Adam Grob of Attikon, who had twice sold dried fruit in the Thurgau, had to pay, for instance, the considerable sum of 75 *Pfund*. Heinrich Müller was fined 3 *Pfund* just for 'tendering forbidden sale of straw in Schaffhausen'.[26] Many such examples can be cited. They show how the country population was deprived of the possibility of self-help in the sense of safeguarding themselves against crises. Its wings were broken. But these examples also reveal the authorities' attitude which underlay these regulations and fines. This attitude is important for our folklorist enquiry because it directly determined the behaviour of the rural population in times of need and in years of good earnings. If the authorities were incapable of adopting measures along the lines of a social policy, such as preventive measures against lack of earnings, unemployment, price rises and fluctuating wages, they were also incapable of transmitting to the rural population engaged in industry their ideals and principles about how it should ensure its survival and behave when confronted with vicissitudes. The government's intellectual and institutional foundations had not been created with that purpose in mind.

We scarcely need to expound any further on how little security the production system of the putting-out industry was able to offer the outworkers at that time. They felt the effects of every fall in prices and every sales stoppage quickly and harshly. They were wholly subject not only to the fluctuations of the textile manufacture, but the rises in the price of food in years of poor harvests also affected their wages' purchasing power. In such times their wages would not rise, and might even drop. The urban putting-out masters were not wholly responsible for this; far more so were the rural carriers and clothiers, as already discussed in the previous chapter. In 1723, for instance, a 'Bericht der Herren Geistlichen, was für Ursachen der Armuth seyen' ('Report by the Gentlemen Clergy about the Origins of Poverty') complained that 'In manufactures where bad wages prevail, the carriers strangely never hand over what is due to the people.' The carriers were admonished on this account to pay the outworkers 'a decent wage' and to allot contracts for work impartially.[27] We must be aware that the outworkers were at the mercy of the clothiers and the carriers, who often used their power to influence village policy. In their desire to make a profit they did not abstain from arbitrary and harsh oppression. The outworkers lived isolated lives and enjoyed no effective protection by the authorities. We will approach this question again from another angle later on.

· The object of these preliminary remarks has been to introduce us to the ecclesiastical and lay authorities' attitude towards poverty, begging, crises and price rises. The religious interpretation of poverty coupled with the Protestant work ethic, the ethical and moral values which were upheld by the puritanical spirit of renunciation of the world, and the economic conditions which developed out of an economic mentality moulded by city-state mercantilism, all these stood in the way of a social policy in the present sense of the term. This we must remember.

Yet many places in the eighteenth century realised that, with the development of industry and the growth of the population engaged in industry, the urban authorities were faced with a completely new situation, and that the prevailing arrangements could no longer meet the new social and economic conditions. However, a long period was needed before this new spirit was able to take these altered conditions into account, until new social and political ideas penetrated civic and economic life and were incorporated into institutions as well. It took even longer for these ideas to be received into popular thinking and to become duly effective in the life of the common people. A development which will have to be followed up in Part two of this investigation.

Having just roughly outlined the preconditions for a specifically folklorist enquiry, we should now ask how the country population responded to the ecclesiastical and lay authorities' policy for the poor. How did the industrialised population live through price rises, crises and lack of earnings? How did it react to poverty and distress and to the vicissitudes of industrial existence?

The ecclesiastical and lay authorities' attitude to poverty, begging and alms had to be implanted in the hearts of the population alongside the Protestant work ethic. The religious interpretation of poverty, outlined above, was modified and recast by its reception among the common people, who imbued it with their own feelings and experiences. The influence of the State Church on its rural subjects should not be underestimated. As we know, the mandates about begging and alms were read out from the pulpit. The schools made use only of religious teaching materials and taught religion almost exclusively. The articles of faith (in question and answer form) were hammered unceasingly into the school children. The minister supervised lessons and teaching, examined the teachers, the pupils and their households. In spite of the might of the State Church and the authority enjoyed within the parish by its representative the minister (he had to be a town burgher), popular piety obeyed its own laws, because it drew its strength from a different set of destinies and experiences – as was the case with the religious interpretation of poverty. The plague of beggars could grow out of all proportion, but the common folk resisted the ecclesiastical and lay authorities' attitude to almsgiving. The traditional popular belief in the power of almsgiving to cancel sin was much too strong for people to be stopped from donating their mite to suppliants. They gave without asking whether the recipient was also entitled to it, 'fancying that almsgiving is a right willed by God, and so handing it out through the window'.[28] Take, for instance, the minister of Gossau who complained bitterly about how badly his flock had received the regulation about begging and almsgiving:

Stubbornly resorting to all sorts of reasons over and against all protests and exhortations, saying . . .; people had different opinions, people were worried about falling into sin, and not a few of them, and not the lowliest either, have the foolish notion that it is because begging has been forbidden that the harvest has turned out so badly and that one disaster follows another. It is incredible how much authoritative words and thoughts are disputed and rejected, in consequence of which many clergymen . . . are looked down on by many and hated.[29]

The flock had their own ideas about poverty as well, in which the comparison between the camel and the eye of a needle played its part. Jakob Stutz records cousin Anneli's joy in her poverty

for she firmly believed that no rich person would enter Heaven, since Holy Writ had said so clearly. 'Listen', she said once, 'I want to tell you in a song how much the Lord God prefers poor people to rich people. Oh, my parents, your sainted grandparents, and all of us sang this song many thousand times as we span and each time the tears rolled down my cheeks.'[30]

What was the range of destinies and experiences available to the population engaged in industry? How are we to calculate the extent of their deprivation? What were the origins of their poverty?

It must be recalled that in the days before world trade the danger of famine was always latent. Even partially failed harvests were enough to throw the affected regions into a state of emergency. Opportunities to import from neighbouring regions were limited. Local economies were very susceptible and prices reacted sensitively and suddenly. In January 1770, for instance, a loaf of bread cost 5 *Schilling* 8 *Heller*, and it rose to 12 *Schilling* 6 *Heller* in January 1771, reaching 15 *Schilling* in April 1771 and dropping again to 6 *Schilling* in August 1772. Price rises and famines like these were part of the normal experiences of a lifetime, like natural catastrophes or epidemics, and they were remembered as admonishments and warnings. People should not ask themselves, wrote minister Schmidlin of Wetzikon, 'why God subsequently [after good years] thins the misapplied surplus in anno 1770 and 1771 with shortages'.[31] It became apparent that their daily bread came from the hand of the Lord: the official price of bread was announced from the pulpit after morning service. During the years of rising prices the people would acknowledge this portentous message with humble resignation. In the starvation year 1817, when the prices were read out in the church of Wetzikon on 6 June, the choir leader, school-master Jenta of Ettenhausen, struck up a song by Schmidlin *Ich sterbe nun* (*I Die Now*) and the parishioners sang it through to the end with tears in their eyes.[32] The spectre of famine was constantly knocking at the door, but poverty and distress cannot be explained by failed harvests and starvation years; they should be seen 'not so much as absolute causes, but as catalysts'.[33]

The parish clergy provided endless warnings about the growing poverty in their parishes in their reports and at synods. Appalling and endless too was the army of anaemic persons who passed their lives in the most terrible poverty. But where were the roots of this poverty to be sought, when hungry years and failed harvests were only direct occasions for, but not the origin of, poverty. The clergy were constantly preoccupied with this question of the origin of poverty, but their social and mental ties frequently prevented them from perceiving the social and economic structure of the countryside. They pointed with moral disapproval at luxury, indulgence in food and drink, at gambling and frequenting public houses, at the irresponsible early marriages and at the absence of savings in years of high earnings. The dean of the Wetzikon Chapter, for instance, named three reasons for poverty with lapidary brevity: 'Sauffen, Spillen, Hoffart' (boozing, gambling, luxury).[34] Minister Bürkli reported the poverty in his Maur parish and was

concerned that it may get much worse, because all fear of God is disappearing . . . partaking in the Sacrament amazingly bad, the Poor of the Parish with the exception of a few will attend no weekly sermons, most of them have not a streak of work in them, they are all drunken: their caps off their heads, beds under their bodies, looms and implements and other things stashed away, sold, house and holding in disarray and, intending to turn begging in town and countryside, yea, even robbing and stealing, etc., into a trade.[35]

Johann Hottinger puts the following admission in the mouths of the Oberland outworkers when writing for the New Year newspaper of the Zurich Hülfsgesellschaft (Help Association) of 1817:

We have previously experienced times of surplus and of rich, excessive earnings, but we were not worthy of this blessing from Heaven. We squandered the money won so quickly and easily on finery, loose living, gambling and wantonness. In our arrogance we looked down on the stout-hearted farmer, who went on winning his bread from the soil in the sweat of his brow, and on whose mercy we are now thrown once more. We brought up our children badly and did not send them to school, simply that they might be able to help us make money early on, which, had we been thrifty and orderly, we would have had more than enough of. We are fickle, lazy and unskilled through our own fault. When our previous livelihood began to falter, we could easily have started gradually earning our keep in another manner, if we had not thoughtlessly lived from day to day, if we had been satisfied with less profit, if we had not found shameful begging and idleness easier.[36]

We are sufficiently familiar with the parish clergy's attitude to the out-workers' manner of living, and with all their reproaches. They are not simply to be dismissed, but must be assessed and referred to differently. The question of the origin of poverty is above all a question of where the poor came from.

The number of those needing protection can be anticipated: widows and orphans, the sick and the invalid, the infirm and the elderly. As we know from the 'Description of the Poor in the Whole Countryside of Zurich', they all tried to manage by doing outwork, but they could not survive without charity. This also applied to the eighteenth century, when the putting-out industry expanded and developed. The wretched wages it paid did not allow for any mishap. If a provider died, or earnings dropped through sickness, the case was desperate. For instance, in 1715 the widow Frey of Wetzikon was promised a subsidy 'to improve her wage' and twelve other persons obtained support for the same reason.[37]

But it was not only those in need of protection; even able-bodied people had difficulty making ends meet and were forced to apply for Relief. We have seen how periodic emigration helped to assuage poverty before the advent of intensive industrialisation. Industrial labour offered these people, living on the margins of the agricultural community (day-labourers, smallholders, villeins, etc.), the chance of earning their livings in their homeland. They developed into a core population which based its existence on outwork alone, without any significant property at all. They managed to get by in good years. But as soon as price rises occurred following bad harvests, or the supply of work dried up, they fell into trouble. They were totally helpless before both price rises and work stoppages. These people lived literally from hand to mouth. Industrial earnings did not adjust to price rises. As we have seen, they even tended to sink in such times. Here is just one example: we have cited the rising price of bread in the years 1770–1 (from 5 *Schilling* to 15 *Schilling*). During this period, the spinners' and weavers' wages dropped and it was only in 1772 that they returned to their 1769 levels.[38] We should not underestimate that section of the population which had on account of its origins no farm to fall back on. In 1696, half a century before the full flowering of the Zurich textile industry, the minister of Zell reported:

In my whole parish, which extends to more than 700 souls, only two households have means . . . the rest have to get by with the greatest difficulty and are loaded down with debts. The common people support themselves as well as possible by spinning wool, but they complain bitterly about their bad pay; that they no longer get the old pay as previously.[39]

In the same year (1696) out of seventy-seven households in Brütten, thirty-three were on the parish and twenty-one were close to so being. But there was no question of failed harvests in that period and there were only a few poor harvests.[40] Minister Köchlin of Brütten describes how in winter the hungry people searched the fields and meadows for anything edible. Now it was June they could concentrate more on the outwork 'since the days are longer and one does not need to heat [one's house] any more, or to search the fields and meadows for so many plants to eat'.[41] These pictures of misery continued into the eighteenth century. The 'Reflexionen der Herren Pflegeren des Almosenamtes über die Armuth auf der Landschaft' ('Reflections of the Gentlemen Administrators of the Alms Office about the Poverty in the Countryside') of 12 April 1723 report that everywhere people were complaining 'about the sadly ever increasing poverty of our people, despite the prosperous times and surplus in food and drink and the flourishing Camerarii and commerce, as a rich and strange Divine blessing'.[42]

We mentioned earlier that the numbers of landless outworkers increased considerably with the advance of industrialisation. This social group was characterised by a strong and natural rise in population. All the reports refer to the great willingness to marry in these circles and to the early marriages (beggars' weddings).

The core population of landless outworkers increased (again following the advance of industrialisation and most especially in times of crisis) with the emergence of another social group. This was the growing number of people who, because of their origins, had some sort of farm to fall back on, but, tempted by cash (and more besides) had divested themselves of this security. They divided their holdings, properties and village rights. While some of them retained enough land to provide at least some of their food requirements, others, however, divested themselves entirely of their ancestral lands and were content with just a vegetable patch. Even this was often neglected when the industry was at its peak. As we know, this subdivision of farms and lands must be viewed as a form of shared inheritance typical to cottage industry. If the subdivision was accompanied by a more intensive use of the soil, the portions of land could still provide an effective safeguard against crises, especially if their owners adhered to subsistence farming and to a peasant economic thinking, and if the property was not too much in debt. But such conditions were not prevalent everywhere. Many families bound themselves for better and for worse to the fate of the putting-out industry. In times of price rises and work stoppages they then ran into trouble.

The authorities were aware of this source of poverty. The 'Report by the Gentlemen Clergy about the Origins of Poverty' of 12 April 1723 mentioned that 'the subdivision of the farms is very harmful'.[43] The government instructed the regional and district governors 'not to permit this sort of division of farms and properties easily or without special reason, but to keep the households together as much as possible'.[44]

We have briefly introduced the people who, on account of their origins, were most liable to sink into distress and misery. They were the families without land, or which had become landless. They based their existence on the putting-out industry and, with their irrational and traditional way of thinking, they trusted to this insecure base. The authorities were helpless before this phenomenon. It had the uncontrollable force of a natural disaster. More and more people allowed cotton yarn to become the thread by which hung their fates. Remember Salomon Schinz's judgement, that the cottage industry had 'as it were planted' these people, and that industrial earnings were 'totally indispensable'. 'Even the property owners or the middle class could not subsist without this sort of income' because they 'would find it impossible to pay the interest on their debts from the income from their farm, but solely . . . by their spinning wheels or looms.'[45] Their existence either lacked or had lost its agricultural basis, and relied instead on earnings from the putting-out industry.

The conditions produced by this development were bound to turn catastrophic in bad years when prices rose or when work or earnings were scant. Let us provide a few statistics showing how many rural inhabitants, able to support themselves in good years, sank into hopeless indigence in years of high prices and in times of crisis. Hans Morf has calculated for the year 1771, when prices rose, that 42,234 rural inhabitants were stripped of all resources, and this number does not include those drawing Relief. The entire rural population amounted at that time to *c.* 140,000 souls (according to Morfit was 137,267 and according to Waser, 143,355).[46] Nearly a third of the rural population was thus driven by the increased cost of living into the arms of hunger and poverty. It should be remembered that this rise in the cost of living was preceded by a period rich in earnings. The period from 1757 to 1765 was commonly known as the golden years. In the Oberland the poverty was much greater. In Bubikon, for instance, 310 persons out of 560 were in need. Fischenthal numbered 1,000 inhabitants, of whom 686 were without means. Sternenberg and Wildberg had to count more than half their inhabitants among the needy. In Wyla 431 persons out of 715 were without means, and so on.[47] In 1790, a year of increased prices, the number of those requiring assistance amounted to 19.69% of the population, according to Bertha Keller's reckoning.[48] The Economic Commission's lists provide the following figures:[49]

Parish	Souls present	Total number of needy
Bäretschwil	2,709	1,417
Bauma	3,039	813
Fischenthal	2,476	860
Mönchaltorf	858	433
Sternenberg	1,248	339
Turbenthal	1,892	819
Wildberg	763	310
Wyla	837	426

These proportions are horrifying, but the bare figures cannot reveal the full extent of the distress, suffering and hopelessness of these anaemic people. We are dealing with a process known as pauperism in the nineteenth century. It has already been mentioned that periods of prosperity spurred on its development. They enticed people into earlier marriages, into splitting up their property, to building new dwellings and houses, and so on. People accepted credit without hesitation,[50] and allowed debts to accumulate, and then in times of crisis were unable to pay the interest. The strong circulation of money favoured credit transactions and drove the price of land up: 'Money is often offered to people to enable them to buy expensive properties, and they become heavily indebted, often having nothing of their own to pay with.'[51] A large proportion of the outworkers found themselves in this situation of permanent debt. It was not just the prevailing housing shortage but also the parish laws tying commonage rights to the house which were responsible for credit being taken out rashly and irresponsibly for extending, altering or rebuilding existing houses. The short payment periods made it more difficult to liquidate debts. Added to this was the outworkers' mental and spiritual approach to their basis of existence, which will be discussed later on.

The outworkers had other habits too, acquired in prosperous times, which did them harm when earnings fell. For instance, an outworker might give up an allotment, which he could have retained at a low rent, or often even for nothing. In times of shortage, then, he would have nothing. He would be forced to buy his most basic necessities at a high price. He would not be able to recover what he had lost: 'These people, raised and constantly living in spinning parlours lack the will, the strength and the skill to enable them to cultivate these allotments.'[52] Further, as people became accustomed to new needs, they forgot their former simple recipes. When poverty and hunger came, people no longer knew how to prepare simple but satisfying meals from cheap ingredients. The members of the Economic Society attempted with paternal concern to instruct the outworkers in the method of preparing cheap nourishing stews in years of famine.

We do not need to cite further examples. It is clear that the outworkers' form and style of life, which was expressed in new habits, needs and forms of behaviour, had a catastrophic effect in times of crisis and heightened despair. However, this is a very superficial way of looking at things and does not do justice to the prevailing conditions. We must start from the outworker's attitude to his existence, to his basis of existence and to life in general.

We mentioned earlier that the outworker bound himself to his industrial earnings with an irrational mental and spiritual attitude. He was indeed used to no longer reckoning, as his peasant neighbours did, by the seasons and harvests, but only by his weekly or fortnightly wages. He met most of his needs through the medium of money. He grew accustomed to this without, however, understanding in any rational way that the fluctuating and uncertain conditions of the early industrial putting-out system demanded new safe-guards, fundamentally different to those of peasant life. The outworker relied blindly on the actual state of the industry and adjusted his way of life to his actual earnings. He paid for his keep out of his wages or used them to pay the rent on his little property. He believed that his life was thereby assured and he did not want anything more. Anything he earned over and above his keep he spent on his new needs, or he might prefer not to work at all. The sources speak out clearly.[53] This behaviour was part of the outworker's way of coming to terms with his new form of existence. He derived his self-esteem in good years from this manner of living. In times of increased prices and work stoppages, however, his self-esteem collapsed. The outworker realised that his work could barely save him from death by starvation, even if he increased his output to breaking point. He no longer mocked the peasants now, but looked longingly at their simple and hard existence. Jakob Stutz wrote about the year of starvation 1817 as follows: 'In those days one heard very little mockery about the peasantry; yea, all the weavers and silk spinners would gladly have been peasants. They were well off, they were safe.'[54] But as soon as the emergency was over, the outworker would return to his former life style, and his mood would lift again.[55]

The outworkers' basis of existence obliged them to experience life in terms of earnings or wages, and not in terms of property, as the peasants did. The question now arises as to why the population engaged in industry did not safeguard their basis of existence against the ups and downs of life in an appropriate form? Why did they oscillate between (relative) excess and starvation, starvation and excess, without finding any middle ground? Why were drastic mood changes inherent to the outworkers' emotional life? The parish clergy was constantly urging the outworkers to save in good years, so that they would have something to fall back on in times of price rises and crisis. But even the most urgent appeals and the most bitter experiences remained ineffectual. It was a very long time before the outworkers (and later the factory workers) invested in rational savings and insurance schemes. It took a long time for ideas about savings and insurance to be received into the popular mentality. Nowadays they are firmly anchored in popular thinking. Present-day life of the common people is characterised by innumerable state, company and private insurance institutions. This is a mental historical process, which must be taken into account by folklorists, because it leads to new relationships and ways of behaving and replaces old ties, both mental and religious, as well as human and social ties.

As far as the outworker under the Ancien Régime was concerned, the preconditions for such a willingness to save and to take out insurance were absent, and they would remain absent until far into the nineteenth century. It should be recalled that the great movements of the nineteenth century to provide insurance, mutual associations and social assistance were supported and driven on by artisan circles, a class which looked back on an old and varied insurance tradition and brought with it both the mental and the social preconditions for accepting the new system. But the putting-out system of early capitalism had no tradition of insurance. It was neither able to offer the outworkers security nor did its human and organisational structure include arrangements which could have provided the outworkers with models of how to safeguard their existence. The authorities did not possess any such institutions either. They merely tried to work in this direction by means of countless prohibitions, which were scarcely suited to implanting the will to save in the population engaged in industry. It was only with the onset of a factory industry that responsible entrepreneurs introduced obligatory banks, sickness and accident funds, and funds against old age and death, etc. Socially conscious parish clergy did not tire of recommending these institutions over and over again. We will pursue this development in Part two, when the artisans' and workers' self-help organisations will also be discussed.

This, however, serves to illuminate only one side of the matter. We must ask ourselves which mental and religious preconditions as well as those of a human and social kind the population engaged in industry brought with it in order to safeguard itself against the vicissitudes of life with new institutions appropriate to their basis of existence.

The perception of industrial life was still taking place through traditional mental images, in which the social 'station' was perceived as part of the Divine order. The outworker felt that the vicissitudes of his insecure existence constituted a fate willed and determined by God. Just as he understood times of prosperity as the blessings of God, so too he experienced crises as the Lord's warning and punishments.[56] Just as he rejected the lightning conductor as an ungodly invention, so too he rejected rational arguments in favour of savings and insurance, and accepted need, poverty, hunger and deprivation with dull resignation, the more so because social and economic inequality were things willed by God.

The popular reception of an insurance philosophy undoubtedly involved a parallel loss of traditional religiosity, as well as an emancipation from traditional mental images and a secularising process. The traditional view of life was not frivolous, but was upheld by a profound trust in God, who feeds everyone.[57] This did not involve only the outworker. It is well known how difficult it is to persuade farmers to understand the sense of taking out insurance for their cattle or against the weather. However, the outworkers' situation was quite different to that of the farmers. The old peasant local community, with its functions encompassing all aspects of life, enjoyed safeguards centuries old (common lands, neighbourhood assistance, all kinds of farming regulations). All these safeguards grew up out of a rural economy and a peasant economic mentality. Rural life is maintained and bolstered by such arrangements. But conditions were quite different for the outworker. He had grown up in the same local peasant community, although he had never enjoyed a secure place on account of his origins, and would never qualify as a full member. When he bound his life to the putting-out industry, the traditional peasant security arrangements lost their value and in part their meaning for him. The old local community with its legal and customary institutions was no longer adequate for the numerically important class of landless outworkers. These people threatened to burst the rural safeguards and so it is not surprising that the farmers tried to shut themselves off from the population engaged in industry. It took a long time, however, for the outworkers to stop thinking along the old lines and to stop looking for security in the old ties, and to create or adopt different institutions, better suited to their basis of existence. The intellectual and institutional preconditions had first to be created from above and from below.

One might well suppose that there were also thrifty and economical outworker families who tried to keep a farm going as their main support and who even achieved modest prosperity.[58] These were, however, people who were both spiritually and materially rooted in their land, and who remained peasants in their behaviour. We will see this more clearly when we examine the outworkers' behaviour in times of price rises and crises, and ask what forms of life emerged from the experiences of such times; what sorts of customary ways of behaviour developed; and how they were manifested in the life and culture of the common people.

The various social groups engaged in cottage industry did not experience the crises and times of poverty in the same way. The families farming smallholdings as well as working for the putting-out industry possessed the most material and spiritual security, allowing them to avoid pauperisation. They did not react as sensitively to the years of price rises because they were able to meet their needs in a traditional and in part still subsistent way, which preserved them from the worst. The work stoppages were far more damaging to them, because the interest on their mortgaged farms could only be paid with industrial earnings. At such times the receiver's hammer hung over them menacingly. The district law court of Wald, for instance, reported on 19 April 1799:

This week alone the law court has dealt with thirteen cases, among which appeared many people who had more than enough to live on in better times, but are now driven with wife and children out of house and home. There is already a pile of new distraints, reminders and summonses here, so that when the legal process starts up again there is another crowd of bankrupts. In our district now all the best men are in the service of the Fatherland, two and three out of every house. Often the old father has to work the little property . . . How can they now help themselves? How are they to bring in the money? . . . We have decided in God's name to stop the reminders this week, until we have asked you! The public prosecutor is asked to stop the horrible legal business for a while at least.[59]

It was characteristic of these smallholder and cottage industry circles that they preferred to suffer the worst 'rather than decide on the painful step of reporting to the parish alms officers for Relief'.[60] They owned, alongside their little smallholding, at most a share in the right to use the commons and had the right to vote in the village community matters. They were rooted in their community, which gave them the self-confidence and spiritual strength to hold out. As soon as they went on the Parish and drew Relief they lost their active right as citizens, with the ensuing social and economic consequences. Johann Hirzel wrote as follows about the landowning outworkers: 'They are too proud to beg, or to request assistance, they sigh in silence over their misfortune and the Father knows their need, who can see into hidden things.'[61] They are generally referred to in the sources as 'silent poor' because of their behaviour.

The 'silent poor' were to be found not only among the landowning outworkers. Many landless people behaved in the same way. They derived from their humble and often sectarian piety the courage and strength to try to bring themselves and their own through the hard times without public or private assistance. They experienced failed harvests, price rises, work stoppages and lack of earnings in a strongly eschatological sense. Johann Hirzel refers with emphasis to these honourably poor outworkers. There was among 'this class of factory workers a further large, large number of righteous, industrious, retiring, and pious Christian individuals and whole families, who were most worthy of respect, trust and also of charitable help in the days of need'.[62] These people, who were 'engaged only in spinning and weaving, but are diligent', worked until they collapsed in times of need in order to offset the rising prices and their falling earnings. Johann Hirzel reports how in 1816 their rate of pay was reduced week by week. 'With steadily weakening forces these poor people now struggle against their growing poverty. Hunger and grief were imprinted on their features. They allowed only a few hours for sleeping, in order to maintain their unhappy lives by means of exhausting labour. But they will have to succumb, if help does not come.'[63]

It is not difficult to recognise that we are dealing here with people who had an intellectual and spiritual anchor, which gave them self-confidence and self-assertiveness. It could be that their smallholding and the position it gave them in the local community guaranteed such an anchorage, it could be that their 'understanding of religion' dictated this attitude. The same intellectual and spiritual foundation had previously, during good times with rich earnings, prevented these people from all too easily repudiating their customary way and form of life. However, it was different for those outworkers who did not have this resource. They were the people who were not only materially dependent on the putting-out industry, but who had also bound themselves intellectually and spiritually to this new form of livelihood. Their self-awareness and self-confidence rose and fell with the possibility of industrial earnings. We have seen how this sector of the population had spent all their earnings in the golden years on distinguishing themselves from their agricultural environment by means of a costly manner of living. When their wages fell, work stoppages occurred or prices increased, they not only possessed no material reserves, but their spiritual resistance was equally exhausted. They had no self-assurance any more, because their self-esteem as a class was undermined. Their behaviour in poverty and hardship was characteristic. They did not belong to the silent poor. They were not at all embarrassed about petitioning the Poor Officers for Relief. L.J. Schweizer, who described the outworkers' poverty in harrowing terms, had to admit

that some of them, who complain the loudest and are already talking about starving to death, did not belong in better times to the retiring, thrifty and orderly fathers of families, and even now are basically not complaining about lack of necessary sustenance, but rather about the removal of the means of continuing their previous expenditure on clothes and soft living.[64]

The will to hold out was foreign to these circles. They showed little inclination to work harder and live more moderately when their earnings dropped. According to the parish report about Bäretswil, it was

chiefly a source of moral impoverishment, causing many people to give up and to lose heart as soon as they have sunk to a certain depth of economic collapse. – They have not enough strength to pull themselves together again – to 'defend' themselves, as they used to call it; so they let everything go as it goes.[65]

These outworkers had as little compunction about approaching the Poor Offices as they had moral reservations about grasping the beggar's staff. The sources speak out frequently and urgently about this. A large proportion of the beggar convoys moving in hard times like a plague of locusts through the country consisted of impoverished and unemployed outworkers. The minutes of the Economic Commission went as follows:

The beggar class consists mostly of the sort of folk who turned out badly during the good times – getting into debt – and were not content with their earnings [from the putting-out industry], who did poor work – cheating – tricking the tradesman in every way, and who have dealt a fatal blow to manufacturing earnings. – These people were the first to be given no work, and took most naturally to begging.[66]

The minister of Fischenthal wrote about the 'actual factory workers' (meaning the landless outworkers):

As these people's earnings were now steadily diminishing, and Want with its fearful consequences overwhelmed them, who could be surprised that among such people a real race of beggars should emerge, being too little used to hardship, and mostly trained in only one manufacture, having grown up in parlours or loom shops many of them were left with neither strength nor ability for farmwork, especially when they were obliged to change all at once to hard physical labour; many of them were also too lazy to learn a new task, and they began to seek what they needed by begging until some of them took up begging as a profession.[67]

Why did part of the outworker population grasp the dishonourable beggar's staff and join the vagrants, the *Lumpenproletariat?* It should be mentioned first that the life of the common people included various practices which made it easier for them to grasp the beggar's staff. Remember how the travelling artisans were allowed by custom to beg? The unemployed outworkers made use of this custom, although not originally associated with it. The source just quoted says of the outworkers that they 'began to travel as journeymen; exchanging travel passes, testimonials and records of their employments and so imposing under various guises on the goodwill of people far and near'. Hawking, a particularly popular and familiar occupation in the Oberland, was also used by the outworkers as an occasion and a cover for begging:

both with and without patents, with only a bit of cotton stuff, some botched filigree work, or even just a couple of flower pots, the beggars travel in large and small troupes through the level regions of the cantons of Zurich, Schaffhausen, Thurgau and St Gall, and even the most remote farmhouses do not escape these travellers' avid gaze. Loaded with money, bread and other foods, the little troupe returns at the end of the week to our beloved homeland, consumes its proceeds gaily and rapidly and once they are used up, this hungry little nation readily undertakes a second flight into Egypt, in order to amass food.[68]

Finally, the seasonal and harvest-time migrations, with their customary practices, also set the outworkers on the road to beggardom.

However, little is explained by these points of contact with traditional forms of mendicancy. A higher degree of mental poverty and spiritual self-abandonment was required to set whole villages in the Oberland in the throes of 'begging fever' and to make them 'move, sack over shoulder, from village to village'.[69] Conditions were particularly bad in the spring of 1817. Thousands of outworkers travelled through the countryside begging in order to avoid starving to death. 'The beggars streamed past like an army', Jakob Stutz recorded, 'their pale, mud-coloured, bloated faces, their wasted bodies, their swollen feet, their leaden tread, oh, what a picture of wretchedness and terrible poverty they made.'[70] In the same year, Johann Schulthess, Canon and Professor of Theology, and member of the Church and Education Council, made a speech before the Zurich Synod in which he asked: 'Whether one would not rather they [the medicant outworkers] underwent physical death than such moral dissolution within their living bodies, God knows; but where the entire civic and ecclesiastical society is concerned, this human horde, which brings only trouble and harm, undoubtedly constitutes an unspeakable evil.'[71]

Were these mendicant outworkers the flotsam and jetsam of industrialisation, as Johann Schulthess and others were ready to admit? Certainly the armies of vagrants were recruited from the many outworkers who were poorly qualified hands, due to age, illness, infirmity or just through lack of skill, and could only spin on the wheel or prepare the raw materials for spinning and weaving. These people were singled out soonest by fate during work stoppages and crises, but especially in the chaos during the Revolution and when hand spinning collapsed. Their work must also have meant little to them, and their earnings everything. Consequently their dwindling earnings caused them the greatest degree of mental anguish. However, these instances do not suffice to explain the phenomenon. Why did mendicancy become a customary form of self-help for a proportion of the outworkers? We must attempt to answer this question by looking at the industrial form of existence.

Anyone who bound his life to the putting-out industry had to come to terms with an altered reality. He had to try to put down roots in a new spiritual and material environment. The transition from a mainly agricultural to an industrial way of life could not take effect without a violent shock to his mental and spiritual system. His traditional ties, assumptions, forms of behaviour and values lost their validity. The fundamental conditions of human life and society were altered. Manners and customs which had previously invested the life of both individuals and the community with a sense of direction and orientation no longer fulfilled their functions in the new form of existence. We have shown this in relation to the most varied spheres of life in the earlier chapters, while taking care to establish that this did not result in a break with tradition. The old adjusted to the new, was reassessed, re-experienced and applied differently. It was not a one-sided process of disintegration, but a new orientation which adjusted itself to the industrial existence. The new orientation was supported and driven by a genuine and strong creative urge, which gave the life of the common people new impulses and found expression in popular culture. It took time for people to become reconciled to industrial conditions of existence. Binding norms of behaviour towards the new environment could be found and confirmed by custom only over a long process, which speeded up in times of prosperity. Earnings from cottage industry also constituted the soil from which the industrial way of life grew. The thicker the layer of humus, the more vigorously the industrial life style could grow on it. We have encountered the self-confidence of the outworkers in times of prosperity, their manner of living, their behaviour towards the agricultural world, their manners and customs, which were mostly viewed as bad habits and dissolute vices by their contemporaries. With their traditional mentality,[72] the outworkers adjusted to this form of existence. The process of coming to terms, adjusting and adapting was, however, not fated to be peaceful and steady. Every price rise, work stoppage and wage reduction immediately swept away the layer of humus in which the outworkers had embedded their existence. The outworkers were obliged to discover that, after their fashionable luxury requirements had been satisfied, soup kitchens and beggary were lying in wait for them. Their self-confidence and self-conscious pride in their social station, which was indeed for many of them only pride in their earnings, gave way abruptly to leaden despair. They were confronted not only with a material but also an intellectual and spiritual void. It was only then that they realised the extent to which they had distanced themselves from the ancient peasant form of existence and its safeguards. They were now completely disorientated. The authorities did not undertake any effective preventive measures (apart from prohibitions and police regulations), and the official arrangements for Poor Relief were not adequate to allay their suffering. In this hopeless situation many outworkers were 'tortured by hunger and reduced by lack of earnings to desperation and to becoming discontented vagrants'.[73] Even when they were obliged only temporarily to resort to this pitiable condition, it brought them into contact with the practices of people who spent all their life on the road. We know the authorities' attitude to beggars and what means they employed to fight them. But mendicancy remained a form of self-help appropriate to the outworkers' social and economic conditions until far into the nineteenth century. In 1831, for instance, the minister of Wyla could still write that the lack of earnings everywhere in the eastern parishes of the canton had resulted in people, especially the weaker, unqualified outworkers, 'sitting together without work and – grumbling – or grasping the beggar's staff – which they were not used to do previously'.[74]

It is clear that the attitude of the ecclesiastical and lay authorities to poverty, outlined at the beginning of this chapter, was responsible for this situation. If the general opinion was that poverty was in some way dishonourable, even sinful, and that even those entitled to alms had to accept their dole in the full glare of publicity, the indigent would not find it any more shaming to be forced to survive for a while by begging in the streets. It must have been less intimidating to ask for food and drink at the doors of the wealthy than to accept one's bread dole before the assembled parishioners while being reminded that by accepting alms one had forfeited the right to vote in the parish.[75] With all its abuses, mendicancy was entwined in the life of the age, which brings us back to our initial questions.

In the early days of industrialisation, price rises and crises, poverty and need, hunger, destitution and mendicancy were all familiar aspects of life. They arose out of the social and economic conditions of the age and their interaction with its social attitudes, its moral values and behaviour. We have tried in this chapter to demonstrate, if only piecemeal, the mutual dependence between social conditions and social behaviour. We took care to emphasise this chronological and mental historical dependence, during which process local fundamental forces also appeared in strength. Conditions in the neighbouring industrial region of Appenzell and Toggenburg were already different. A different economic and social structure had given rise to an industrial population which 'had not been reduced by manufacturing to the degree of distress into which the spinners and weavers of the Zurich region had fallen'.[76] It would, however, be wholly mistaken to blame the putting-out industry for these conditions. We cannot emphasise this enough: cottage industry and the putting-out system should not be looked at from the point of view of uprooting. The cotton industry provided thousands with work and a livelihood, gave them a home, even when they did not have an inch of land, and saved thousands of people from the bitter fate of emigration, by establishing the material preconditions for a settled life and for founding families of their own. The changeover from a mainly peasant life and way of thinking to an industrial one has profound repercussions and involves wide spheres of life. Time is needed to adjust both materially and spiritually to the new industrial conditions of existence, especially since this existence is constantly being put in doubt by serious crises. It is only when industrial existence, with all its unstable factors, acquires adequate and serviceable safeguards, anchored in tradition and in the community, that the process of adjustment can succeed. We will return to this question in the Conclusion.

The manufacture of cotton yarn through the putting-out system altered the economic structure in many areas of the Zurich countryside. It need scarcely be mentioned that this process, accomplished in periods of prosperity in an unbridled, unsupervised and unpredictable manner, was not accomplished harmoniously. It too needed time in which to accommodate the social and economic spheres. Every common body reacted differently, according to its own legal, social and economic peculiarity. Each common body had pressing reasons of its own for establishing a social and economic equilibrium within the changed economic structure. It is understandable that this could lead to crises and desperate human situations. But we cannot lay the blame for this wholly on the putting-out industry, given that this, with its human and organisational structure and its mental, legal and economic foundations, was but a product of the Ancien Régime, of city-state mercantilism. If we use hindsight to assess the situation in terms of our modern social consciousness, we find that the responsibility for poverty, crises and mendicancy lay with the political and social structure of the Ancien Régime. We have spotlighted a few instances illustrating this. There remains the task of briefly describing the outworkers' fate in the stormy period around the turn of the century.

The transition from the eighteenth to the nineteenth century was a fateful and dramatic time for the whole of Europe. They were years of upheaval and transformation for State, economy and society, years which speeded up the flow of history like a waterfall. This applied particularly to the old Confederation and the Zurich city-state. The Helvetic Revolution brought about the collapse of the Ancien Régime and civic, social and economic life was fundamentally transformed, although various reactionary movements delayed and restricted this process. It constitutes an eminently important historical hiatus and has up till now hardly been mentioned in this investigation, because it belongs in time and content to Part two of this work and only there can its significance for our enquiry be given its full due.

These fateful and portentous years brought the population engaged in industry an excess of poverty and misery. It was directly hit by the evils of war and invasion, the political revolutions and all the muddle and confusion of the age, but this was not all. These years also ushered in a technological revolution of truly epoch-making significance, which shattered the very foundations of the outworkers' life and existence: spinning jennies arrived in Switzerland from England, causing the hand spinning industry to collapse. The economic and social conditions of the outworkers, described in this chapter, deteriorated completely during the course of this development.

This important transition has already been dealt with in numerous specialised studies, so we will limit ourselves to a few key words. Nor do we need to discuss the rise and development of machine spinning or of factory industry in Switzerland, since Part two will begin with these. We assume that the reader is familiar with the historical events.

The first machine-spun English yarn arrived in Switzerland in 1790, causing the price of all coarse-plied yarns to drop. This dealt a severe blow to the unqualified workers, who could only spin coarse yarn on the wheel. However much they strained and toiled, trying to make up for their falling wages by increasing their output, these people sank more and more deeply into abject poverty. They could work their fingers to the bone, but the number of distraints increased, and the troupes of unemployed and unfed beggars grew larger. Anyone who could replaced his spinning wheel with a loom, or tried to earn a miserable living by spinning fine yarns. The most finely plied yarns could not as yet be produced mechanically, which was vitally important for the skilled spinners, the *Briefgarn* or *Löthligarn* spinners, as they were called. These people were not as severely affected by the wage reductions as the spinning-wheel workers, a circumstance which helped to relieve the poverty in the Oberland, where most of the hand spinners lived. All the same, political events and sabre-rattling led to a fall in demand for fine cloth and consequently for fine-spun yarn. The effect was traumatic. Alongside the depressed prices came the evils of war and occupation during the Revolution. French rule brought with it import prohibitions and sales stoppages: both trade and manufacturing were disrupted. The industrially employed population found itself in a desperate situation: 'Our Revolution and lack of manufacturing earnings have caused not just a mass of people to sink into oppressive poverty – but also a large number into idleness and disorderliness – especially the young people.'[77] We have already seen instances of their need. As the English spinning machine was improved, even the finer sorts of yarn were affected by the falling prices.

The continental blockade throttled the import of English machine-spun yarns, which delayed the collapse of hand spinning. Its death was granted a last reprieve and the home industry won the time to change over to machine production.[78] However, the economic decrees and customs restrictions of the Napoleonic era threatened to throttle the manufacture. Bankruptcy loomed above many merchant houses, even old and respected ones. The outworkers were obliged to get by on only a fraction of their previous wages, if they could find any work at all. They suffered terrible poverty and hardship, especially in 1812 when a new series of price rises broke out. All official and private attempts at procuring work proved inadequate. People tried to encourage the manufacture of silk, woollen cloth and linen and to get the industry going again. They strove to propagate and subsidise sheep breeding and hemp and flax growing, and so on. However, none of these efforts was noticeably successful. It was inevitable that the economic and social conditions which had evolved in the eighteenth century, when the cottage industry was at its peak, should now completely deteriorate. Shocked and horrified contemporaries watched the cotton manufacturing industry, the State's foster-mother, dwindle and the hard-working spinning population sink into terrible poverty. Now everyone was aware of the dark side to the over-expanded cottage industry, about which so many clear-sighted patriots had warned:

Are not the following, to wit, the accumulation of the population to such a degree that it is out of all proportion to the produce of the soil; the exaggerated expansion of a manufacture which in good times cripples people, robbing them of their moral and physical strength, and in bad times, delivers them over to misery and indigence, which has the most destructive effects on bringing up children and makes us more dependent politically and economically, all evils which balance out, and even tip the scales against, all the advantages ensuing from them, however great these may seem.

This entreaty and question was posed anonymously in a script published in 1806, and continued as follows: 'But, it will be replied, since the evil is now here, we ought to provide assistance for so many more or less underfed persons, and wherever possible also try to bring about a less sudden and devastating collapse of our prosperity.'[79]

These words reveal a sense of responsibility towards the population engaged in industry, whose diligence and skill had contributed so much to the prosperity of town and State. They are evidence of a real social political understanding, of the realisation that the authorities were responsible for the prevailing and future social and economic conditions. While this may seem obvious to us, it is not so at all. For instance, a letter was sent on 4 April 1815 from the president of the Educational Council to the government which included these amazingly injudicious sentences:

Without doubt the whole or the greater part of the factory workers, and the part of our canton who live from factory earnings, have frequently given civic and church officials a lot of serious trouble. Ever since our land has been populated by such people out of all proportion to its size and produce, it has been on the whole a frivolous, carefree and decadent horde, able to earn its living with ease, which has given rise by means of premature and multiple reproduction to a more spineless and impoverished race, but has failed to increase the State's inner strength. During the price rises of the seventies and subsequently, whenever trade and commerce break down, the State has already borne the burden of ensuring the survival of such a huge number of people, who, once their earnings (which are dependent on foreign countries) dwindle and disappear, no longer know how to find their necesssary support.[80]

The landless outworkers were not the only ones to be driven to poverty and starvation by the collapse of the hand spinning industry and by market stagnation and falling prices following the political disorder; the outworkers who owned farms were also in a hopeless situation. As we know, these farms were enormously indebted. When the interest could no longer be earned, an enormous number of people were driven from their houses and farmsteads. The outworkers' hitherto great creditworthiness soon disappeared. Cassandra-like wails could be heard all over the place, complaining that the cotton manufacturing industry was mortally wounded and that it would never recover.[81] This would incite the creditors to move against debtors who could not pay with the utmost harshness, the more so in that many of the creditors were also under pressure. Nor can we avoid the reproach that many a town burgher sought, by mercilessly calling in their debts, to take revenge on the rural population for the Helvetic Revolution and the political and social defeat, and the shame they had suffered.

The outworkers' attitude to their basis of existence had hardened into customary behaviour, and this proved to be just as destructive. The Oberland spinners found it very difficult to quit the trade they had exercised for so long, which had fed them until now but could do so no longer, and to earn their living in a different employment. They were unable to grasp that the foundations on which they had built their lives were collapsing. It was feared 'that they run the risk of seeking refuge from their poverty by taking desperate measures rather than by changing to another trade'.[82] The outworkers refused to believe the first rumours about the English spinning jenny. The devil himself could not invent a spinning wheel that could turn by itself, let alone a person. What did England matter to us: 'We're in our country, and they're in theirs!'[83] It was only when spinning machines were set up in the Zurich countryside and in the Oberland that the outworkers realised what had happened to them. Dazed, they took on board the fact that they could now hang their spinning wheels up above the chimney. Incapable of recognising the signs of the times, the population engaged in industry directed its blind, uncomprehending hate against the spinning jennies. It resulted in unrest and menaces in the Oberland. There was an acute danger of the machines being attacked.[84]

Towards the end of the eighteenth century the Zurich domestic weavers were producing mostly fine muslin wares (in conjunction with the embroiderers of St Gall and Appenzell). The disruption caused by the Revolution and the Napoleonic wars drove this luxury industry into the ground. After the Battle of Leipzig and the lifting of the continental blockade the frontiers opened up again to the import of raw materials and the export of finished wares. A strong demand had built up for coarse cotton cloth, called calico (the Zurich hand weavers called it *Galli* for short). The mechanisation of spinning increased and cheapened the production of thread, which resulted in broad sections of the population being able to afford rough cotton cloth. As well as this, a new technical invention called the flying shuttle was adopted in the industrial regions of Zurich around 1800, which made weaving cotton cloth cheaper. A new, faster bleaching process had the same effect. The strong demand for coarse cotton cloth after the war was a very important feature of the changeover from hand spinning to machine spinning. It helped to ease the process of adjustment to a new sort of employment for the outworkers. The majority of the hand spinners were spurred on to earn their livings as domestic weavers by the big demand for weavers and their high earnings. Nor did the changeover turn out to be too difficult, since weaving the coarse calico cloth did not demand a lot of skill. Apart from this, technical improvements to the weaving process contributed towards making it possible to learn the technique in a few weeks.[85] The Zurich fine-ware industry soon went over to producing coarse calico. The years 1813 to 1815 brought rich earnings for the industrial population:

Now the complaints and cries of woe about the war, price rises and pestilence and so on were stilled, and instead jubilation and joy, dancing and merriment, not on account of peace, but because of the good wages, with people being paid as much as between 1 *Thaler* and 3 *Gulden* for a small piece of calico. Oh, how the manufacturing people lived it up then, as if it would last for ever.[86]

Cotton manufacture flourished like a hot house plant. Although its bloom lasted only a few years, it had a fateful importance for the Zurich outworkers and for the Oberland people especially. There were compelling reasons for changing over, and the change itself was made very much easier by the factors mentioned above. English machine-spun thread was not as yet produced in sufficient quantity to flood the European markets. There was a huge demand for thread, and hand-spun yarn could also be sold in insignificant quantities alongside the native machine-spun yarn. Outworkers who had lost their livelihoods, and who could not possibly have been employed in the newly built machine spinning shops, were able to survive again.[87] It was only then that the loom travelled out of the villages into the homesteads and hamlets. The busy clatter of the loom could now be heard in the remotest corners of the gullies, on the slopes and crannies of the Oberland hills and mountains. Within a few years there was hardly a house in these regions which did not have one or more looms in it. It was a matter of life and death to be able to go on doing outwork, especially for the hamlets and homesteads which had risen up during the wave of industrial settlement in the eighteenth century. They had been founded on earnings from cottage industry and could not exist without them. They were too far away from the newly arisen and growing machine spinning shops, which relied on the rivers for their power, for their inhabitants to earn their livelihoods in such enterprises.

It is obvious that this changeover from domestic spinning to domestic weaving led to various changes to people's traditional way of life, to their social life, to their settlements and homes. The new tools, techniques and aids of the work as well as its new noises had a direct effect on the groups working and living under cottage industrial conditions. But in any case, even in places where previously spinning but no weaving had been done, the inhabitants were already familiar with these working and living conditions.

Calico wares were produced through the putting-out system as well. The rural inhabitants' newly acquired freedom of trade and manufacture now enabled them to ascend the social scale and become independent putters-out. They made capable use of this freedom. A large number of rural manufacturers inserted themselves into the manufacturing industry, often employing only a few hand-loom weavers, working hard and travelling long distances on foot to distribute the warps, marketing the wares themselves. Especially after 1820, small putting-out establishments of this kind sprung up like mushrooms. In the Hinwil district, for instance, there were around fifty such enterprises in 1839,[88] thus providing the human and organisational structure of the putting-out system with a new social structure. The family and neighbourly relations between employee and employer were strengthened, allowing a better grasp of the putting-out hierarchy. It was increasingly possible to change putting-out masters. People were no longer tied for better or worse to one particular putting-out establishment. Conversely, social distinctions within the parish were growing more marked, giving rise to an industrial aristocracy, which later also included the entrepreneurial factory manager families (some of the rural putting-out masters also became factory owners). The possibilities for social advancement through the newly acquired freedom of trade and manufacture put new stimulus into the social life of the rural parishes. We can only mention all these aspects in passing, because the development and history of cottage industry in the nineteenth century does not belong to our theme, and will receive full treatment in Part two of our investigation.

The collapse of hand spinning and the transition to machine spinning and more domestic weaving did not, however, occur peacefully. The period of rich earnings only lasted a short while; it was paid for with harsh crises and years of starvation. Many factors contributed to this: more and more English machine-spun thread was flooding the European markets. The English textile industry managed to increase its production considerably by improving its looms and preparatory processes, a development which not only robbed all the outworkers of their livelihood, but also put several machine spinning shops in the Zurich countryside out of business. Only efficient factory works, well managed and equipped with good machinery, were able to withstand the competition. In 1816 various European states introduced protective tariffs. The Federal cantons were unable to counter these restrictions with their own customs policy. On top of this, 1816 was a year when the harvest failed quite spectacularly. The price of food soared in the winter of 1816–17. Many examples have already been cited concerning 1817, the year of starvation. The industrial regions in particular suffered unspeakable hardship. Countless people died from lack of food or fell sick from eating unsuitable food.

So it was against this dreadful background that the textile industry's first great transition took place: a major turning point in the history of the industry and of technology in general. The economic and social structure of the putting-out system, which had developed over 200 years and was maintained by a suitable economic and social mentality, underwent a profound convulsion following this collapse. But the forces which had driven, directed and supported this development were also capable of completing the process of transition and of ensuring the continuation of the Zurich textile industry: the inventiveness, the entrepreneurial spirit, the energy and trading skills of the putting-out and manufacturing masters overcame all the difficulties. New machines were invented and constructed in their own country, new markets were discovered and won outside Europe. Conversely, it was the industrial population's own stubborn and unshakeable adherence to their particular work and basis of existence, in spite of all the crises and hardship, which made the transition easier. Their diligent and skilled hands remained within the cotton manufacturing industry, and raised it to new heights in the twenties, when new improvements were implemented.

To sum up: in the industrial regions of the Zurich countryside a population evolved over the generations which knew that its existence was inseparably bound up with the putting-out system. It clung with all the tenacity of its traditional way of life and of thinking to the very basis of its existence, a basis which was as much material as mental and spiritual. The scope of the industrial population's fateful involvement in the putting-out system was revealed in times of crisis: the traditional attitudes of the population engaged in industry, which were bound up in community and custom, had resulted in their accepting poverty, hardship and crises as familiar and unavoidable features of their lives. It was their irrational moral and religious precepts guiding their lives which bound them to their industrial employment, and which let them cling to it even during times of poverty and hardship. Just as a mountain farmer clears his fields and meadows of the debris left by the floodwaters, and as a miner goes down the same pit in which his father and brother may have lost their lives, so too did the outworker cling to his cotton threads, which appeared to guarantee him life and livelihood, as they had done for his father and grandfather. When this thread snapped in times of crisis, the outworker accepted it with dull resignation, gathering up the torn strands again when things improved.

Like peasants, miners and sailors, the outworkers were distinguished at the onset of industrialisation by their resigned attitude towards the dangers and risks of their profession. These were not natural catastrophes such as floods, hail and storms, but sales stoppages, crises, slumps and the rising cost of living. Their resignation was, as we have seen, based on religious and ideological grounds. The outworker of the eighteenth century was scarcely aware of the concept that he should take out adequate safeguards against the vicissitudes of his profession, let alone demand civic, mutual or private supervisory and insurance institutions. Manufacturing and factory laws, accident and health protection, savings, sickness, old-age and widows' funds, trades union combinations to protect the workers' interests, self-help organisations in general and much more – all these are part of the history of the nineteenth century. They are not to be found under the Ancien Régime – only their first stirrings are evident. Behind these institutions stands a truly exciting slice of mental, cultural, state, social and economic history, which will be extensively discussed in Part two of this investigation.

Let us recapitulate: much as the outworkers' insistence on adhering to an insecure way of life may be incomprehensible to us with our modern perception of society, we should not overlook the fact that the outworkers' mentality and attitude to life, bound up as it was in community and tradition, ensured the continuity of the Zurich textile industry. We have shown in this chapter how the industrial population overcame serious crises and emergencies without losing hold of their industrial basis of existence. They were often forced to change and to adapt. Their firm hold, together with the acquired ability to change and adapt, also made it possible and necessary for the industrial population of the Zurich countryside to withstand the worst and most fundamental upheavals in their existence around the turn of the eighteenth century and so ensure the continuation of the Zurich textile industry. The old domestic spinning industry collapsed, but the putting-out system was able to adjust and flourish anew, and machine spinning developed in spite of all competition. The newly strengthened textile industry encouraged new branches of the industry to develop along industrial lines, a process commonly known as the 'Industrial Revolution'.

If the industry allowed people to put down roots in their homeland, it was, on the other hand, the workers who enabled the industry to become firmly established and settled, and so ensured that it would survive difficulties and crises. Industrial landscapes with all their cultural wealth arose.

7 ♣ Conclusion

The last chapter ended with a complementary relationship – let us pick it up again: on the one hand the putting-out industry gave people a homeland in the comprehensive sense of the term; on the other hand these people ensured that the textile industry found stability within their economic and cultural area, in spite of all crises. The 'industrial landscape' grew out of this complementary relationship. What do we understand by the term?

'Industrial landscape' is a cultural and morphological term. The cultural landscape is stamped with visible signs of the putting-out industry. We have learnt about them during our research. They are the changes to settlement, buildings and home life – changes to husbandry, use of the soil and field patterns (Chapter 4). On top of this there are the thousand and one things which spring to the traveller's eye as he journeys through the industrial regions of the Zurich landscape; it could be the spinning work place beside every village well, the rotting and abandoned weaving equipment, the broken spinning wheels near the woodpile – or it could be the yarn and cloth dealers with their packs on their backs, whom he meets on the road, the mules laden with cotton bales or the spinner-girls in their fasionable clothes. They all tell him that he is passing through a bit of country in which the putting-out system is at home.

When the putting-out system is at home in a landscape, it is clear that the term 'industrial landscape' involves more than just these external signs. Behind these signs stands a reality: the forms of popular life and culture, which are ineluctably bound to the putting-out industry; forms of life and social life adjusted to and appropriate to an industrial basis of existence. These forms of life lay at the centre of our investigation. We have tried to show in all kinds of spheres how the basic conditions of human life and social life are changed when existence is founded wholly or partially on an industrial base. Instead of summing up let us recall the following key words: the changes in people's attitude to marriage and the marriage contract, to the structure and cohesion of the family, and the early industrial demographic movements (Chapter 2); the changes to people's diet, clothing, and the whole range of their needs, the function of fashion and luxury in their new life style, the altered forms of

184

community and sociability and the new cultural wealth (Chapter 3); the Protestant work ethic and the outworkers' attitude to work, the effect of putting-out work on the life and culture of the common people (Chapter 5); the behaviour of the industrially employed population towards their basis of existence in times of poverty, hardship and crisis (Chapter 6). This reality lay behind the visible signs which marked a particular cultural environment as an 'industrial landscape'.

With this, man, the creator and upholder of cultural existence, steps into the limelight. Industry is rooted in people – it is implanted in their hearts. This is a fact which had particular significance for those sectors of the population which were employed in industry, which were forced to settle elsewhere. These people carried with them as invisible baggage their skills, experience and their ways of living, behaving and thinking, taught them by their industrial basis of existence, and they transplanted the industry to their new homeland. A. Karasek-Langer[1] has provided us with telling examples from the most recent past of this sort of industrial transplantation.

Industry is rooted in people. Their traditional ways of living and thinking, bound up in community and custom, shaped their environment into an 'industrial landscape'. When we use this term, we recognise that 'in the functional combination of the various elements constituting a living cultural unity', industry is the 'dominant element'.[2] Implicit in this term is also the further profession that industrialisation cannot and should not be seen from the point of view of destruction and accumulation.[3] While the life and culture of the common people were indeed altered by industrialisation, they were not displayed and destroyed, but shaped anew. The term 'industrial landscape' vouches for this. This thesis has already been advanced in our Introduction and we hope it is sufficiently supported by the results of the present enquiry.

These final remarks lead us to a brief outlook: the Zurich Oberland along with other parts of the Zurich countryside were already industrial landscapes before factory industry took over in the nineteenth century. The radical change from a predominantly agricultural to an industrial way of living and thinking had already taken place. The new living conditions had already gained a sufficient hold on the life and culture of the common people. The first slumps, which accompanied the process, had been surmounted. The factory industry of the nineteenth century found a population whose social structure, manner of living, economic management and whole mental and spiritual attitude demonstrated their familiarity with industrial conditions and terms of existence, quite apart from the preconditions present in this population regarding the techniques of work and their attitude to work. The factory industry found that the ground had already been prepared and that it could simply be grafted onto the putting-out industry.

The changes to the life of the common people under the influence of the putting-out industry, which we have tried to analysis in this thesis, constituted important preconditions and foundations for the subsequent factory industry. We hope that our analysis has made this sufficiently clear. It is evident that the upheavals brought about by factory industry were less radical than they would have been if the factory industry had broken into an unprepared peasant and farming world. The changes to people's way of life under the influence of factory industry were not as massively fundamental as they had been with the preceding putting-out industry, as long as they took place in fully developed industrial regions like the Zurich countryside.

One fatefully significant circumstance attending the changeover from cottage industry to factor industry was the cottage industry's refusal to collapse and to leave the field wholly to the factory industry. It survived varying fortunes, enduring all sorts of changes, right up until the twentieth century. For generations many families had a dual industrial basis of existence: some family members would earn their living in the textile factories while the others worked at home, at their looms or embroidery frames. If the family still owned a smallholding, it would be farmed in common, if individual family members did not perform all or part of this task. Even when the factory industry was not able to become established in several regions with an old putting-out industry, it would still draw the inhabitants in its wake. Workers of both sexes would climb down from their mountainous and hilly zones and make the weary journey through wind and rain at all times of the year to the factory in the valley. This dual industrial basis of existence made the process of transition easier and had an equalising effect, dampening the reaction against the new employment possibilities, which unfolded with the factory industry. Within the social structure of the industrial landscape such families formed a counterweight against the families which earned their livings exclusively in factory halls and spent their lives in the new boarding houses.

The changes in people's way of life under the influence of the factory industry were nevertheless comprehensive enough. They will provide the theme for the sequel to this book. From the old roots of the putting-out industry sprouted both an established entrepreneurial class and a settled working class. The Zurich textile industry developed in a new century, throbbing with new ideas and harnessed to an altered political, economic and social order. The life and culture of the common people were altered still further, supported by a population whose manner of living and thinking, bound up in community and tradition, fettered them to the textile industry. Anybody walking today through the Zurich Oberland would be aware of this with every step he took, noticing, too, how the factory industry had been grafted onto the old putting-out industry. Standing alongside the boarding houses and factory works are the *Flarz* houses and the outworker cottages of the eighteenth century. As well as the factory workers returning home from work, one may now and again still meet an outworker doing her work in front of her house.

Industrialisation is unquestionably one of the most astonishing phenomena of our most recent history. Its effects cannot be overlooked and may scarcely be overestimated. We expressed our conviction in the Introduction that it is a common duty of all the arts disciplines dealing with the present age to research this phenomenon. This investigation should contribute to this from the historical and folklorist view point. The theme of 'Industrialisation and Everyday Life' has an urgent immediacy, especially for the underdeveloped countries, over whom industry is breaking like a tidal wave. For this reason we think it important to study the process of development in the old industrial landscapes of Europe, that we may more fully understand the present.

Postscript

Ulrich Pfister

Rudolf Braun's work on the social and cultural impact of cottage industry in the canton of Zurich before 1800 belongs to a group of studies which appeared around 1960 and opened the field of regional studies in social and economic history.[1] A common feature of them was their stress on structures and processes bearing on the lives of the great mass of ordinary people, such as the family, demography, work conditions, popular culture and mentality. All were usually based on a detailed scrutiny of primary source material available for a limited regional context.

Whereas in France the Annales movement paved the way for this new paradigm and the Anglo-Saxon community itself had a long-standing heritage in social and economic history, such a background was lacking in German historiography.[2] Hence, it is of little surprise that Rudolf Braun's *Industrialisierung und Volksleben* has many of its roots outside historiography and, as the reader will note in the Introduction, rather in the specific Swiss academic tradition of *Volkskunde* (folklore).[3] Thus, while being in general a study in the history of mentality, this work nevertheless stands outside the corresponding tradition initiated by French writers.[4] However, it does not merely form an application of concepts derived from *Volkskunde*, but breaks new ground by focussing less on cultural tradition (as was the usual approach of the discipline) than on cultural change and innovation associated with the emergence of industrial structures.[5]

As a consequence of its unique background this study, despite its academic popularity, has tended to remain outside the mainstream of social historical writing. While it paved the way for numerous quantitative and structure-oriented works, the author himself always stressed the importance of the complementary use of qualitative information by the historian.[6] Hence, considered in the context of the emerging saturation of the discipline with quantitative work, Braun's study can also be regarded as a forerunner of 'thick description' as a specific methodology in historiography.[7]

Apart from its general value Braun's work is of particular importance in a specific research field, namely the study of rural handicraft industry before the advent of the factory, that is, of *proto-industrialisation*. Coined by Franklin

188

Mendels in 1972 this term has been broadened conceptually and has been discussed in a vast number of studies since.[8] Together with a few other seminar works,[9] Braun's book served as a point of departure for the later discussion. In order to appreciate its impact in more detail, and to point to more recent extensions and revisions, the following discussion will be based on the well-known conceptual framework introduced by Mendels.[10] Each point (the framework consists of four definitions and six hypotheses) will be introduced briefly and will be discussed with reference to the study in question. It should be pointed out, however, that this procedure is only used to put Braun's work into a broader perspective; it does not form this book's conceptual background.

Definition 1 Proto-industrial production is oriented towards manufactured exports into markets beyond a regional context.

Definition 2 Proto-industrialisation is marked by the participation of rural households in the production of manufactured goods, that is, by the phenomenon of cottage industry.

Braun's book is one of the first modern studies which focusses on industrialisation before industrialisation, that is, on forms of handicraft production of industrial products by individual households with the help of relatively primitive technologies. It thus marks a break with traditional studies of the origins of industrialisation, which usually began their analysis with the introduction of the factory system. As a consequence, the current characterisation of export-oriented manufacture in rural households as a distinct social and economic phenomemon reflects in part the emphases of Braun's study, which later investigation was to replicate elsewhere.[11] In the light of recent doubts about the utility of the two definitional criteria in question,[12] Braun's documentation of a specific type of social behaviour among rural workers engaged in export-oriented production of manufactures still retains much analytical value, at least for those features of proto-industrialisation with which he is concerned.

Definition 3 Proto-industry implies the differentiation between, on the one hand, farmers producing a commercialised surplus, and, on the other, poor farmers and cottagers seeking additional income either as agricultural labourers or as workers in manufacturing. This differentiation may occur either in a local context (village, region) or in a supra-regional context (between regions, within nations or even internationally).

Together with the work of Thirsk,[13] Braun's analysis of the distinctive features of the Oberland of the canton of Zurich as compared to the rest of the canton (mainly the Unterland; see Chapter 1 of this book) has sometimes been regarded as telling evidence for the thesis of regional differentiation or bifurcation as an integral aspect of proto-industrialisation.[14] His main stress is on the following causal chain believed to be decisive for the emergence of cottage industry in the Oberland: originally, the hilly character and the infertile soils made the region unsuitable for the usual field rotation system with corporate land use, as practised in the relatively flat Unterland. The consequent dominance of separate ownership and individual land use (*Egartenwirtschaft*) prevented the formation of close village communities which could have restricted the use of commons and have erected barriers against immigration. This in turn led to the emergence of a rural proletariat which was only able to make ends meet with the help of earnings derived from manufacturing work.[15] This process as a whole suggests the presence of certain structural features which can be regarded as characteristic of proto-industrial regions.

Stimulated by studies such as Braun's, later authors have elaborated on the regional aspect of proto-industrialisation by using a systematic comparative approach. Mendels, in particular, developed the notion of a typical proto-industrial region being subdivided into first, a flat, rich agricultural area with large concessions and possibly impartible inheritance; secondly, a hilly area with poor soils, a predominance of dairy farming associated with proto-industry, partible inheritance and labour migration into the richer area; and, thirdly, a larger town between these two complementary rural areas providing the commercial and entrepreneurial skills required for the operation of the economic links between the two.[16]

Despite the similarities between Braun's thesis and the bifurcation model set out above, the canton of Zurich does not seem to fit very well into the latter.[17] The Unterland never was a rich and market-oriented grain producing area; grain for the town of Zurich and the Oberland was imported from southern Swabia which also offered an important seasonal labour market for many poor people south of the Rhine. Obviously, the region complementary to the Oberland (according to the model set out above) was not the Unterland but southern Swabia, and both were separated by the Unterland, dominated by subsistence agriculture supported by modest levels of proto-industrial textile production at certain times (before the end of the seventeenth and during the last years of the eighteenth centuries). This suggests that processes of regional differentiation associated with cottage industry were of greater complexity than proponents of the bifurcation thesis have concluded, on the basis of Braun's work.

Definition 4 Proto-industrialisation is a regional phenomenon and has to be analysed on this level of aggregation.

As mentioned at the outset the present book was among the first explicitly to practise local history from the perspective of concepts of social and economic history;[18] it thus played a considerable role in orienting research on proto-industry towards a regional approach.

To turn to the hypotheses within Mendel's framework, the majority relate to problems of organisation in the proto-industrial system, capital accumulation, the acquisition of industrial knowledge by entrepreneurs and the importance of the emergence of commercial agriculture (in the context of regional bifurcation) as a precondition for later urbanisation. Following the folklorist approach of Braun's work these are not treated in much detail in his book. On the other hand, it has made important contributions to the topics of the demography of proto-industrial populations (hypothesis 1 in Mendel's framework) and of their cultural behaviour (hypothesis 5). The following discussion relates exclusively to these two points.

The first hypothesis states that proto-industrialisation had the effect of breaking up the system of the European pattern of late marriage which had previously prevailed,[19] and thus provided the base for significant population growth. On the one hand, this was because incomes from cottage industry allowed people to divide farms among their offspring without endangering their subsistence, so that more people could marry; on the other hand, people could marry at younger ages because earnings from manufacturing work allowed marriages to be concluded without a significant agricultural base (through inheritance, for example).

The present study was among the first to formulate this hypothesis and to attempt its verification by demographic evidence (Chapter 2 above).[20] At the time of its first appearance this thesis stood in marked contrast to established wisdom, which held that the great demographic transition was initiated by a decline of mortality rather than by a rise in nuptiality and a corresponding increase in fertility.[21] In the meantime, however, the evolution of demographic research techniques has made it possible to demonstrate that the marriage rate was of considerable importance in population dynamics of the eighteenth century.[22]

While some other studies have confirmed the patterns postulated by Braun and Mendels,[23] quite a number of empirical studies have come to negative conclusions with respect to the hypothesis in question. As a consequence, some authors have tended to discard the hypothesis altogether, whereas others have tended to look for conditions under which the mechanisms in question operate or do not operate; the main specifying factors which have been suggested are the type of proto-industrialisation, the speed of its expansion, the nature of its association with agriculture or the sexual division of labour.[24] As for the canton of Zurich, a recent study has shown that the pattern postulated above and in Chapter 2 in Braun's work does hold for the inner part of the Oberland during the rapid expansion of proto-industry in the second half of the eighteenth century, but not so for the outer areas of the Oberland (with, admittedly, more modest levels of proto-industrialisation), and for earlier periods. It suggests that a pattern of rising marriage and fertility rates emerges only where cottage industry leads to a definitive break-up of agrarian structures, and to the emergence of a rural proletariat largely dependent on earnings from manufacturing.[25]

The other hypothesis addressed here states that proto-industrialisation facilitates the formation of a qualified labour force which can easily be integrated into an industrial factory system.

Beyond the question of technical skills this hypothesis addresses more immaterial aspects of the quality of a labour force such as work discipline. It is perhaps in this field that Braun's study has proven most stimulating; it is also here that it still goes clearly beyond more economistic approaches, such as the one advocated by Mendels. In fact a substantial part of Braun's book (notably Chapters 3 and 5) consists of a detailed analysis of the mentality displayed by proto-industrial populations.

What becomes clear is that their ways of behaviour do not resemble very much those of industrial workers. Work has still an eminently social character; it is done in work groups of neighbours, of young people (*Lichtstubeten*) or in the family. Likewise, it principally serves certain social goals which are partly new (fulfilment of subsistence needs, acquisition of consumption goods associated with social prestige), rather than the maximisation of income. On the other hand, Braun points to a number of new elements within the culture of rural working classes which, while often being rooted in traditional folk culture, take on a new meaning through the fact that these groups are largely devoid of an agricultural base and, therefore, develop new means of status allocation and documentation. An often-cited example is the individualisation of courtship customs brought about by a progressive weakening of familial control over marriage arrangements based on the disposition of agricultural property (Chapter 2).

While Braun's approach is basically descriptive in character (see notably the statement at the beginning of Chapter 3), later authors, Medick in particular, have attempted to link systematically the mental structures of proto-industrial populations to the specific proto-industrial family economy.[26] Even these extensions, however, rely in part on empirical evidence provided by the present study. Perhaps the most important revision of these attempts at more conceptional coherence is Medick's contention that the separation of the proto-industrial worker from an agricultural base does not necessarily individualise courtship and marriage choice; rather, the temporal necessity to maximise the familial production of manufactures creates the base of new objective criteria in marriage choice (e.g. work capacity). Since little empirical material bearing on this issue is available, however, it is difficult to decide between these two positions.

To conclude, the juxtaposition of Braun's work with a major recent analysis of the concept of proto-industrialisation shows that it raised a number of issues which, while extended and modified since, have mostly not yet been resolved. Its frequent citation as a source of theoretical statements or, indeed, of empirical evidence, is witness to its lasting relevance in the field of research on proto-industrialisation.

Appendix: a note on the administrative structure and social stratification in the countryside of Zurich during the Ancien Régime

Ulrich Pfister

The territory of the canton of Zurich was acquired by the town of Zurich during the late Middle Ages mostly through purchase or mortgaging by declining feudal powers. During the Reformation a vast amount of church property was secularised and seized by the town. The latter was ruled by two town councils (a large and a small one, the latter being the governing body) with two Mayors at its head. It is the small council which is usually addressed as Your Worship in the sources quoted by the present book. The rural territory was administered by governors (*Land-* and *Obervögte* for the secular property, *Amtsmänner* for former church property; the translation invariably uses the term governor) chosen from among the members of the town council for a limited period of years.

On the local level, a clear distinction must be made between the village community and the church parish. The latter often encompassed several villages and, particularly in the Oberland, hamlets and scattered farmsteads not belonging to a commune. Its chief officer was the minister who, from the late sixteenth century onwards, had to be a burgher of the town of Zurich. He and the church elders (*Ehegaumer*) chosen from among the parishioners formed a supervisory body (the *Stillstand*) watching over the moral life in the parish and administrating church funds, particularly with regard to Poor Relief.

The intermediary between the village community and the political administration represented by the governor was the bailiff (in the sense of an administrator; *Untervogt*) who usually was a member of the local upper class, i.e. a wealthy farmer. Other positions usually taken by the village notables were the adminstrator of the village funds (*Seckelmeister*), the bailiffs and jurymen in the district courts as well as the lower officer ranks in the militia.

As elsewhere, the rural upper class can be broadly defined as the farmers possessing at least one plough-team (full farmers). Apart from this group, half farmers (those possessing only one animal capable of being used for draught purposes), smallholders and landless day-labourers are social classes which are frequently mentioned in the present context.

The interests of the local village community, and in particular those of the upper class, become visible in the entry charters (*Einzugsbriefe*) quoted extensively in Chapter 1 of this study. Usually demanded by the village notables (who form the delegation) from the governor and the town government, they gave a commune the right to raise a fee from immigrants and stipulated rules regarding the use of village property (the commons), the division of holdings and the erection of new houses. However, and this is a distinctive feature of areas where dispersed settlement predominated (as in the Oberland) and where, correspondingly, village communities were weak, the rural upper class, if it was able to organise itself at all, had to seek other ways to safeguard its interest in restricting access to pasture and wood. Hence, church parishes were used as the channel to formulate demands for entry charters.

A consequence of the restriction of mobility by entry charters was a stronger division between burghers of the village commune and non-burghers or villeins (*Hintersässen*), i.e. persons living in a commune without having paid the entry fee and in principle being denied the access to wood and pasture. If they were poor they burdened the Relief funds of both Church and State, which explains in part why they were strongly resented by the rural upper class.

Notes

Introduction

1. This aim is summarised in the title of an essay by Max Silberschmidt: 'Zur Geistesgeschichte der industriellen Revolution', *Schweizerische Hochschulzeitung*, 29, no. 6 (1956).

2. See A. Karasek-Langer's fundamentally important remarks in 'Neusiedlung in Bayern nach 1945', *Jahrbuch für Volkskunde der Heimatvertriebenen*, 2 (1956), pp. 65ff.

3. See R. Weiss, *Volkskunde der Schweiz*, Erlenbach and Zurich 1946, pp. 15 and 23ff.

4. It should be mentioned here that the *Tüchler* (clothiers) employed by a putting-out enterprise were often called *Fabrikanten* (manufacturers) in contemporary sources. In the same way, outworkers employed in the putting-out industry were described as *Fabrikarbeiter* (factory workers) in eighteenth-century sources (students of public affairs, economists and physiocrats in the eighteenth century were already trying to differentiate between 'factory' and 'manufacture', etc.). In this enquiry we have quoted the contemporary term 'factory', without pointing out each time that it refers here only to conditions within the putting-out industry. We refer the reader to the appropriate entries in various encyclopaedias.

5. Walter Bodmer's *Schweizerische Industriegeschichte*, Zurich 1960, appeared shortly before this enquiry was printed. We were not able to make use of this work, but would like to take this opportunity to refer to it.

6. See Bibliography.

1 The preconditions for industrialisation

1. See State Archive of Zurich (hereafter St.A.Z.) F I 354ff, *Beschreybung der Armen uff der ganzen Landschaft Zürich*, 1649, 1600, 1680, 1700.

2. See St.A.Z. A 99, *Gemeindegüter und Einzugsbriefe*, viz., Töss 1630, Unterhittnau 1638, Pfäffikon 1739, Illnau-Otikon 1730, etc. See too F. Meier, *Geschichte der Gemeinde Wetzikon*, Zurich 1881, p. 151.

3. St.A.Z. A 124.

4. Limited quantities of hemp and flax may have been imported from the Thurgau and the Rhine valley, and from Swabia. See J. Ebel, *Schilderung der Gebirgsvölker der Schweiz*, 2 vols., Leipzig 1789, 1802, vol. 1, p. 268.

5. Let us refer the reader to the various works on economic history by A. Bürkli-Meyer, O. Haegi, W. Honegger, B. Keller, E. Künzle, and others.

6. See J.C. Hirzel, 'Beantwortung der Frage: Ist die Handelschaft, wie solche bey uns beschaffen, unserem Lande schädlich oder nützlich, in Absicht auf den Feldbau und die Sitten des Volkes?', *Magazin für die Naturkunde Helvetiens*, 3 (1788), p. 118.

7. There was also a modest number of manufacturers in the town, but they do not concern us here.

8. A. Bürkli-Meyer, *Die Zürcherische Fabrikgesetzgebung vom Beginn des 14. Jahrhunderts an bis zur Schweizerischen Staatsumwälzung von 1798*, Zurich 1884, whose collection of laws and directives provides impressive documentation of how the economic order slowly altered. This process was carried out in the field of force between the old artisan and guild order and the new forces in the putting-out industry.

9. See G. Finsler, *Zürich in der zweiten Hälfte des achtzehnten Jahrhunderts*, Zurich 1884, p. 185.

10. St.A.Z. F I 354ff; the subsequent references are all quoted from this Poor Register. Details of year and place are given in brackets in the text to allow the source to be pin-pointed easily.

11. We shall retain only these simple facts at this stage, putting off all enquiries about the origins of these conditions so as not to pre-empt our conclusions.

12. This involved not only political and economic dependence on the town, but also, as alms recipients, the loss of communal rights. Alms recipients lost their active rights as members of the village commune. See H. Strehler, *Beiträge zur Kulturgeschichte der Zürcher Landschaft*, Part II: 'Aberglaube, Armut und Bettel', in *Zürcher Taschenbuch auf das Jahr 1935* (1935), p. 95.

13. Even small local improvements in the labour market had a restricting effect. Within the catchment area of the Wald weekly market with its peasant yarn manufacture in 1649, for instance, hemp and flax were still being spun throughout. However, this tells us nothing about the level of poverty in the Wald region, but rather, something about the rates of pay for spinning in the putting-out industry and about the growth of the putting-out system.

14. St.A.Z. A 99/1. A petition by the parish assembly of Unterdürnten of 1 Nov. 1661 to their governor about raising the entry fee and ratifying their suggestions concerning the use of the commonalty.

15. Strehler, *Beiträge zur Kulturgeschichte der Zürcher Landschaft*, Part II, p. 83.

16. St.A.Z. A 99/1.

17. See the harvest records in minister Ulrich of Lufingen's diary for 1685–1710; quoted in part by H. Morf, *Neujahrsblatt der Hülfsgesellschaft von Winterthur*, vol. 12: *Aus der Geschichte des zürcherischen Armenwesens*, Winterthur 1873, p. 31. Morf also cites figures for the extent of the impoverishment. In 1700 the ratio of families receiving Poor Relief to other families in the better-off parishes was 1:8. This ratio could climb as high as 2:5. The average for the whole canton was at most 1:5. Morf writes that 'it should not be overlooked that people could be left without help who would nowadays have a prior claim to charity' (p. 32).

18. In so far as he owned any such rights. In the sixteenth century the poor of the village commune still had a distinguishing mark fixed to their shoulder. Strehler, *Beiträge zur Kulturgeschichte der Zürcher Landschaft*, Part II, p. 95.

19. We do not need to analyse the deep-seated social effects of this sort of emigration more closely at this stage.

20. See for instance H. Bernhard, *Wirtschafts- und Siedlungsgeschichte des Tösstales*, Diss., Zurich, 1912, p. 59; popular literature is particularly prone to cite this as the origin.

21. F. Wyss, 'Die Schweizerischen Landsgemeinden', *Zeitschrift für schweizerisches Recht*, 1 (1852), p. 24.

22. *Ibid.*, p. 25.

23. This development was accompanied by an alteration to the community as a legal person. The communities became independent and the matters within their jurisdiction grew in number. We will discuss this in detail further on. We also refer the reader to the various monographs, especially the one by F. Wyss. He points out the reactionary character of process in question in a passage of such fundamental significance that we quote it here: 'From the middle of the fifteenth century to the middle of the sixteenth, it is very evident that the foundations, on which the inner condition of the communities had until then rested, had collapsed. This was a consequence of weakened domanial rights and the rise and increased power of the peasantry, and was particularly apparent in the changeover from feudal tenure to actual proprietory rights, liable only to rent, or, at least in an approximation to the latter, in an abolishment or reduction of serfdom, in a narrowing of the gaps between the several classes of the peasantry in a fragmentation of formerly closed and tied estates, in a loosening of the formerly strict village regulations about the number and location of houses, in a frequent change of residence and a facilitation of new settlement. These facts were actively interrelated with the political and even the religious movements of the age. They were manifestations which have appeared successfully and lastingly in other states only in this century, and closer analogies have been found amongst us again more recently. From the middle of the sixteenth century and especially in the seventeenth century the attempt was made within the actual community to protect the interests of the surviving larger landed estates and the previous use of the commonalty, which had been endangered by these changes, and to introduce to this purpose a new form of community right with a new set of tighter restrictions' (*ibid.*, p. 5).

24. The Zurich government had made sure of the right to determine and control restrictions on settlement in the villages (private and legal concerns were entwined).

25. C.G. Schmidt, *Der Schweizer Bauer im Zeitalter des Frühkapitalismus*, Berne 1932, p. 48: 'That the peasants as a rule demanded a high entry fee from all those who wanted to settle in their midst as members of the community, in order to protect the form of economy particular to their locality from external influence, is a circumstance which has particular interest for economic history, since it shows how the peasants' subjective aims, in our case their "esprit de rétrécissement" (hidebound spirit) . . . was upheld by the objective lay-out of the economy, in our case, by the communal decrees, ratified by the authorities, about taking on new citizens. It betrays how their mentality relied on the "economic order".'

26. St.A.Z. A 99/6. Also called *Dorfbrief* (village charter), viz., Wildberg 18 Feb. 1642.

27. St.A.Z. A 99/2, Unterhittnau 16 March 1638.

28. St.A.Z. A 99/1, Bäretswil and Adetswil 30 July 1565.

29. St.A.Z. A 99; compare too Bernhard, *Wirtschafts- und Siedlungsgeschichte des Tösstales*, p. 53. We have not followed up the question about the origins of the scarcity of common property. Its beginnings go back to the cultivation of the Oberland. Seigneurial rights and, as we will see, natural conditions were contributory factors. We have also abstained from establishing figures for any particular year about the level of entry fees levied by the different community of the Zurich countryside.

30. See Chapters 2 and 4.

31. The extent to which the entry charters of the Oberland parishes differ from the stereotype formulas of the other entry charters is revealing.

32. St.A.Z. A 99/1.

33. The church parish is not identical with the village community, nor did they usually coincide, and their lands were separate. After the Reformation and its re-organisation, the care of the poor devolved, along with other duties, on the church parishes. According to Wyss the right of membership in the church parish was 'necessarily tied to membership of the secular parish, or to one of the many such village communities belonging to the church parish' ('Die Schweizerischen Landsgemeinden', p. 46).

34. St.A.Z. A 99/1. The permitted entry fee was also an entry fee to the church parish. We must bear these connections in mind when we come to discuss the religious and ecclesiastical attitudes of those people who had fallen into industrial dependence.

35. *Ibid.*, A 99/1, A 99/3. Wildberg also did not have an entry charter 18 Feb. 1643.

36. *Ibid.*, A 99/3.

37. *Ibid.*, A 99/2.

38. *Ibid.*, A 99/2, 5 May 1643.

39. *Ibid.*, A 99/4.

40. *Ibid.*, A 99/4. There can have been no answer to this renewed petition either. The State Archive contains no relevant entry permit. See Hirzel, 'Beantwortung der Frage', p. 79.

41. The term villein (*Hintersässe*) refers to a class of disenfranchised non-burghers who have not paid the entry fee and who are in principle denied access to the use of the commons (see also Appendix, p. 194). In our age, in which the parish is an independent legal person, villeins no longer come under the landlord's protection; see Wyss, 'Die Schweizerischen Landsgemeinden', p. 47.

42. St.A.Z. A 99/2, compare Hinteregg, 3 Jan. 1654.

43. See Meier, *Geschichte der Gemeinde Wetzikon*, pp. 159, 169ff and 197.

44. Their share in the parish facilities: schools, pastoral care, cemetery, etc.

45. St.A.Z. A 99/4, 17 Oct. 1621. The wording of the petition of 5 Oct. 1708 of the church parish of Bäretswil stresses in any case the protective character of the villeins' fees: 'In the meantime your church parish Bäretswil has been burdened with so many villeins that from now on each one will have to pay 3 *Pfund* of villeins' fees (*gelt*) every year (Art. 4)' (A 99/1).

46. St.A.Z. A 99/4. This is only one of many such references in the sources, and it shows with the utmost clarity that there had been people since the beginning of industrialisation who owned nothing except what they earned through the industry. We stress this circumstance all the more, because the general opinion in the literature is that the early outworkers as well as the factory workers of the nineteenth century were exclusively small farmers who did industrial work on the side.

47. See Wyss, 'Die Schweizerischen Landsgemeinden', p. 26.

48. St.A.Z. A 99/1, request for an entry charter by the community of Unterdürnten of 1 Nov. 1661.

49. *Ibid.*, A 99/1, an entry charter of 15 Feb. 1638 for the community of Bäretswil. See too the entry charter of Kempten, Art. 6, quoted by Meier, *Geschichte der Gemeinde Wetzikon*, p. 158.

50. Meier, *Geschichte der Gemeinde Wetzikon*, p. 157.

51. St.A.Z. A 99/2, entry charter for Hinteregg of 20 Dec. 1654. The wording was almost identical in the charter for Kempten; Meier, *Geschichte der Gemeinde Wetzikon*, p. 160, viz., 'If someone sells his half of a house and two households are living in one dwelling, then no more members of the village community should dwell in this house than there would be in an undivided one.' Entry charter of 24 April 1600, St.A.Z. A 99/1. Although the legal function of the house had its roots in the agricultural history of the Middle Ages, it should be noted that there was something fundamentally new about tying the commonage rights to the house. The medieval system of labour dues with its manorial law courts and distribution of the produce survived only very exceptionally in the Zurich countryside. When the villagers set up barriers against immigration, they referred back simply to old legal thinking. For the legal function of the house, cf. P. Leumann, *Das Haus als Träger von markgenossenschaftlichen Rechten und Lasten*, Diss., Zurich

1939; K.S. Kramer, 'Haus und Flur im bäuerlichen Recht', *Bayrische Heimatforschung*, 2 (1950), and K.-S. Krauer, *Die Nachbarschaft als bäuerliche Gemeinschaft: Ein Beitrag zur rechtlichen Volkskunde mit besonderer Berücksichtigung Bayerns*, München-Pasing 1954.

52. Wyss has shown that this fundamental trend was fully in tune with the *Zeitgeist* and was paralleled in the towns by the development of their civic rights ('Die Schweizerischen Landsgemeinden', p. 15). When the right to vote was coupled with the commonage right, so that it shared the same material preconditions, then it was impossible for individuals to enjoy civic rights. The problem lay principally with the adult children of parish members who could not fulfil the material preconditions of membership. Did they form a new circle, separate from the villeins, because they were able to vote in certain parish matters? This poses the question about the historical emergence of personal rights of citizenship. One would have to research each case; how far and when each parish was able to achieve an actual separation of the commonage community and the political community. Such an arrangement opened the door wide to disputes about inheritance, which constituted a considerable force for change. See too J.C. Nüscheler, *Beobachtungen eines redlichen Schweizers aus vaterländischer Liebe entwarfen*, Zurich 1786, pp. 8 and 12.

53. St.A.Z. A 99/5. The petition by the village community of Töss, viz., of 28 Jan. 1630, speaks of 'new immigrants, in whole and half houses on account of the commonage and rather fine common property'; see too the sources quoted in n. 51 above.

54. *Ibid.*, A 99/2. 4 June 1679. The petition of 28 Oct. 1654 by Hinteregg already contains this condition. The petition of Unterdürnten of 1 Nov. 1661 goes as follows: 'As hitherto the household dwellings were not split in two and it was not permitted that even only two households should live under one roof, so it should remain this way in the future' (A 99/1).

55. We are unable to establish how far this was influenced by old seigneurial rights.

56. St.A.Z. A 99/1.

57. Such a subdivision of holdings was performed by the community of Unterwetzikon in 1714, probably as a result of disputes over inheritance. See Meier, *Geschichte der Gemeinde Wetzikon*, p. 183.

58. St.A.Z. A 61, sub Neftenbach, taken from *Neujahrsblatt der Hülfsgesellschaft von Winterthur*, Morf, vol. 12, p. 19.

59. *Ibid.*, A 99/1, Unterdürnten, 1 Nov. 1661.

60. See Schmidt, *Der Schweizer Bauer*, pp. 47 and 54.

61. Bernhard, 'Wirtschafts- und Siedlungsgeschichte des Tösstales', p. 87.

62. *Ibid.*, p. 24. See too p. 26, where the morphological and geographical conditions of the upper Tösstal are assessed from the point of view of building techniques.

63. Hirzel, 'Beantwortung der Frage', p. 73. We have not followed up the history of settlement in the Oberland any further. Research into houses and settlements had stressed the importance of the natural conditions for the form of settlement. Our region lies in the rainy zone of the northern pre-Alpine area, which is typified by single farmsteads. Historical forces play their part alongside these natural influences. Seigneurial factors also contributed to the land clearance and settlement of the Oberland: the more so since the Oberland region was opened up relatively late. Of most significance for us is the fact that even before industrialisation the Oberland was a landscape of isolated farms. Hamlets and villages arose where conditions permitted. There is plenty of evidence for this. J. Ebel describes the eastern part of the canton of Zurich as follows: 'Previously this whole mountainous part of the Allmann was extremely wild, rough and sparsely populated; by the end of the fifteeenth century wolves and bears still inhabited its wooded mountains': *Gebirgsvölker*, vol. 2, p. 46.

64. Meier, *Geschichte der Gemeinde Wetzikon*, pp. 171ff.

65. Hermann Lussi, *Chronik der Gemeinde Fischenthal*, Wetzikon and Rüti 1932, pp. 104ff. See too Bernhard, 'Wirtschaft- und Siedlungsgeschichte des Tösstales', p. 58 (with bibliographical references); S. Schinz, *Das höhere Gebirge des Kanton Zürich, und der ökonomisch-moralische Zustand der Bewohner, mit Vorschlag der Hülfe und Auskunft für die bey mangelnder Fabrikarbeit brotlose Übervölkerung* (Synodalrede), Zurich 1817, pp. 6ff; and Hirzel, 'Beantwortung der Frage', p. 75.

66. Thus have we avoided mentioning Zurich's policy concerning manufacture, finance and trade. The disavantageous results this policy would have on the economic situation of the Zurich countryside are well known. Nor have we mentioned tithes, which must be named as a factor contributing to industry, since earnings from the putting-out industry, which were not based on land, were not liable to paying tithes.

67. See Chapter 4 especially.

68. Paul Kläui and Edward Imhof, eds., *Atlas zur Geschichte des Kantons Zürich*, Zurich 1951, Plate 35. Valid figures for winter employment are presented on this map. Had valid figures also been compiled for the summertime, the highly industrialised regions would stand out much more clearly. For instance, beneath the list of figures for the Grüningen district one may read that 'According to the unanimous reports by the officials, it may be calculated that at least a quarter of the 8,992 spinners were employed in agriculture throughout the summer.' For Kyburg one may read that 'In the upper district in summertime a quarter of the spinners are to be subtracted on account of field-work. In the lower district in summertime spinning almost completely stops.' In the arable and wine growing regions this stands out even more clearly and is noted in many reports: Horgen, for instance: 'The farmers' sons and daughters spin throughout the winter on account of the good wages, but they stop when spring comes again.' Or about Rafz, where 117 persons spin in the winter, the following applies: spinning 'lasts only for the winter, and with spring and the beginning of the grape growing season it ceases'. St.A.Z. A 76. The cotton cottage industry is the only one represented on the map.

69. Hirzel, 'Beantwortung der Frage', p. 74.

70. Kläui and Imhof, eds., *Atlas*, Plate 40. We are aware that very different motives applied when emigration was considered. The 1734 to 1744 map only deals with emigration to North America.

71. Hirzel, 'Beantwortung der Frage', p. 80.

2   Changes to the structure of family and population in the industrial regions

1. It has been mentioned that this social restructuring of the Zurich countryside reaches far back into the pre-industrial era. Undoubtedly such rural, but not peasant, sections of the population developed their own life style, which was reflected in the customs and life of the common people of the Oberland. One has only to think of seasonally restricted work in the fields and the woods, of seasonal emigration and homecoming, etc. But these people will scarcely have developed a class feeling of their own. They lacked important preconditions for this. For instance, they did not enjoy a common and unifying basis of life. They lacked the will to express class consciousness in cultural terms. There was no room for this sort of cultural determinism there, where people were vegetating at the margins of the peasant community in poverty and hardship and whose whole energy was directed towards securing their basic needs from day to day. Poverty and hardship do not make a class on their own. But these are problems which require a more rigorous investigation than we can give them here, given that it is doubtful if the available sources would permit this sort of investigation.

2. Courtship, marriage, inheritance, etc., are included in this, in their manifold local variations.

3. J.C. Hirzel, 'Beantwortung der Frage: Ist die Handelschaft, wie solche bey uns beschaffen, unserem Lande schädlich, oder nützlich, in Absicht auf den Feldbau und die Sitten des Volkes?', *Magazin für die Naturkunde Helvetiens*, 3 (1788), p. 129.

4. See J.C. Nüscheler, *Beobachtungen eines redlichen Schweizers aus väterlandischer Liebe entworfen*, Zurich 1786, p. 12, in which the problem of the communal right in relation to the division of inheritance is mentioned. See too Chapter 4.

5. Hirzel, 'Beantwortung der Frage', pp. 129 and 104.

6. C. Meiners, *Briefe über die Schweiz*, Part III, Tübingen 1791, p. 47.

7. Hirzel, 'Beantwortung der Frage', p. 77. The increase in marriages cannot of course be considered in isolation, but must be set in relation to the population increase.

8. Viz., O. Haegi, *Die Entwicklung der Zürcher-Oberländischen Baumwollindustrie*, Diss., Berne 1924, p. 34.

9. S. Schinz, *Das höhere Gebirge des Kanton Zürich, und der ökonomisch-moralische Zustand der Bewohner, mit Vorschlag der Hülfe und Auskunft für die bey mangelnder Fabrikarbeit brotlose Übervölkerung* (Synodalrede), Zurich 1817, p. 8.

10. *Ibid.*, p. 17.

11. *Vaterländische Erinnerungen an meine Mitlandleute der äussern Rhoden, über das Verhältnis der Landes-Produktion, gegen unsere angewohnten Bedürfnisse*, 1811, p. 131.

12. Hirzel, 'Beantwortung der Frage', p. 130.

13. H. Strehler, *Beiträge zur Kulturgeschichte der Zürcher Landschaft*, Part II: 'Aberglaube, Armut und Bettel', in *Zürcher Taschenbuch auf das Jahr 1935* (1935), p. 83.

14. Nüscheler, *Beobachtungen*, p. 17.

15. Schinz, *Das höhere Gebirge*, p. 11.

16. Johann Hirzel, *Rede über den physischen, ökonomischen und sittlich-religiösen Zustand der östlichen Berggemeinden des Kanton Zürich* (Synodalrede), Zurich 1816, p. 16.

17. J. Schulthess, *Beherzigung des vor der Zürcher Synode gehaltenen Vortrags*, Zurich 1817, p. 52.

18. Hirzel, *Rede über den physischen, ökonomischen und sittlich-religiösen Zustand*, pp. 24ff. Many laws forbidding early marriages are found in the mandates of the seventeenth century. The mandate of 1676 requires country people to produce at least 100 *Gulden* at their wedding, or at least an assurance of being able to earn their own living (Strehler, *Beiträge zur Kulturgeschichte der Zürcher Landschaft*, Part II, p. 92). See too Schulthess, *Beherzigung*, p. 60.

19. Quoted by F. Meier, *Geschichte der Gemeinde Wetzikon*, Zurich 1881, p. 461. Johann Schulthess quotes as follows from a country minister's visitation notes (no reference supplied): 'My church elders, noticing that it is mostly young married couples who are suffering from the present shortage, who were indeed driven into marriage by necessity or without sufficient fortune; and knowing that in the bordering countries of Germany, no one is allowed to marry who does not have his own house, have already asked me whether our government could not also introduce a law to prevent such marriages: for the restriction in the matrimonial laws is not adequate for this.'

20. Schulthess, *Beherzigung*, pp. 54ff. See too pp. 68ff.

21. See, for instance, H.F.K. Gunther, *Das Bauerntum als Lebens- und Gemeinschaftsform*, Leipzig 1939, Chaps. 13 and 14.

22. See H. Strehler, *Beiträge zur Kulturgeschichte der Zürcher Landschaft*, Part I: *Kirche und Schule im 17. und 18. Jahrhundert*, Lachen 1934, p. 62: 'For all the wantonness and early marriages these *Licht-* and *Bett-* or *Gadenstubeten* can be held responsible. It is because of them that in many villages a wreath is now seldom worn at weddings. The mandate of 1647 included the following "We hereby prohibit to no less a degree . . . *Lichtstubeten* and similar nocturnal junketings" ' (St.A.Z. III AAb.1).

23. See, too, 1650 mandate: *Sabbath und Sittenmandat für die Landschaft* (Sabbath and

Moral Mandate for the Countryside), Art. 18; 1652 mandate: *Satzungen und Ordnungen wider die unzeitigen Ehen und anderen Leichtfertigkeiten* (Legislation and Ordinances against the Untimely Marriages and Other Wantonness); 1668 mandate: *Wider die Hurerey und Ehebruch, unzeitige Ehen, Frühzeitigen Beyschlafs und anderen Leichtfertigkeiten* (Against Whoredom and Divorce, Untimely Marriages, Premature Cohabitation and Other Wantonness), etc.: St.A.Z. *Zürcher Mandate* 1631–71 and 1671–1700, III AAb.1.

24. J. C. Nüscheler, *Über die Revision der Matrimonialgesetze im Kanton Zürich*, Zurich 1831, pp. 16 and 26.

25. *Ibid.*

26. *Ibid.*, p. 13: Nüscheler goes on to say 'That it would be possible to put an end to the *zu Licht gehen*, even after the Revolution, is proven by the example of a respectable parish, which had nearly exhausted its Poor Relief funds during the expensive period of 1816–17 and the parish inhabitants were often obliged to pay taxes, so the parish overseers looked for ways of reducing their expenditure and found that the parish assistance for illegitimate children was very significant, and that the *zu Licht gehen* was the main reason for this heavy expense, hence the decision on the part of the parish council to put a stop to the *zu Licht gehen* in their parish.' The parish councillors directed parents to save money by 'keeping their sons at home and fathers and mothers supervising their daughters, so that no so-called "Lights" are able to come to them at night time. But in order to put a stop to the existing nocturnal gatherings, these gentlemen officials had to make the biggest sacrifice; taking it in turns to do a few circuits around the parish with a contingent of parishioners on Sunday and Saturday nights to places where the *zu Licht gehen* generally took place – warning the night gatherers and sending them home' (p. 32).

27. *Ibid.*, pp. 29ff.

28. Hirzel, 'Beantwortung der Frage' p. 122.

29. See Hans Bächtold, *Die Gebräuche bei Verlobung und Hochzeit*, Basle 1914, pp. 123ff. 'The Zurich matrimonial law book of 1719 recognises a public announcement, pledge or written note as evidence that a marriage oath has been given' (p. 125). It thus cannot be stated that industrialisation destroyed the Christian basis of marriage.

30. Nüscheler, *Matrimonialgesetze*, pp. 16ff, incl. p. 19.

31. Schulthess, *Beherzigung*, pp. 19–20.

32. See, for instance, Gunther, *Das Bauerntum*, Chaps. 13 and 14.

33. In peasant circles, people married the farm. Gotthelf provides instructive examples of this.

34. Schulthess, *Beherzigung*, p. 19.

35. Nüscheler, *Matrimonialgesetze*, p. 31.

36. G. Meyer von Knonau, in his book *Der Kanton Zurich*, St Gall and Berne 1844, vol. 1, p. 196, provides statistics about the origin of domestic servants around 1836. Of serving girls, etc., 156 originated from the Bulach district, 147 from Andelfingen, 109 from Regensberg (three mostly agrarian districts), 32 from Uster and 19 from Hinwil (two industrial districts).

37. Meiners, *Briefe*, p. 48; see too J. Ebel, *Schilderung der Gebirgsvölker der Schweiz*, Leipzig 1798, vol. 1, p. 280, about Appenzell.

38. Quoted in H. Krebser, *Das erste Bevölkerungsverzeichnis der Gemeinde Wald aus dem Jahre 1634* (off-print from *Von euserer Walder Heimat*), Wald 1952, p. 8.

39. Parish roll of the Wald church, 1739, St.A.Z. E II 264a: the numbers refer to the households.

40. Krebser, *Das erste Bevölkerungsverzeichnis*, p. 11.

41. Parish roll of the Wald church, 1739, St.A.Z. E II 264a.

42. See Chapter 4.

43. St.A.Z. E II 264a, parish roll of Bäretswil 1723.

44. Nüscheler, *Beobachtungen*, pp. 18ff.

45. *Ibid.*, p. 19; Chapter 4 deals extensively with these questions.

46. Hirzel, 'Beantwortung der Frage', p. 28.

47. Schinz, *Das höhere Gebirge*, p. 8.

48. Schulthess, *Beherzigung*, p. 39.

49. U. Brägger, *Leben und Schriften des armen Mannes im Toggenburg*, 3 vols., Basle 1945, vol. 3, p. 157.

50. Hirzel, 'Beantwortung der Frage', pp. 121ff. See too Chapter 4, where further comparisons are to be found. Johann Heinrich Waser (1742–80), an important statistician of his time, stood in strong opposition to the regime and was sentenced and put to death because he had allegedly stolen legal documents establishing seigneurial rights over significant parts of the territory of the town of Zurich.

51. G. Meyer von Knonau, *Die Volkszählung des Kantons Zürich am 9., 10., und 11. Mai 1836 – ein Nachtrag*, Zurich 1837, p. v.

52. H. Krebser, 'Aus der früheren Industriegeschichte von Wald', *Volksblatt vom Bachtel*, 32 (Heimatblatt), 19 Aug. 1949.

53. Meyer von Knonau, *Volkszählung*, p. vi. We have had occasion to mention the problem of living space several times already. We have related the constituent factors to industrialisation. See the section on luxury and the standard of living in Chapter 3.

54. Hirzel, 'Beantwortung der Frage , p. 77.

55. Meiners, *Briefe*, p. 47.

56. *C.* sixty-five years old. She wove in her parents' home in Kaltbrunn until 1910.

57. Brägger, *Schriften*, vol. 1, p. 126.

58. Schulthess, *Beherzigung*, p. 57.

59. As people's needs increased and they expected a higher standard of living, marriages became less fertile.

60. See *Schweizerisches Idiotikon*, 13 vols., Frauenfeld 1891ff, vol. 6, pp. 1496ff, where the other meanings of the word are listed. See also F. Stalder, *Versuch eines Schweizerischen Idiotikons*, Aarau 1812.

61. J. Stutz, *Gemälde aus dem Volksleben*, Part III, Zurich 1836, p. 1.

62. J. Stutz, *Lise und Salome, die beiden Webermädchen*, Zurich 1847, pp. 11 and 79.

63. G. Finsler, *Zürich in der zweiten Hälfte des achtzehnten Jahrhunderts*, Zurich 1884, p. 253.

64. Nüscheler, *Beobachtungen*, pp. 38ff.

65. Hirzel, 'Beantwortung der Frage', p. 146.

66. Hirzel, *Rede über den physischen, ökonomischen und sittlich-religiösen Zustand*, p. 15.

67. This refers to the 'Erneuerte Schul- und Lehrordnung für die Schulen der Landschaft Zurich, vom 26. Weinmonat 1778'.

68. St.A.Z. III AAb.1, our text has been cut.

69. Hirzel, *Rede über den physischen, ökonomischen und sittlich-religiösen Zustand*, p. 15.

70. Hirzel, 'Beantwortung der Frage', p. 78, see Schulthess, *Beherzigung*, p. 58.

71. Minister Irminger of Henggart 1783, quoted in A. Bollinger, *Die Zürcher Landschaft an der Wende des 18. Jahrhunderts – nach Berichten der ascetischen Gesellschaft*, Diss., Zurich 1941, p. 69.

72. Hirzel, *Rede über den physischen, ökonomischen und sittlich-religiösen Zustand*, p. 15.

73. Schinz, *Das höhere Gebirge*, p. 11.

74. Pastoral letter about the education of children in the countryside, 1777, p. 47.

3   Life and society of the population engaged in industry

1. J.C. Nüscheler, *Beobachtungen eines redlichen Schweizers aus vaterländischer Liebe entworfen*, Zurich 1786, p. 16.

2. J.C. Hirzel, 'Beantwortung der Frage: Ist die Handelschaft, wie solche bey uns beschaffen, unserem Lande schädlich, oder nützlich, in Absicht auf den Feldbau und die sitten des Volkes?', *Magazin für die Naturkunde Helvetiens*, 3 (1788), p. 130.

3. Extracts from the *Stillstand* notices of the church parish of Wald, *Walder Ortschronik*, MS 21.

4. It can also be tied to the family and even become the object of free purchase. The development must have been similar to that of the communal membership right. The question is not relevant to our theme.

5. R. Weiss, *Volkskunde der Schweiz*, Erlenbach and Zurich 1946, p. 128.

6. See, for instance, *Zeitbeobachtungen über das schweizerische Baumwollgewerbe, dessen Folgen und Aussichten*, Switzerland 1806, no author cited, p. 10: 'But it is just as true that through the influence of cotton the population in various regions has accumulated to such a degree, that it is out of all proportion to the produce of the soil.'

7. *Vaterländische Erinnerungen an meine Mitlandleute der äussern Rhoden, über das Verhältnis der Landes-Produktion, gegen unsere angewohnten Bedürfnisse*, 1811, p. 21.

8. For how far this applies to the Oberland, see Chapter 4.

9. Reports by the Ascetische Gesellschaft quoted by C.G. Schmidt, *Der Schweizer Bauer im Zeitalter des Frühkapitalismus*, Berne 1932, p. 80. n. 174. Charitable farmers of Ottenbach provide for the beggar children (1692) 'with a crust of bread, a gift of flour, a beaker of milk, a bit of turnip, a gift of *Anken*, a little basket with fruit, with a half measure of peas'. See too H. Morf, *Neujahrsblatt der Hülfsgesellschaft von Winterthur*, vol 12: *Aus der Geschichte des zürcherischen Armenwessens*, Winterthur 1873, p. 28. An experienced countryman tells a young peasant lad: 'You have surely already heard about corn, wheat, barley, beans, oats, rye, peas and then also about white and yellow turnips, about cabbage and savoys and potatoes: these are most of the things which one grows in the fields for people and cattle'; see *Unterricht über den Landbau in einem freundlichen Gespräch zwischen einem alten, erfahrenen Landmann und einem jungen Bauernknab, zum Gebrauch unserer Landschulen*, Zurich 1774, p. 41.

10. Federal Councillor Forrer has elevated this motto to a state maxim in one of his speeches' 'No one shall starve, no one shall go without a decent dwelling and clothing, that is what the State is for.'

11. See H. Strehler, *Beiträge zur Kulturgeschichte der Zürcher Landschaft*, Part II: 'Aberglaube, Armut and Bettel' in *Zürcher Taschenbuch auf das Jahr 1935* (1935), p. 96; about food in general: H. Messikommer, *Aus alter Zeit: Sitten und Gebräuche in Züricher Oberland*, 3 vols., Zurich 1909–11, vol. 1, pp. 11, 31, 40ff.

12. Salomon von Orelli describes the peasants and landowners of the Wädenswil region: 'The country farmers remained fairly loyal to their fathers' way of life; since they mostly inhabited the higher regions, far away from the villages, they did not encounter those among the village inhabitants who were employed in manufacture on a daily basis, and so were less influenced by their customs, especially as they seemed despicable to them. Their houses remained as they should be, large but real farmhouses, and they fashioned their clothes according to the old shapes and from cheap material. They mostly ate the food they produced themselves: they imbibed cider, curds and home-made wine during their heavy field-work. Coffee was revolting to them, too thin and not as stimulating as a drink, and as a foodstuff, it seemed fully nonsensical to them. They belittled in all earnestness those who spent their good money on those sorts of fancy foods; but they did not mind in the least selling their milk at a right high price to those *Caffeeschleker*, as they called them. There were just as many rich persons of this class as there were among the manufacturers, but their money had not been acquired over such a short time. Their wealth was based on frugality, moderation and thrift, wherever they were to be found.' Salomon von Orelli. *Abschriften nebst Manuskripten über den Stäfner Handels*, St.A.Z. B X 39, p. 6 (quoted by D. Fretz, *Neujahrsblatt der Lesegesellschaft Wädenswil, Lesegesellschaft Wädenswil*, Wädenswil 1939, Chap. 2, n. 26).

13. H. Spoerry-Jaeggi, *Die Baumwollindustrie von Wald*, Wald 1935, p. 25.

14. Elisabeth Hess: born 25 Oct. 1864, died 12 March 1948; handwritten *curriculum vitae, Walder Ortschronik*, MS 43.

15. Heinrich Hess: born 1874, died 1919: 'Mein Lebenslauf', *Walder Ortschronik*, MS 8.

16. 'Etwas aus der guten alten Zeiten', *Volksblatt vom Bachtel*, 12 and 13 (Heimatblatt), Oct. 1944; informant H. R. born 1876.

17. *Brief an einen Bürger des Kanton A., über die Bedürfnisse der Zeit und des Vaterlandes*, 1811, p. 11.

18. *Vaterländische Erinnerungen*, p. 115.

19. *Zeitbeobachtungen*, p. 17.

20. St.A.Z. A 76.

21. S. Schinz, *Das höhere Gebirge des Kanton Zürich, und der Ökonomisch-moralische Zustand der Bewohner, mit Vorschlag der Hülfe und Auskunft für die bey mangelnder Fabrikarbeit brotlose Übervölkerung* (Synodalrede), Zurich 1817, p. 8.

22. Parish report of 1702, quoted by Herrmann Lussi, *Chronik der Gemeinde Fischenthal*, Wetzikon and Rüti 1932, p. 105.

23. Hirzel, 'Beantwortung der Frage', p. 64; the author talks about the eastern side of the Zürichsee.

24. *Ibid.*, p. 68; the western side of the Zürichsee is being discussed.

25. *Ibid.*, pp. 78 and 139.

26. C. Meiners, *Briefe über die Schweiz*, Part III, Tübingen 1791, p. 59.

27. Report by the Ascetische Gesellschaft, Wallisellen 1788, quoted by A. Bollinger, *Die Zürcher Landschaft an der Wende des 18. Jahrhunderts – nach Berichten der ascetischen Gesellschaft*, Diss., Zurich 1941, p. 75.

28. Report by the Ascetische Gesellschaft, quoted by *ibid.*, p. 78.

29. Minister Holzhalb, Wallisellen 1788, quoted by *ibid.*, p. 78.

30. J. Schulthess, *Beherzigung* p. 57. Re the chicory-water, see Messikommer, *Aus alter Zeit*, vol. 1, p. 42.

31. J. Stutz, *7×7 Jahre – aus meinem Leben, als Beitrag zur näheren Kenntnis des Volkes*, Pfäffikon 1853, pp. 361ff.

32. Meiners, *Briefe*, p. 60.

33. This fact is well documented; see, for instance, *Zeitbeobachtungen*, p. 14.

34. H. Krebser, 'Aus der früheren Industriegeschichte von Wald', *Volksblatt vom Bachtel*, 32 (Heimatblatt), 19 Aug. 1949.

35. Hirzel, 'Beantwortung der Frage', p. 130.

36. See *ibid.*, p. 45: 'At the same time most of the farms [in the Oberland] consist of meadows, which are ploughed up every so often, and planted with corn, oats, beans, but preferably with potatoes. These are just as much at home here and form the most important agricultural produce. For this reason it was also here that the first ordinances respecting the tithes payable on potatoes had to be drawn up in 1750 for Fischenthal and in 1774 for Wald.'

37. H. Krebser, 'Aus der früheren Industriegeschichte'; see too F. Meier, *Geschichte der Gemeinde Wetzikon*, Zurich 1881, p. 528.

38. The geographical situation of the Oberland also contributed towards this changeover. The heavy rainfall of the lower Alpine zones is not suitable for growing wheat.

39. H. Krebser, *Wald im Zürcher Oberland*, Wald 1951, p. 30, with many further references. See too J. Stutz, *Lise und Salome, die beiden Webermädchen*, Zurich 1847, p. 61: 'On the scrubbed table boiled potates were steaming, white and red ones, nearby stood a green dish with milk curds, and a prettily carved oak beaker with caraway seeds and salt. That was the whole meal.'

40. See Schinz, *Das höhere Gebirge*, p. 9.

41. Hirzel, 'Beantwortung der Frage', pp. 80ff.

42. Schinz, *Das höhere Gebirge*, p. 20.

43. Meiners, *Briefe*, p. 56.

44. Schulthess, *Beherzigung*, p. 39.

45. *Zeitbeobachtungen*, p. 10.

46. Johan Hirzel, *Rede über den physischen, ökonomischen und sittlich-religiösen Zustand der östlichen Berggemeinden des Kanton Zürich* (Synodalrede), Zurich 1816, p. 14.

47. U. Brägger, *Leben und Schriften des armen Mannes in Toggenburg*, 3 vols., Basle 1945, vol. 1. p. 331.

48. Hirzel, *Rede über den physischen ökonomischen und sittlich-religiösen Zustand*, p. 14.

49. Stutz, *7×7 Jahre*, p. 409.

50. See Weiss, *Volkskunde der Schweiz*, pp. 140ff.

51. When domestic spinning changed over to domestic weaving, a change in everyday clothing also took place. The oldest and most worn clothes were good enough for working at the loom, and old domestic weavers would emphasise how much domestic weaving had spared their clothes; slippers and an old apron had sufficed for it.

52. A report by the Ascetische Gesellschaft, quoted by Bollinger, *Die Zürcher Landschaft*, p. 54.

53. See Schmidt, *Der Schweizer Bauer*, p. 24.

54. This spirit of the age is already documented in the term *Buss-Mandat* (Penance Ordinance).

55. St.A.Z. III AAb.1.

56. Johann Kaspar Escher, 'Bemerkungen über die Regierung der Grafschaft Kyburg', *Archiv für Schweizerische Geschichte*, 4 (1846), p. 262.

57. Report by the Ascetische Gesellschaft, quoted by Schmidt, *Der Schweizer Bauer*, p. 35.

58. Report by the Ascetische Gesellschaft, quoted by *ibid.*, p. 101 n. 211.

59. *Zeitbeobachtungen*, p. 12.

60. *Unterricht über den Landbau*, p. 68.

61. Meiners, *Briefe*, p. 60.

62. Hirzel, *Rede über den physischen, ökonomischen und sittlich-religiösen Zustand*, p. 14.

63. Report by the Ascetische Gesellschaft, quoted by Bollinger, *Die Zürcher Landschaft*, p. 30.

64. Salomon von Orelli, see above, quoted by Fretz, *Neujahrsblatt der Lesegesellschaft Wädenswil*, vol. 11, Chap. 2, n. 14.

65. Brägger, *Schriften*, vol. 3, p. 157.

66. Quoted in Meier, *Geschichte der Gemeinde Wetzikon*, p. 436. Village mockery and keeping the utmost distance between two groups within the local community shows how far the sense of village community had disintegrated.

67. *Ibid.*, p. 526.

68. Schinz, *Das höhere Gebirge*, p. 20.

69. Stutz, *7×7 Jahre*, p. 202.

70. Report by the Ascetische Gesellschaft, quoted in Schmidt, *Der Schweizer Bauer*, p. 101 n. 211.

71. Stutz, *7×7 Jahre*, p. 466. The miller-girl is Jakob's godmother. Jakob Stutz came from a propertied family. His father ran a yarn business as well as the farm. Nevertheless, Jakob's mother's clothes were 'the peasant costume of the times, bodice and skirt, which were nothing less than lovely and very uncomfortable to boot. For all that, they clung firmly to the traditional fashion, decrying everything new as sinful and never thinking that their clothes had also once been the latest fashion. The only thing they allowed themselves was to change their red stockings for white ones and their high *Stöckli* shoes for ones with lower heels.' (*Ibid.*, p. 13).

72. *Brief an einen Bürger*, p. 11.

73. See Michael Bösch, *Freymüthige Gedanken über den sittlichen Verfall seines Vaterlandes*, Lichtensteg 1784, p. 21.

74. The discussion about luxury reached a high point in the second half of the eighteenth century. The second discussion followed a century later.

75. Leonhard Meister: Professor at the Carolinum in Zurich; Johann Heinrich Pestalozzi: important publicist and pedagogue of the Enlightenment.

76. L. Meister, in *Aufwandgesetze. Sammlung einiger Schriften, welche bei der Aufmunterungsgesellschaft in Basel eingelaufen sind über die Frage: Inwiefern ist es schicklich, dem Aufwande der Bürger, in einem kleinen Freystaate, dessen Wohlfahrt auf die Handelschaft gegründet ist, Schranken zu setzen?*, Basle 1781 (ZBZ xviii. 1774), p. 16.

77. J. H. Pestalozzi, in *ibid.*, pp. 10ff.

78. See the statements about fashion: Meister, in *ibid.*, p. 48.

79. Meister, in *ibid.*, pp. 16ff and 35.

80. Pestalozzi, in *ibid.*, p. 13.

81. *Vaterländische Erinnerungen*, p. 115.

82. Meister, in *Aufwandgesetze*, p. 22.

83. Pestalozzi, in *ibid.*, p. 14.

84. *Ibid.*, p. 33.

85. Meister, in *ibid.*, p. 53.

86. Pestalozzi, in *ibid.*, p. 23.

87. *Ibid.*, p. 33.

88. Anonymous prize-winner, in *ibid.*, p. 16; see too p. 14.

89. Michael Bösch, minister of Wildhaus, *Freymüthige Gedanken*, p. 12.

90. Meister, in *Aufwandgesetze*, pp. 50ff.

91. Pestalozzi, in *ibid.*, pp. 17ff.

92. *Ibid.*, p. 15.

93. Meister, in *ibid.*, p. 60; Pestalozzi, in *ibid.*, p. 29; Anonymous, in *ibid.*, pp. 19 and 64.

94. Meister, in *ibid.*, p. 49.

95. Pestalozzi, in *ibid.*, p. 55; the extent to which the author had to take censorship into account is uncertain.

96. Anonymous, in *ibid.*, pp. 24ff.

97. *Ibid.*, pp. 9ff.

98. Meister, in *ibid.*, p. 63. Pestalozzi also reassesses the old notion of luxury and the class concepts behind it (see *ibid.*, p. 9).

99. Nowadays a mink coat or a SS-type Jaguar are factors determining their owner's social standing, and important for establishing his credit-worthiness. In the last analysis, the American's question 'How much are you?' illustrates this notion of class.

100. Schmidt, *Der Schweizer Bauer*, pp. 62ff.

101. According to Fritz Rudolf Staehelin's verbal testimony (investigator in farmhouse research for the canton of Zurich), the outworkers must thus have made increased demands on dwellings in the Zurich countryside. But precise information is hard to gather (when houses are knocked down the panelling, for instance, ought to be dated). See Chapter 4.

102. Jakob Stutz also mentioned the *Steckliherren* in *7×7 Jahre*, pp. 121 and 275.

103. Salomon von Orelli, *Abschriften nebst Manuskripten über den Stäfner Handels*, St.A.Z. B×39, quoted in Fretz, *Neujahrsblatt der Lesegesellschaft Wädenswil*, vol. 11, pp. 39ff. The Stutz family prove that not all clothiers felt obliged to lead this life style.

104. Schinz, *Das höhere Gebirge*, p. 10.

105. *Zeitbeobachtungen*, p. 17.

106. See for instance Jakob Stutz, *7×7 Jahre*, pp. 289ff, where the girl reapers, who move to Uster and Greifensee, carry a heavy barley loaf on their heads on the way home, a pretty bunch of blossom in their pinnies and holding their sickles carefully wrapped in straw. When Jakob went to fetch the hired reapers from the mountains to Felmis, the whole gathering of reapers was as joyful 'as if they were going to a wedding'.

107. Salomon von Orelli, *Abschriften nebst Manuskripten über den Stäfner Handels*, St.A.Z. B×39, quoted in Fretz, *Neujahrsblatt der Lesegesellschaft Wädenswil*, vol. 11, p. 167 n. 12.

108. St.A.Z. E II 120; see the visitation report for Wald of the same year.

109. St.A.Z. E II 127. The Sabbath and Moral mandates forbade *Lichtstubeten*. For instance, Art. 18: among other things are to be forbidden 'the *Lichtstubeten* and other similar frivolous gatherings in day or night time including the *Weydstubeten* (meadow rooms)'.

110. See Strehler, *Beiträge zur Kulturgeschichte der Zürcher Landschaft*, Part II, pp. 60ff; we have culled the following material from these source references. On this point we refer the reader to the visitation reports of Freiamt-Kap. 1699, Bauma 1701, Bubikon 1707.

111. St.A.Z., 1685, E II 122, p. 1375.

112. Quoted in Meier, *Geschichte der Gemeinde Wetzikon*, p. 437; see too Messikommer, *Aus alter Zeit*, p. 122.

113. Messikommer, *Aus alter Zeit*, p. 126.

114. Strehler, *Beiträge zur Kulturgeschichte der Zürcher Landschaft*, Part II, p. 60.

115. Stutz, *7×7 Jahre*, p. 182.

116. K. Meuli, 'Maske, Maskereien', in *Handwörterbuch des Deutschen Aberglaubens*, 10 vols., Berlin 1927–42, vol. 6, p. 1818.

117. E. Strübin, *Baselbieter Volksleben*, Basle 1952, p. 136.

118. St.A.Z. III AAb.1.

119. Strehler, *Beiträge zur Kulturgeschichte der Zürcher Landschaft*, Part II, p. 63.

120. St.A.Z., Freiamt-Kap. 1682, E II 122, p. 546.

121. *Ibid.*

122. J.C. Nüscheler, *Über die Revision der Matrimonialgesetze im Kanton Zürich*, Zurich 1831, p. 5.

123. St.A.Z. Winterthurer-Kap. 1669, E II 118, p. 459.

124. St.A.Z., Freiamt-Kap. 1682, E II 122, p. 546.

125. See Strehler, *Beiträge zur Kulturgeschichte der Zürcher Landschaft*, Part II, p. 58.

126. Extracts from the *Stillstand* records of the church parish of Wald, *Walder Ortschronik*, MS 21.

127. *Walder Stillstandsakten* 1760; *Walder Ortschronik*, MS 21.

128. *Walder Stillstandsakten* 1752; *Walder Ortschronik*, MS 21.

129. Escher, 'Bemerkungen', p. 258.

130. Hirzel, 'Beantwortung der Frage', pp. 145ff.

131. Hirzel, *Rede über den physischen, ökonomischen und sittlich-religiösen Zustand*, p. 14; see too *Zeitbeobachtungen*, p. 12.

132. St.A.Z. A·124, 1761, quoted in Meier, *Geschichte der Gemeinde Wetzikon*, p. 436.

133. J.H. Heidegger, *Der vernünftige Dorfpfarrer*, Zurich 1791, pp. 18ff; the following extracts too.

134. The term originates from Heidegger himself, who called his minister a 'Religions- und Volksglückseligkeitslehrer' (teacher of religion and national happiness).

135. See Fretz, *Neujahrsblatt der Lesegesellschaft Wädenswil*, vol. 11, pp. 12ff.

136. Hirzel, 'Beantwortung der Frage', p. 76.

137. Stutz, *7×7 Jahre*, p. 122.

138. See *ibid.*, pp. 125, 388 and 426.

139. *Ibid.*, pp. 121ff; the other extracts too.

140. Schulthess, *Beherzigung*, p. 39.

141. As in all true story-telling and singing gatherings, individual members emerge as choir leaders and as special story-telling types (see Stutz, *7×7 Jahre*, p. 97). These spinning gatherings would often lock themselves within such a mythical circle. Stutz provides examples of this in his chapter on spinning parlours.

142. Stutz, *7×7 Jahre*, p. 119.

143. *Ibid.*, p. 99.

144. *Ibid.*, p. 137.

145. Schulthess, *Beherzigung*, p. 54.

146. Stutz, *7×7 Jahre*, p. 119. See St.A.Z. III AAb.1. The mandate of 7 July 1658 includes the following: 'And we also want to include that, in the present harvest time, the young folk, lads and daughters be diligently watched and carefully kept in by all masters and wives, that they may have no opportunity to meet up at night in one place, but be kept apart.'

147. Hirzel, 'Beantwortung der Frage', p. 146.

148. G. Finsler, O. Hunziker, H. Morf, H. Strehler, J. Studer, and others.

149. Nüscheler, *Beobachtungen*, p. 26.

150. Re the obligation to attend church services (*Kirchenzwang*) see, for instance, the *Stillstandsakten* for Wald of 21 March 1756. 'By order of His Lordship Governor Grebel in Grüningen, Heinrich Honegger from Hittenberg, soldier, and Jakob, tailor, of Selmatt were forcibly brought by virtue of the Chancery ordinance before His Reverence by the district summoner and condemned to sit three days in the tower and the tailor to get twelve strokes on the *Stud*. Which two were earnestly spoken to, on account of failing to attend public church services, etc., about the parable in Matt. 22, 1.' (*Walder Ortschronik*, MS 22).

151. The source references are provided in Chapter 1.

152. See Weiss, *Volkskunde der Schweiz*, p. 306.

153. Hirzel, *Rede über den physischen, ökonomischen und sittlich-religiösen Zustand*, p. 14; see re peasant piety: 'Zwölf Fragen nach bäuerlicher Frommigkeit und Sittlichkeit', answered by A. Brunner, Rotwasser-Laupen (Wald parish), in *Schweizerische Theologische Zeitschrift*, 3 (1911).

154. Hirzel, *Rede über den physischen, ökonomischen und sittlich-religiösen Zustand*, p. 10.

155. Weiss, *Volkskunde der Schweiz*, p. 306.

156. St.A.Z., Egg 1674, E II 120.

157. See Stutz, *7×7 Jahre*, pp. 338ff.

158. Hirzel, *Rede über den physischen, ökonomischen und sittlich-religiösen, Zustand*, p. 10.

159. See Strehler, *Beiträge zur Kulturgeschichte der Zürcher Landschaft*, Part II, p. 94;

and R. Weiss 'Vom Standort des Lehrers in userer Zeit', *Schweizerische Lehrerzeitung*, 1 (1957), p. 4.

160. H. Escher, *Synodalrede über die Besten Mittel zur Beförderung eines verbesserten Zustands der zürcherischen Kirche*, Zurich 1774, pp. 12ff.

161. Hedwid Strehler is an exception. In her chapter on teaching ('Der Unterricht') she follows up the question of the tools of instruction (*Beiträge zur Kulturgeschichte der Zürcher Landschaft*, Part II, pp. 105ff). We have summarised a few of her conclusions. The *Namenbüchlein* (illustrated primers) began with twenty-four little pictures illustrating the alphabet. Then came exercises using syllables, which were often combined to form the most nonsensical words, such as 'enheiten', 'elkeit', 'zigster', 'samstes'. They would finish off with reading exercises in the form of the most varied Christian prayers and the Ten Commandments. During the Reformation Leo Jud compiled a big Catechism as a book of comprehensive religious instruction for the common people and a smaller, easier one for the young. The big Leo Jud Catechism was replaced in 1639 by the *Fragstücklein*. They were called, after the Jud Catechism, the 'Little Catechism' or the 'little *Lehrmeister*'. A special edition of references was printed in the *Zeugnisbuch* in 1628, assembled by Bäumler. In 1639 H.C. Suter divided the enlarged Bäumler Catechism (with the extensive references) into forty-eight *Pensa*, introducing each *Pensum* with a few verses from the Lobwasser Book of Psalms, and adding a Catechism song, summarising the content of all the foregoing *Pensa*. This book was known from then on as *Die Zeugnisse*, and is in fact the *Zeugnisbuch* in the extended and present meaning of the term. The first of the ninety-three questions in the *Fragebüchlein* run as follows:

> Question 1: What is your only and greatest solace in life and death?
> Answer 1: Life Everlasting.
> Question 2: Who gives you Life Everlasting?
> Answer 2: God alone, through Jesus Christ.
> Question 3: What is God?
> Answer 3: God is the eternal, highest and greatest good, from whom we receive all good things.
> Question 4: Is there then but one God or are there many gods?
> Answer 4: There is but one single true God (. . . and so on).

The big Catechism is constructed along the same lines.

162. See Stutz, *7×7 Jahre*, pp. 93ff.

163. Escher, *Synodalrede*, p. 24. In the Stutz household were found, for instance, *Himmelsleiter, Das Paradiesgärtlein, Das wahre Christentum, Der grosse Habermann, Die Kreuzschule, Krafts Handbuch*, etc.: see Stutz, *7×7 Jahre*, p. 244. See too Messikommer, *Aus alter Zeit*, p. 20 and Strehler, *Beiträge zur Kulturgeschichte der Zürcher Landschaft*, Part II. p. 70, in which various books of moral instruction are briefly described.

164. The Lobwasser Psalms were the most popular of all the editions available. L. Meister wrote in 1782 that 'People in the Zurich countryside use (during church services) the Lobwasser Psalms with melodies by Gaudimel; it appears that it is difficult to introduce other holy songs.' (*Kleine Reisen durch einige Schweizer Kantone*, Basle 1782, p. 177). In 1792 Minister Dälliker of Buchs noticed that 'the old remain eternally loyal to their "*Ambrosius Lobesan*" ' (quoted in Fretz, *Neujahrsblatt der Lesegesellschaft Wädenswil*, vol. 11, p. 158 n. 67). Among others were Kaspar Bachofen's *Musikalisches Halleluja oder schöne und geistreiche Gesänge mit neuen und anmutigen Melodien* (*Musical Halleluja or Beautiful and Spiritual Songs with New and Cheerful Melodies*), which appeared in Zurich in 1758 and in 1767, in the 7th and 8th editions respectively, and Johann Schmidlin's *Singendes und spielendes Vergnügen Reiner Andacht oder gestliche Gesänge nach der*

Wahl des Besten gesammelt, zur Erweckung des innern Christentums eingerichtet und mit musikalischen Kompositionen begleitet (*Enjoyable Songs and Music for Pure Contemplation or Holy Songs Assembled by Choosing the Best, Arranged to Arouse the Inner Kingdom of God and Accompanied by Musical Compositions*), published in Zurich in 1758 and 1767, in the 2nd and 3rd editions respectively (see Fretz, *Neujahrsblatt der Lesegesellschaft Wädenswil*, vol. 11, p. 22). We include folk-tales, ballads, etc., under the rubric 'oral-literature'. The story of Genoveva, for instance, as well as stories about bandits, murder and love in the form of 'folk-songs', which Bas-Anneli, for instance, knew an awful lot of. 'Bas Anneli could not sing, so she just declaimed the songs' (Stutz, *7×7 Jahre*, p. 59).

165. J.H. Pestalozzi, *Sämtliche Werke*, ed. A. Buchenau, E. Spranger and H. Stettbacher, 28 vols., Berlin 1927–76, vol. 10, pp. 272–85.

166. *Ibid.*, p. 287.

167. See Fretz, *Neujahrsblatt der Lesegesellschaft Wädenswil*, vol. 11, p. 65.

168. Strehler, *Beiträge zur Kulturgeschichte der Zürcher Landschaft*, Part II, p. 120.

169. *Ibid.*, p. 121. See too Fretz, *Neujahrsblatt der Lesegesellschaft Wädenswil*, vol. 11, pp. 19ff.

170. Fretz, *Neujahrsblatt der Lesegesellschaft Wädenswil*, vol. 11, p. 21.

171. Salomon von Orelli, *Abschriften nebst Manuskripten über den Stäfner Handels*, St.A.Z. B×39, quoted in *ibid.*, p. 22.

172. *Ibid.*, p. 27.

173. The text was published by Orell-Gessner in Zurich, and it is significant that the *Textbüchlein* (little text book) was got up to resemble the town *Kantatentextbüchlein*, which were used for concerts.

174. Fretz, *Neujahrsblatt der Lesegesellschaft Wädenswil*, vol. 11, p. 30.

175. *Ibid.*, p. 32.

176. *Ibid.*, p. 38.

177. *Ibid.*, p. 39. It should be stressed that not all clothiers in the Zurich territory counted as representatives of new ways of life and as transmitters of new luxury and cultural goods. There were many who were still anchored to their farms and who also held firmly and conscientiously to traditional ways of life, with the 'morals-enforcing plough' (Pestalozzi, *Werke*, vol. 10, p. 275). We have already mentioned the Stutz family, where we saw how stubbornly Jakob's mother remained loyal to the traditional costume.

178. Pestalozzi, *Werke*, vol. 10, p. 294.

179. Fretz, *Neujahrsblatt der Lesegesellschaft Wädenswil*, vol. 11, p. 42.

180. Breitinger's verdict took place in the Examinatorenkonvent, quoted in *ibid.*, p. 43. Fretz remarks that Breitinger distorted the situation: 'Voltaire had already mostly been translated into German for those who just wanted to get to know him out of a desire to be in fashion . . . There was something hiding in these people, which could indeed erupt unpleasantly, but was none-the-less based on a healthy talent and not just on superficial imitation.'

181. *Ibid.*, p. 47, and see too L. Weisz, 'Die literarischen Gesellschaften des alten Zurichs', *Neue Zürcher Zeitung*, 15 and 16 Nov. 1933.

182. Salomon von Orelli, *Abschriften nebst Manuskripten den Stafner Handels*, St.A.Z. B×39, quoted in Fretz, *Neujahrsblatt der Lesegesellshaft Wädenswil*, vol. 11, p. 53. With this kind of people, Fretz wrote, the performances must always have been tragedies, featuring men and 'female persons'.

183. Quoted in *ibid.*, p. 52.

184. *Ibid.*, pp. 64ff.

185. *Ibid.*, pp. 87ff.

186. See *Ibid.*, Chap. 4; Wolfgang von Wartburg, 'Zürich und die französische

Revolution' *Baseler Beiträge zur Geschichtswissenschaft*, 60, (1956), and A. Custer, *Die Zürcher Untertanen und die französische Revolution*, Diss., Zurich 1942, p. 69. A. Custer quotes a saying by the big farmer Dänliker, to wit: 'the members of the reading and music societies with their round hats are the originators of all evil'.

187. See Fretz, *Neujahrsblatt der Lesegesellshaft Wadenswil*, vol 11, pp. 67ff, 69 and 71.

188. We are unfortunately obliged to refrain from investigating the form, activity and development of the Wädenswil Reading Society any further. Fretz parades every detail before us; the details are important.

189. The following quotations are taken from the archive of the Ascetische Gesellschaft, III, no. 85, Zurich Central Library.

190. We mentioned the cultural gap between the lake districts and the Oberland when discussing luxury and clothes.

191. Quoted in Krebser, *Wald im Zürcher Oberland*, p. 27. The other details are also to be found in it.

192. *Volksblatt vom Bachtel* (Heimatblatt), 29 Aug. 1874.

193. G. Peterhans-Bianzano, *Ins Zürcher Oberland*, Winterthur 1925, p. 27.

194. In the second half of the nineteenth century craftsmen and workers tried to make the cultural wealth of their age accessible within their own circles and organisations. These efforts towards self-education all experienced the same fate again, they were partly drawn within the sphere of influence of the international worker associations, which identified their striving towards intellectual independence with the class struggle.

195. Quoted in Custer, *Die Zürcher Untertanen*, p. 51.

196. See the chapters in *ibid.*, entitled 'Die französische Revolution und die schweizerische Freiheitstradition' and 'Patriotismus'.

197. See the chapter in *ibid.*, entitled 'Revolutionäre und obrigkeitstreue Gesinnung im Volke', pp. 86ff and n. 184.

198. Brägger, *Schriften*; R. Weiss, *Häuser und Landschaften der Schweiz*, Erlenbach and Zurich 1958, pp. 209ff. Uli Brägger was an outworker and a yarn dealer. We know that his thirst for education was stilled in an urban educational circle. Salomon Schinz, provides us with a very fine picture of the Oberland population (*Das höhere Gebirge*, pp. 9ff) in which its restless nature also has a place: 'On the whole this little mountain populace comes closest in its arrangements, its way of life and its customs to the description of the inhabitants of the Allmann mountains drawn up by Herr Deacon Hirzel. They are not lacking in abilities in the slightest, but rather in opportunities to develop or train them. Inquisitive, lively, often judging people and things very accurately, proud and headstrong [perhaps because of the isolated situation of many dwellings, or the result of inadequate education], cheerful, often even horribly frivolous; for all that not easy to deal with and lead, especially where people want to treat them harshly and condescendingly. Otherwise sensitive and often movingly devoted to those who show them honest goodwill, and dedicated whole-heartedly to their mountains and their free way of life! But all this is also being modified by the variety of employment and situations.'

199. A. Hauser discovered this house motto while out walking and we include it here with his amiable permission.

4 The impact of industrialisation on the house and the rural economy

1. For a more extensive treatment of this topic, see F.R. Staehelin, 'Geschichtliche Wandlungen der Zürcher Hauslandschaft um 1800', unpublished master thesis,

University of Zurich, Zurich n.d. [late 1950s]; a copy of the manuscript has been deposited in the Zurich Central Library.

2. See St.A.Z. B IX 74, p. 251. See too Hans J. Wehrli, 'Über die landwirtschaftlichen Zustände im Kanton Zürich in der zweiten Hälfte des 18. Jahrhunderts' (Nach den Berichten der ökonomischen Kommission der Naturforschenden Gesellschaft), *XCV Neujahrsblatt zum Besten des Waisenhauses in Zurich für das Jahr 1932* (1932), p. 8.

3. St.A.Z. B IX 74, p. 251; elsewhere: 'In Regensdorf the village rights are responsible for the houses having to be built against one another.' B IX 74, p. 252.

4. See Chapter 1.

5. St.A.Z. B IX 74, p. 253.

6. See H. Bernhard, *Wirtschafts- und Siedlungsgeschichte des Tösstales*, Diss., Zurich 1912, p. 86.

7. See *ibid.*, Tab. 3, App. 11.

8. See *ibid.*, Tab. 4, App. 12.

9. See *ibid.*, pp. 1 and 75.

10. See *ibid.*, pp. 87ff with illustrations and especially Tab. 5, App. 13.

11. See *ibid.*, Tab. 2, App. 10.

12. See *ibid.*, Tab. p. 61. Based on the collections of 1787. The spinners in the lower parishes were really only employed at spinning during the idle times in winter.

13. Johann Caspar Hirzel, *Der philosophische Kaufmann*, Zurich 1775, pp. 103ff.

14. See Bernhard, 'Wirtschafts- und Siedlungsgechichte', pp. 74ff, as well as Tab. 5, App. 13, in which many further examples are to be found.

15. See *ibid.*, Tab. 5, App. 13.

16. *Volksblatt vom Bachtel* (Heimatblatt), 12 and 13 Oct. 1944.

17. J. Ebel, *Schilderung der Gebirgsvölker der Schweiz*, Leipzig 1798, vol. 1, p. 252.

18. J.C. Hirzel, 'Beantwortung der Frage: Ist die Handelschaft, wie solche bey uns beschaffen, unserem Lande schädlich, oder nützlich, in Absicht auf den Feldbau und die Sitten des Volkes?', *Magazin für die Naturkunde Helvetiens*, 3 (1788), p. 77.

19. See Staehelin, 'Geschichtliche Wandlungen', pp. 36ff.

20. This example can be found with all the relevant source references, photographs and plans of the foundations, in *ibid.*

21. J.C. Nüscheler, *Beobachtungen eines redlichen Schweizers aus vaterländischer Liebe entworfen*, Zurich 1786, p. 19.

22. Staehelin, 'Geschichtliche Wandlungen', p. 55, with photographs.

23. St.A.Z. A 99/3; likewise a projected entry charter from Ober-Mettmenstetten *c.* 1686 (undated): 'Upon one whole village right there may be built no more than two living rooms and two hearths.' St.A.Z. A 99/3.

24. Hirzel, 'Beantwortung der Frage', p. 128; see too p. 78; likewise C. Meiners, *Briefe über die Schweiz* Part III, Tübingen 1791, p. 49.

25. Nüscheler, *Beobachtungen*, pp. 19ff. The author continues by citing a rather wicked example to illustrate the moral perils to which the children were exposed in these living conditions.

26. St.A.Z. A 99/3 sub Maschwanden.

27. *Ibid.*, sub Mettmenstetten-Dachelsen.

28. *Ibid.*, B IX 96 sub Anleitung für die Landgemeinden . . ., p. 4.

29. Meiners, *Briefe*, p. 49. For this description the author will have had the lake parishes in mind, but it applies just as much to the Oberland. See too Hirzel, 'Beantwortung der Frage', p. 65: 'These [factory earnings] are also to be thanked for the numbers of well-built, stone-clad houses, and the general introduction of tile roofs' (the east side of the Zurich Lake is referred to here).

30. Ebel, *Gebirgsvölker*, vol. 2, p. 46. The farm 'Ragenbuch' in the parish of Fischental, high up on the way to the Strahlegg, even today still possesses a gorgeous living room stove, with splendid painted tiles. It was built in 1699 by the renowned potter David Pfau for a client in Winterthur and is supposed to have been moved to the 'Ragenbuch' farm in 1795. See Staehelin, 'Geschichtliche Wandlungen', p. 37.

31. St.A.Z. B ×39, p. 4.
32. *Ibid.*, B IX 111, p. 1.
33. *Ibid.*, N 37 a/1 sub Hombrechtikon.
34. *Ibid.*, N 37 a/1 sub Männedorf.
35. Hirzel, *Der philosophische Kaufmann*, pp. 103 and 101.
36. See Meiners, *Briefe*, p. 54.
37. See *ibid.*, pp. 49ff.
38. Hirzel, 'Beantwortung der Frage', p. 46, see too pp. 80ff.
39. St.A.Z. N 37 a/1 sub Schönenberg.
40. Hirzel, 'Beantwortung der Frage', p, 122.
41. *Ibid.*, p. 126.
42. Meiners, *Briefe*, p. 51.
43. Both of these quotations are taken from, Hirzel, 'Beantwortung der Frage', p. 124.
44. *Ibid.*, p. 83.

5   Work in the putting-out industry and its effect on the life of the common people

1. St.A.Z. F I 354ff.
2. Max Weber, *Gesammelte Aufsätze zur Religionssoziologie*, 3 vols., Tübingen 1920–1, vol. 1, p. 26.
3. G. Finsler, W. Köhler and A. Ruegg, eds., *Ulrich Zwingli*, Zurich 1918, pp. 263ff (a selection from his writings commissioned by the church council of the canton of Zurich).
4. A. Niederer, *Gemeinwerk im Wallis*, Basle 1956, p. 48.
5. St.A.Z. *Zürcher Mandate* 1671–1700, III AAb.1.
6. Quoted in J.C. Hirzel, 'Beantwortung der Frage: Ist die Handelschaft, wie solche bey uns beschaffen, unserem Lande schädlich, oder nützlich, in Absicht auf den Feldbau und die Sitten des Volkes?', *Magazin für die Naturkunde Helvetiens*, 3 (1788), p. 108.
7. St.A.Z. F I 354ff.
8. Look up 'müssig, Müssiggang' in the various dictionaries of proverbs.
9. Jakob Stutz, *7 ×7 Jahre – aus meinem Leben, als Beitrag zur näheren Kenntnis des Volkes*, Pfäffikon 1853, p. 212.
10. *Ibid.*, pp. 125ff.
11. *Ibid.*, pp. 121ff.
12. See *Grütlikalender für das Jahr 1925*; we refer deliberately to this source and not to Robert Seidel, because this reference reveals how such songs of praise and hymns to work entered the genre of popular calendars, thus becoming reading matter for the common people.
13. *Bericht über einige Industrieverhältnisse im Kanton Zurich*, Zurich 1833, p. 26.
14. Hirzel, 'Beantwortung der Frage', p. 109.
15. *Ibid.*, pp. 106ff. Elsewhere, Hirzel wrote: 'But if we want to return to the reason for and origin of this flouishing wealth, then we must stay with the holy Reformation, and give honour to the Reformer Zwingli, the founder and originator of the same' (p. 105).
16. Quoted in *ibid.*, p. 108.

17. *Ibid.*, pp. 98ff.

18. Let it be emphasised that we are not concerned with the purely technical side of the spinning and weaving work. These questions are dealt with in the rich literature on the subject: Emil Künzle, Oskar Haegi, Walter Honegger, Heinrich Spoerry-Jaeggi and others (see Bibliography). Besides the purely scientific works, we recommend in particular the description of domestic spinners and weavers provided by J.W. Goethe in *Gedenkausgabe der Werke, Briefe und Gespräche* (24 vols., Zurich 1949, vol. 8, Book 3, Chap. 5). In this, Goethe provides a detailed description of the spinning and weaving work processes. His account is based on the knowledge he had acquired among the Zurich cottage workers. See F. Berthau, *Goethe und seine Beziehung zur schweizerischen Baumwollindustrie*, Wetzikon 1888.

19. Niederer, *Gemeinwerk im Wallis*, p. 8.

20. See C.G. Schmidt, *Der Schweizer Bauer im Zeitalter des Frühkapitalismus*, Berne 1932, pp. 36ff; and E. Strubin, *Baselbieter Volksleben*, Basle 1952, p. 52.

21. See R. Weiss, *Volkskunde der Schweiz*, Erlenbach and Zurich 1946, p. 102.

22. Archive of the Ascetishe Gesellschaft, III, no. 77, Zurich Central Library, quoted in A. Bollinger, *Die Zürcher Landschaft an der Wende des 18. Jahrhunderts – nach Berichten der ascetischen Gesellschaft*, Diss., Zurich 1941, p. 31.

23. Strubin, *Baselbieter Volksleben*, p. 32.

24. Archive of the Ascetische Gesellschaft, quoted in Bollinger, *Die Zürcher Landschaft*, p. 31.

25. Hirzel, 'Beantwortung der Frage', p. 83.

26. J.C. Hirzel quoted this saying and reported that this still youthful manufacturer had had to alter his wares a good ten times (*ibid.*, p. 153).

27. The coarse dry yarn was spun on a wheel and measured by the pound. For this reason it was called Pound-yarn as well as wheel-yarn. The fine, damp yarn, *Lödli* (*Löthli*) yarn, or *Brief* (stocking) yarn, was spun by hand on a spindle. It was measured by the *Schneller*. One *Schneller* represented a thousand turns around a reel of 7/4 ells circumference (105 cm.). This yarn was also called *Schneller* yarn. See A. Bürkli-Meyer, *Die Zürcherische Fabrikgesetzgebung vom Beginn des 14. Jahrhunderts an bis zur Schweizerischen Staatsumwälzung von 1798*, Zurich 1884, pp. 34 and 47.

28. Jakob Stutz, *Gemälde aus dem Volksleben*, Part III, Zurich 1836, chapter 'Die Spinnstube – umgefähr ums Jahr 1807', pp. 3ff.

29. See the governmental factory ordinance of 1717; quoted in Bürkli-Meyer, *Zürcherische Fabrikgesetzgebung*, pp. 28ff.

30. Goethe, *Gedenkausgabe der Werke*, vol. 8, Book 3, Chap. 5.

31. Similar conditions governed weaving and the cottage industrial processes preparatory to spinning or weaving, which we do not discuss at this stage.

32. The visitation acts of the Wetzikon chapter, 1771/2; quoted in H. Strehler, *Beiträge zur Kulturgeschichte der Zürcher Landschaft*, Part I: *Kirche und Schule im 17. und 18. Jahrhundert*, Lachen, 1934, p. 101.

33. *Zeitbeobachtungen über das schweizerische Baumwollgewerbe, dessen Folgen und Aussichten*, Switzerland 1806, p. 14.

34. Archive of the Ascetische Gesellschaft, quoted in Bollinger, *Die Zürcher Landschaft*, p. 70.

35. St.A.Z. reports by ministers and the Poor Officers about 'the influence of the factory conditions on Poor Relief and about the social position of the factory worker', 1857: N 37 a/1, sub Männedorf.

36. Hans Kunz, 'Meine Vorfahren und die Geschichte der Textilindustriearbeiter im Zürcher Oberland', Prüfungsarbeit am Seminar Unterstrass 1946; *Walder Ortschronik*, MS 12, p. 12.

37. *Zeitbeobachtungen*, p. 14.
38. S. Schinz, *Das höhere Gebirge des Kanton Zürich, und der ökonomisch-moralische Zustand der Bewohner, mit Vorschlag der Hülfe und Auskunft für die bey mangelnder Fabrikarbeit brotlose Übervölkerung* (Synodalrede), Zurich 1817, p. 12.
39. J.H. Pestalozzi, *Wirtschaftliche und soziale Schriften*, p. 446.
40. Niederer, *Gemeinwerk im Wallis*, p. 10.
41. Hirzel, 'Beantwortung der Frage', p. 48.
42. Stutz, *7 × 7 Jahre*, p. 27.
43. 'Protokoll des Fabrikdirektoriums 6', p. 114, quoted in A. Künzle, *Die Zürcherische Baumwollindustrie von ihren Anfängen bis zur Einführung des Fabrikbetriebes*, Diss., Zurich 1906, p. 44.
44. Bürkli-Meyer, *Zürcherische Fabrikgesetzgebung*, p. 38. A mandate of 23 June 1733, 'Regarding the dishonest workers', provides the following excerpt: 'That the silk, wool and cotton which have been distributed round the countryside by the citizen tradesmen to be combed, spun and woven are not to be considered as entrusted property, nor to be in any way sold, purchased or pawned, nor may money, food or other goods be lent against them.' *Ibid.*, p. 42.
45. Johann Schulthess, *Beherzigung des vor der Zürcher Synode gehaltenen Vortrags*, Zurich 1817, p. 41.
46. St.A.Z. N 37 a/1.
47. It is an unsigned report by the commission to the government council, printed in Zurich 1833, p. 18.
48. H. Spoerry-Jaeggi, *Zeit des Übergangs von der Heimindustrie des Zürcher Oberlandes zum industriellen Betrieb*, Wald 1927, p. 17.
49. See Jakob Stutz, *Lise und Salome, die beiden Webermädchen*, Zurich 1847, p. 15.
50. Factory Ordinance of 16 August 1717, Bürkli-Meyer, *Zürcherische Fabrikgesetzgebung*, p. 38.
51. The quoted material is taken from Bürkli-Meyer's text. Details about the technicalities of the work are of no importance to our enquiry and are not explained.
52. *Ibid.*, p. 14.
53. *Ibid.*, pp. 28ff.
54. *Ibid.*
55. J.H. Pestalozzi, 'Schriften zur Stäfener Volksbewegung' ('writings about the Stäfa Rising'), in *Sämtliche Werke*, ed. A. Buchenau, E. Spranger and H. Stettbacher, 28 vols., Berlin 1927–76, vol 10, pp. 282ff.
56. St.A.Z. B IX B 62 V, vol. 31, III, quoted in O. Haegi, *Die Entwicklung der Zürcher-Oberländischen Baumwollindustrie*, Diss., Berne 1924, p. 17.
57. Niederer, *Gemeinwerk im Wallis*, p. 11.
58. R. Weiss calls it an 'ineradicable human characteristic', *Volkskunde der Schweiz*, p. 15.
59. Parish curate Wegmann, 1768; quoted in R. Weiss, 'Vom Standpunkt des Lehrers in userer Zeit', *Schweizerische Lehrerzeitung*, 1 (1957).
60. Niederer, *Gemeinwerk im Wallis*, p. 49.
61. Although every local paper carries a business column, they have stayed this way up to the present day. In the autumn of 1955 a winder told me worriedly that there was almost no yarn left in the store and that there would certainly be a work stoppage. I explained to her that there might be little yarn in the store, but that on the world market, there was not too little but too much cotton. The American cotton policy was not yet determined, but people were reckoning on a fall in prices. For this reason our manufacture was delaying buying yarn and was laying in only as many supplies as were absolutely necessary.

62. Stutz, *7×7 Jahre*, p. 145.

63. St.A.Z. N 37 a/1.

64. See Bollinger, *Die Zürcher Landschaft*, pp. 31ff, and in general R. Weiss, *Das Alpenerlebnis in der Literatur des 18. Jahrhunderts*, Zurich 1933.

65. *Zeitbeobachtungen*, p. 11.

66. Stutz, *7×7 Jahre*, p. 355.

67. Stutz, *Gemälde aus dem Volksleben*, p. 37.

68. Archive of the Ascetische Gesellschaft, quoted in Bollinger, *Die Zürcher Landschaft*, p. 54.

69. Johann Hirzel, *Rede über den physischen, ökonomischen und sittlich-religiösen Zustand der östlichen Berggemeinden des Kanton Zürich* (Synodalrede), Zurich 1816, p. 12.

70. Weiss, *Volkskunde der Schweiz*, p. 31.

71. From a lecture given by Hans-Rudolf Schinz before the Naturforschende Gesellschaft Zurich 1782/3, quoted in D. Fretz, *Neujahrsblatt der Lesegesellschaft Wädenswil*, vol. 11: *Die Entstehung der Lesegesellschaft Wädenswil*, Wädenswil 1939, p. 26.

72. Quoted in *ibid.*, Chap. 1, n. 74.

73. Stutz, *Gemälde aus dem Volksleben*, p. 74.

74. We will discuss these problems in detail in a sequel to this thesis. Likewise, many things concerning cottage industry will only be mentioned there. For instance, child labour and the physical damage inflicted by industrial work.

75. Stutz, *Lise und Salome*, p. 35.

76. See H. Strehler, *Beiträge zur Kulturgeschichte der Zürcher Landschaft*, Part II: 'Aberglaube, Armut und Bettel', in *Zürcher Taschenbuch auf das Jahr 1935* (1935), p. 90. 'The reason for being incapable of working is given with horrifying frequency as dim or poor sight or even full blindness.'

77. Zurich Central Library, II, no. 101.

78. Zurich Central Library B 6a, both quotations in Bollinger, *Die Zürcher Landschaft*, p. 55.

79. U. Brägger, *Leben und Schriften des armen Mannes im Toggenburg*, 3 vols., Basle 1945, vol. 1, p. 246.

80. H. Messikommer, *Aus alter Zeit: Sitten und Gebräuche im Züricher Oberland*, 3 vols., Zurich 1909–11, vol. 1, p. 25.

81. Stutz, *7×7 Jahre*, p. 578; he refers to doing two jobs at once (*Doppelarbeit*).

82. Hirzel, *Rede über den physischen, ökonomischen und sittlich-religiösen Zustand*, p. 11.

83. The weaver was more exposed to this dichotomy due to his greater isolation. He was also isolated by the clatter of his loom.

6 The outworkers' attitude to poverty and crises

1. See Werner Sombart's essay regarding this methodological problem, 'Die Arbeiterverhältnisse im Zeitalter des Frühkapitalismus', *Archiv für Sozialwissenschaft und Sozialpolitik*, 44 (1917), pp. 19ff.

2. We would refer the reader to the following monographs: Alice Denzler, *Geschichte des Armenswesens im Kanton Zürich im 16. und 17. Jahrhundert*, Diss., Zurich 1920; Bertha Keller, *Das Armenwesen des Kantons Zürich vom Beginn des 18. Jahrhunderts bis zum Armengesetz des Jahres 1836*, Diss., Zurich 1935; as well as the works by Hedwig Strehler and H. Morf.

3. C.G. Schmidt, *Der Schweizer Bauer im Zeitalter des Frühkapitalismus*, Berne 1932, p. 51.

4. This and the next quotation is taken from St.A.Z. III. AAb.1, Almosenordnung 1693.

5. See M. Adler, 'Fabrik und Zuchthaus', *Kultur- und Zeitfragen*, 10, p. 13.

6. Quoted in H. Morf, *Neujahrsblatt der Hülfsgesellschaft von Winterthur*, vol. 12: *Aus der Geschichte des zürcherischen Armenwesens*, Winterthur 1873, p. 13.

7. St.A.Z. A 61/6, Bettelmandat 5 Feb. 1700.

8. *Ibid.*, II AAb. 1, Almosenordnung 1693.

9. *Ibid.*

10. This comes from the foreword to two competition essays submitted to the Aufmunterungsgesellschaft in Basle on the theme of poverty, mendicancy and charity: *Ueber Armuth Betteley und Wohltätigkeit* – a collection of a few essays submitted to the Aufmunterungsgesellschaft in Basle in 1779, Basle 1780.

11. See, for instance, Werner Sombart, 'Die Arbeiterverhältnisse', p. 26; J.A.C. Brown, 'Psychologie der industriellen Leistung', in *Rowoholts deutsche Enzyklopädie*, vol. 30, p. 10.

12. Max Weber, *Gesammelte Aufsätze zur Religionssoziologie*, 3 vols., Tübingen 1920–1, vol. 1; R.H. Tawney, *Religion and the Rise of Capitalism*, Harmondsworth 1938. The foreword to Tawney's work contains further bibliographical references.

13. Weber, *Gesammelte Aufsätze zur Religionssoziologie*, vol. 1, p. 208.

14. See Keller, *Das Armenwesen*, p. 7.

15. Zurich Central Library, *Zürcher Freitagszeitung* 1816, no. 38.

16. Foreword to the competition essays of the Basle Aufmunterungsgesellschaft 1779.

17. Keller, *Das Armenwesen*, pp. 105ff.

18. *Ibid.*, p. 7.

19. St.A.Z. NN 36, p. 49.

20. *Ibid.*, N 37a/1, sub Bäretswil.

21. Zurich Central Library, *Neujahrsblatt der Zürcherischen Hülfsgesellschaft* 1817.

22. See A. Bürkli-Meyer, 'Die Einführung der mechanischen Baumwollspinnerei', *Fortschritt*, Organ des kaufmännischen Vereins Zürich [1885], p. 8.

23. J.H. Pestalozzi, *Sämtliche Werke*, ed. A. Buchenau, E. Spranger and H. Stett-bacher, 28 vols., Berlin 1927–76, vol. 10, pp. 272ff.

24. C. Meiners, *Briefe über die Schweiz*, Part III, Tübingen 1791, p. 555.

25. See Pestalozzi, *Werke*, vol. 10, pp. 272ff.

26. The official accounts by the district governor of Kyburg for 1795, quoted in Morf, *Neujahrsblatt der Hülfsgesellschaft von Winterthur*, vol. 12, p. 64.

27. St.A.Z. A 61/6, 12 April 1723.

28. *Ibid.*, sub Steinmaur.

29. *Ibid.*, A 61/5a, sub Gossau.

30. Jakob Stutz, *7×7 Jahre – aus meinem Leben, als Beitrag zur näheren Kenntnis des Volkes*, Pfäffikon 1853, p. 73.

31. F. Meier, *Geschichte der Gemeinde Wetzikon*, Zurich 1881, p. 526.

32. *Ibid.*, p. 529.

33. H. Strehler, *Beiträge zur Kulturgeschichte der Zürcher Landschaft*, Part II: 'Aberglaube, Armut und Bettel', in *Zürcher Taschenbuch auf das Jahr 1935* (1935), p. 85; see too Morf, *Neujahrsblatt der Hülfsgesellschaft von Winterthur*, vol. 12, pp. 30ff.

34. St.A.Z. E II 43, Synodalakten, 31 Oct. 1732.

35. *Ibid.*, A 61/6, sub Maur.

36. Zurich Central Library, *Neujahrsblatt der Zürcherischen Hülfsgesellschaft* 1817, p. 14.

37. Stillstandsprotokoll Wetzikon, p. 129; quoted in Keller, *Das Armenwesen*, p. 50.

38. St.A.Z. B IX 70, p. 54.

39. *Ibid.*, A 61/5, sub Zell.

40. See Morf, *Neujahrsblatt der Hülfsgesellschaft von Winterthur*, vol. 12, p. 30.

41. St.A.Z. A 61/5a, sub Brütten.

42. *Ibid.*, A 61/6.

43. *Ibid.*

44. *Ibid.*, B V 113, p. 34, 17 April 1723.

45. S. Schinz, *Das höhere Gebirge des Kanton Zürich, und der ökonomisch-moralische Zustand der Bewohner, mit Vorschlag der Hülfe und Auskunft für die bey mangelnder Fabrikarbeit brotlose Übervölkerung* (Synodalrede), Zürich 1817, p. 8.

46. Morf, *Neujahrsblatt der Hülfsgesellschaft von Winterthur*, vol. 12, p. 44.

47. St.A.Z. B IX 72, pp. 503ff.

48. See Keller, *Das Armenwesen*, p. 95.

49. St.A.Z. B IX 72, pp. 503ff.

50. See *ibid.*, B IX 96, sub Preisfrage 1803, p. 4.

51. *Ibid.*, A 61/6, 12 April 1723.

52. *Ibid.*, NN 36, p. 49.

53. See Sombart, 'Die Arbeiterverhältnisse', p. 26.

54. Stutz, *7×7 Jahre*, p. 468.

55. *Ibid.*, p. 487.

56. See E. Strübin, *Baselbieter Volksleben*, Basle 1952, p. 115.

57. See Stutz, *7×7 Jahre*, p. 409.

58. See, for instance, St.A.Z. N 37/a1, sub Dürnten.

59. Quoted from H. Spoerry-Jaeggi, *Zeit des Übergangs von der Heimindustrie des Zürcher Oberlandes zum industriellen Betrieb*, Wald 1927, p. 41.

60. L.J. Schweizer, *Über den zunehmenden Verdienstmangel in den östlichen Gemeinden des Kanton Zürich*, Zurich 1831, p. 7.

61. Johann Hirzel, *Rede über den physischen, ökonomischen und sittlich-religiösen Zustand der östlichen Berggemeinden des Kanton Zürich* (Synodalrede), Zürich 1816, p. 17.

62. *Ibid.*, p. 16.

63. *Ibid.*, p. 18; see too Schinz, *Das höhere Gebirge*, p. 12, and Schweizer, *Über den zunehmenden Verdienstmangel*, p. 9, *inter alia*.

64. Schweizer, *Über den zunehmenden Verdienstmangel*, p. 7.

65. St.A.Z. N 37/a1, sub Bäretswil; *ibid.*, sub Rüti.

66. *Ibid.*, B IX 96; directions for the country parishes of the canton of Zurich, as to how the smallholders, day-labourers and factory workers may be employed so that they are able to provide themselves and their families with what they need – without resorting to begging. From the essays submitted to the Naturforschende Gesellschaft in Zurich answering their competition question set for 1803; selected and published 1804, p. 15.

67. Schinz, *Das höhere Gebirge*, p. 12.

68. Hirzel, *Rede über den physischen, ökonomischen und sittlich-religiösen Zustand*, p. 13.

69. H. Messikommer, *Aus alter Zeit: Sitten und Gebräuche im Züricher Oberland*, 3 vols., Zurich 1909–11, vol. 1, p. 62.

70. Stutz, *7×7 Jahre*, p. 464.

71. Johann Schulthess, *Beherzigung des vor der Zürcher Synode gehaltenen Vortrags*, Zurich 1817, p. 37.

72. Kurt Stavenhagen would refer here to a 'phenomenally unhistorical' mentality.

73. Hirzel, *Rede über den physischen, ökonomischen und sittlich-religiössen Zustand*, p. 14.

74. Schweizer, *Über den zunehmenden Verdienstmangel*, p. 5.

75. In 1862 the *Volksblatt vom Bachtel*, for instance, could still print the following notice on 15 June: 'The alms recipient Heinrich Honegger-Kuhn of Blattenbach, factory worker at present in the boarding house in Stuck, is with reference to article 29 of the Poor Law forbidden from visiting taverns and gambling. The Alms Office.' It is obvious that this sort of Poor Relief tended to encourage rather than hinder begging.

76. Pestalozzi, *Werke*, vol. 10, pp. 282ff.

77. St.A.Z. B IX 96, sub Anleitung für die Landgemeinden . . ., p. 15.

78. Between 1808 and 1810 the employment level was satisfactory; see Spoerry-Jaeggi, *Zeit des Übergangs*, p. 60.

79. *Zeitbeobachtungen über das schweizerische Baumwollgewerbe, dessen Folgen und Aussichten*, Switzerland 1806, pp. 15ff.

80. St.A.Z. U 28.

81. See, for instance, *Zeitbeobachtungen*, p. 4. 'I hereby acknowledge that I do not consider any arrangement, and even less any sort of political change, adequate to set our cotton manufactures on a secure and solid basis, and to keep them as flourishing as they have been up till now, not just for a few years but for later ages as well. My opinion is that the present situation principally involves staving off the collapse as long as possible and, when the blow can no longer be averted, making it less shattering.'

82. A letter from Conrad Escher von der Linth to Johann Rudolf Steinmüller, dated 29 Dec. 1803, in *Mitteilungen zur Vaterländischen Geschichte*, published by the Historischer Verein in St Gall, 23 (1889), p. 354. The author discusses the 'Kellenland' (Oberland) in this.

83. See Jakob Stutz, *Gemälde aus dem Volksleben*, Part III, Zurich 1836, pp. 39ff.

84. Meier, *Geschichte der Gemeinde Wetzikon*, p. 269, and others.

85. See Stutz, *7×7 Jahre*, p. 577.

86. See *ibid.*, p. 390.

87. G. Meyer von Knonau writes in his work *Der Kanton Zürich*, St Gall and Berne 1844, vol. 1, p. 301: 'In 1827 there were 1,450 male and 1,150 female spinners in the various spinning factories, as well as 2,400 under-age persons of both sexes, with a total of 5,000 people employed.' As we will see in Part two, the first factory workers were mostly recruited from among former cottage workers, especially from the landless hand spinners.

88. A list of the business houses and factories in the canton of Zurich 1837 to 1870; quoted from O. Haegi, *Die Entwicklung der Zürcher-Oberländischen Baumwollindustrie*, Diss., Berne, 1924, p. 61.

7   Conclusion

1. See A. Karasek-Langer, 'Neusiedlung in Bayern nach 1945', *Jahrbuch für Volkskunde der Heimatvertriebenen*, 2 (1956).

2. R. Weiss, *Häuser und Landschaften der Schweiz*, Erlenbach and Zurich, p. 317.

3. We refer once again to Karasek-Langer's programmatic remarks in 'Neusiedlung in Bayern nach 1945'.

Postscript

1. In France the basic study in this tradition is Pierre Goubert, *Beauvais et le Beauvaisis de 1600 à 1730*, Paris 1960; in England J. D. Chambers, 'The Vale of Trent', *Economic History Review*, Supplement 3 (1957).

2. For a survey of German historiography after the Second World War, see Georg G. Iggers, *New Directions in European Historiography*, Middleton, Conn., 1975.

3. See the paradigmatic work by Rudolf Braun's teacher Richard Weiss, *Volkskunde der Schweiz*, Erlenbach and Zurich 1946.

4. For a very influential work from this background which appeared at the same time as Braun's study, see Philippe Ariès, *Centuries of Childhood*, New York 1965; first ed. 1960.

5. See Hermann Bausinger, Utz Jeggle, Gottfried Korff and Martin Scharfe, *Grundzüge der Volkskunde*, Darmstadt 1978, Chap. 3.

6. See Rudolf Braun, 'Proto-industrialization and Demographic Changes in the Canton of Zurich', in Charles Tilly, ed., *Historical Studies of Changing Fertility*, Princeton, 1978, pp. 289–334, notably p. 334.

7. The term has been coined by Clifford Geertz, 'Thick Description: Towards an Interpretative Theory of Culture', in *idem*, *The Interpretation of Culture*, Boston 1973, pp. 3–30; the recent discussion on its use in historiography has been triggered by Lawrence Stone, 'The Revival of the Narrative: Reflections on a New Old History', *Past and Present*, 85 (1980), pp. 3–24.

8. Franklin Mendels, 'Proto-industrialization: The First Phase of the Industrialization Process', *Journal of Economic History*, 32 (1972), pp. 241–61; for a systematic overview, see *idem*, 'Des industries rurales à la proto-industrialisation: Historique d'un changement de perspective', *Annales, E.S.C.*, 39 (1984), pp. 997–1008; Maxine Berg, Pat Hudson and Michael Sonenscher, 'Manufacture in Town and Country Before the Factory', in *idem*, eds., *Manufacture in Town and Country Before the Factory*, Cambridge 1983; Peter Kriedte, Hans Medick and Jürgen Schlumbohm, *Industrialisation before Industrialisation: Rural Industry in the Genesis of Capitalism*, Cambridge and Paris 1982.

9. Notably Chambers, 'The Vale of Trent'; Joan Thirsk, 'Industries in the Countryside', in F.J. Fisher, ed., *Essays in the Economic and Social History of Tudor and Stuart England*, Cambridge 1961, pp. 70–88; Eric L. Jones, 'Agricultural Origins of Industry', *Past and Present*, 40 (1968), pp. 58–71.

10. Mendels, 'Des industries rurales'.

11. The emergence of export-oriented textile production in the canton of Zurich dates back into the late sixteenth century, and since its beginnings a substantial part of the workforce was located in the countryside; see Walter Bodmer, *Die Entwicklung der schweizerischen Textilindustrie im Rahmen der übrigen Industrien*, Zurich 1960.

12. Eckart Schremmer, 'Proto-industrialization: A Step toward Industrialization', *Journal of European Economic History*, 10 (1981), pp. 653–71, argues in favour of a perspective which does not distinguish between crafts producing for local markets and export-oriented production; and Pierre Deyon, 'Fécondité et limites du modèle protoindustriel: premier bilan', *Annales, E.S.C.*, 39 (1984), pp. 870ff, as well as Berg *et al.*, 'Manufacture in Town and Country', stress the importance of towns and of their interactions with the countryside in the process.

13. Thirsk, 'Industries in the Countryside'.

14. The concept of regional bifurcation has been introduced into the discussion on proto-industry by Jones, 'Agricultural origins of Industry'; for the most authoritative recent discussion of the topic see Gay L. Gullickson. 'Agriculture and Cottage Industry: Redefining the Causes of Proto-industrialization', *Journal of Economic History*, 43 (1983), pp. 831–50.

15. The importance of the absence of a control on the supply of rural labour as a precondition of proto-industrial growth (in contrast to guild regulations in towns) is particularly emphasised by Kriedte *et al.*, *Industrialization before Industrialization*.

16. Mendels, 'Des industries rurales', pp. 990ff; a more extensive discussion is provided in *idem*, 'Seasons and Regions in Agriculture and Industry during the Process of Industrialization', in Sidney Pollard, ed., *Region und Industrialisierung*, Göttingen 1980. pp. 177–95; the above sketch also contains elements stressed by Thirsk, 'Industries in the Countryside'.

17. For the following, see Thomas Meier, *Handwerk, Hauswerk, Heimarbeit: Nicht-agrarische Tätigkeiten und Erwerbsformen in einem traditionellen, Ackerbaugebiet des 18. Jahrhunderts (Zürcher Unterland)*, Zurich 1986; and Peter Giger, 'Zürcher Korn markt-politik im 18. Jahrhundert', unpublished master thesis, University of Zurich 1985.

18. For another early study in proto-industrialisation using a regional approach, see Herbert Kisch, 'The Textile Industries in Silesia and the Rhineland: A Comparative Study in Industrialization', *Journal of Economic History*, 19 (1959), pp. 541–64. Later studies by the same author (following a genuine approach to proto-industrialisation based on marxist theory and development economics) have been collected in *idem, Die hausindustriellen Textilgewerbe am Niederrhein vor der industriellen Revolution: Von der ursprünglichen zur kapitalistischen Akkumulation*, Göttingen 1981.

19. See J. Hajnal, 'European Marriage Patterns in Perspective', in David V. Glass and D.E.C. Eversley, eds., *Population in History*, London 1965, pp. 101–43.

20. Further evidence has been added in Braun, 'Proto-industrialization and Demographic Changes'.

21. See the contributions of Habakkuk and McKeown and Brown in Glass and Eversley, eds., *Population in History*.

22. For England, see Edward A. Wrigley and Roger S. Schofield, *The Population History of England, 1541–1871*, London 1981.

23. See, notably, David Levine, *Family Formation in an Age of Nascent Capitalism*, New York 1977.

24. A survey of the evidence is given in Mendels, 'Des industries rurales', Appendix. Outstanding attempts at a revision are Gay L. Gullickson, 'Proto-industrialization, Demographic Behaviour and the Sexual Division of Labour in Auffay, France', *Peasant Studies*, 9 (1982), pp. 105–18; and Myron P. Gutmann and René Leboutte, 'Rethinking Proto-industrialization and the Family', *Journal of Interdisciplinary History*, 14 (1984), pp. 587–607.

25. Ulrich Pfister, 'Proto-industrialization and Demographic Change: The Canton of Zurich Revisited', to appear in *Journal of European Economic History*.

26. Hans Medick, 'The Proto-industrial Family Economy: The Structural Function of Household and Family during the Transition from Peasant Society to Industrial Capitalism', *Social History*, 3 (1976), pp. 291–315; see also Kriedte *et al., Industrialization before Industrialization*, Chaps. 2 and 3.

Sources and bibliography

Sources

State Archive of Zurich

Unpublished sources

Almosenamt (Alms Office): 1520–1790 (A 61).

Baumwollenfabriken (Cotton Factories): Etat der Baumwollenfabriken 1717–87 (A 76).

Zürich, Stadt und Landschaft: Gemeindegüter und Einzugsbriefe (Communal Property and Entry Charters): 1529–1791 (A 99).

Ämter, Vogteien und Herrschaften (Administrative Districts): *Landvogtei Grüningen* (A 124).

Ratsurkunden (Town Council Documents): 1720–8 (B V 113).

Protokoll der Ökonomischen Kommission (Minutes of the Economic Commission): 1787–9 (B IX 70); 1791–3 (B IX 72); 1807–10 (B IX 74).

Abhandlungen über landwirtschaftliche Gegenstände (Treatises on Agricultural Subjects) (B IX 96).

Kurze Beschreibung der Unruhen in unserem Lande (Brief Description of the Troubles in our Country): 1794/5 (B IX 111).

Abschriften nebst Manuskripten über den Stäfner Handel (Writings and Manuscripts about the Stäfa Rising), by Salomon von Orelli (B X 39).

Protokoll der Examinatoren (Minutes of the Examiners): 1731–49 (E II 43).

Visitationsakten des Antistitialarchivs (Visitation Records of the Antistitial Archive) (E II 112–209).

Bevölkerungsverzeichnisse der Landgemeinden (Population Registers of the Country Parishes) (E II 210–70a).

Zivilstandsbücher der Landgemeinden (Civil Status Books of the Country Parishes) (E III).

Beschreybung der Armen uff der ganzen Landschaft Zürich (Description of the Poor in the Whole Countryside of Zurich): 1649 (F I 354), 1660 (F I 355), 1680 (F I 356), 1700 (F I 357).

Einfluss der Fabrikverhältnisse auf das Armenwesen und über die soziale Stellung der Fabrikarbeiter (Influence of Factory Conditions on Poor Relief and concerning the Social Position of the Factory Workers) (N 37 a).

Protokoll der Kommission zur Steuerung der Verdienstlosigkeit (Minutes of the Commission for Reducing Unemployment) 1816–19 (NN 36).

Fabrikarbeit der schulpflichtigen resp. minderjährigen Jugend (Factory Work by Young People of School-Going Age or Underage) 1805–1913 (U 28).

Published sources

Zürcher Mandate 1631–71 and 1671–1700 (III AAb. 1).

Zurich Central Library

Unpublished sources

Archiv der Ascetischen Gesellschaft (Archive of the Ascetic Society).

Published sources

Aufwandgesetze. Sammlung einiger Schriften, welche bei der Aufmunterungsgesellschaft in Basel eingelaufen sind über die Frage: Inwiefern ist es schlicklich, dem Aufwande der Bürger, in einem kleinen Freystaate, dessen Wohlfahrt auf die Handelschaft gegründet ist, Schranken zu setzen?, Basle 1781 (ZBZ XVIII. 1774), (prize-winners: L. Meister, J.H. Pestalozzi, Anonymous).

Bericht über eninige Industrieverhältnisse im Kanton Zürich, author not attributed, Zurich 1833.

Bösch, M., *Freymüthige Gedanken über den sittlichen Verfall seines Vaterlandes,* Lichtensteg 1784.

Brägger, U., *Leben und Schriften des armen Mannes im Toggenburg,* 3 vols., publ. by Samuel Voellmy, Basle 1945.

Brief an einen Bürger des Kanton A., über die Bedürfnisse der Zeit und des Vaterlandes, author not attributed. 1811.

Ebel, J., *Schilderung der Gebirgsvölker der Schweiz,* 2 vols., Leipzig 1798, 1802.

Escher, H., *Synodalrede über die besten Mittel zur Beförderung eines verbesserten Zustands der zürcherischen Kirche,* Zurich 1774.

Escher, J.K., 'Bemerkungen über die Regierung der Grafschaft Kyburg', *Archiv für Schweizerische Geschichte,* (1846).

Heidegger, J.H., *Der vernünftige Dorfpfarrer,* Zurich 1791.

Hirzel, Johann, *Rede über den physischen, ökonomischen und sittlich-religiösen Zustand der östlichen Berggemeinden des Kanton Zürich* (Synodalrede), Zurich 1816.

Hirzel, J.C., *Der philosophische Kaufmann,* Zurich 1775.
Beantwortung der Frage: Ist die Handelschaft, wie solche bey uns beschaffen, unserem Lande schädlich, oder nützlich, in Absicht auf den Feldbau und die Sitten des Volkes?', *Magazin für die Naturkunde Helvetiens,* 3 (1788).

Meiners, C., *Briefe über die Schweiz,* Part III, Tübingen 1791.

Meister, L., *Kleine Reisen durch einige Schweizer Kantone,* Basle 1782.

Nüscheler, J.C., *Beobachtungen eines redlichen Schweizers aus vaterländischer Liebe entworfen,* Zurich 1786.
Über die Revision der Matrimonialgesetze im Kanton Zürich, Zurich 1831.

Pestalozzi, J.H., *Sämtliche Werke,* ed. A. Buchenau, E. Spranger and H. Stettbacher, 28 vols., Berlin 1927–76.

Schinz, J.H., *Versuch einer Geschichte der Handelsschaft der Stadt und Landschaft Zürich,* Zurich 1763.

Schinz, S., *Das höhere Gebirge des Kanton Zürich, und der ökonomisch-moralische Zustand der Bewohner, mit Vorschlag der Hülfe und Auskunft für die bey mangelnder Fabrikarbeit brotlose Übervölkerung* (Synodalrede) Zurich 1817.

Schulthess, J., *Beherzigung des vor der Zürcher Synode gehaltenen Vortrags,* Zurich 1817.

Schweizer, L.J., *Über den zunehmenden Verdienstmangel in den östlichen Gemeinden des Kanton Zürich,* Zurich 1831.

Stutz, J., *Gemälde aus dem Volksleben*, Part III, Zurich 1836.
Lise und Salome, die beiden Webermädchen, Zurich 1847.
7×7 Jahre – aus meinem Leben, als Beitrag zur näheren Kenntnis des Volkes, Pfäffikon 1853.
Über Armuth Betteley und Wohlthätigkeit – Sammlung einiger bey der Aufmunterungsgesellschaft in Basel, im Jahr 1779 eingekommener Schriften, Basle 1780.
Unterricht über den Landbau in einem freundlichen Gespräch zwischen einem alten, erfahrenen Landmann und einem jungen Bauernknab, zum Gebrauch unserer Landschulen, author not attributed, Zurich 1774.
Vaterländische Erinnerungen an meine Mitlandleute der äussern Rhoden, über das Verhältnis der Landes-Produktion, gegen unsere angewohnten Bedürfnisse, author not attributed, 1811 (XXXI. 26813).
Zeitbeobachtungen über das schweizerische Baumwollgewerbe, dessen Folgen und Aussichten, author not attributed, Switzerland 1806.

Main Bibliography (Other references to be found in the notes.)

Adler, M., 'Fabrik und Zuchthaus', *Kultur- und Zeitfragen* 10.
Bernhard, H., *Wirtschafts- und Siedlungsgeschichte des Tösstales*, Diss., Zurich 1912.
Bodmer, W., *Schweizerische Industriegeschichte*, Zurich 1960.
Bollinger, A., *Die Zürcher Landschaft an der Wende des 18. Jahrhunderts – nach Berichten der ascetischen Gesellschaft*. Diss., Zurich 1941.
Brepohl, W., 'Industrielle Volkskunde', in Karl G. Sprecht (ed.), *Soziologische Forschung unserer Zeit – Leopold von Wiese zum 75. Geburtstag*, Köln 1951.
Brown, J.A.C., 'Psychologie der industriellen Leistung', in *Rowohlts deutsche Enzyklopädie*, vol. 30.
Bürkli-Meyer, A., *Die Zürcherische Fabrikgesetzgebung vom Beginn des 14. Jahrhunderts an bis zur Schweizerischen Staatsumwälzung von 1798*, Zurich 1884.
'Die Einführung der mechanischen Baumwollspinnerei', *Fortschritt, Organ des kaufmännischen Vereins Zürich* [1885].
Custer, A., *Die Zürcher Untertanen und die französische Revolution*, Diss., Zurich 1942.
Denzler, A., *Geschichte des Armenwesens im Kanton Zürich im 16. und 17. Jahrhundert*, Diss., Zurich 1920.
Finsler, G., *Zurich in der zweiten Hälfte des achtzehnten Jahrhunderts*, Zurich 1884.
Fretz, D., *Neujahrsblatt der Lesegesellschaft Wädenswil*, vol. 11: *Die Entstehung der Lesegesellschaft Wädenswil*, Wädenswil 1939.
Furger, F., *Beiheft zur Vierteljahresschrift für Sozial- und Wirtschaftsgeschichte*, ed. Prof. Below, vol. 11: *Zum Verlagssystem als Organisationsform des Frühkapitalismus im Textilgewerbe*, Stuttgart 1927.
Haegi, O., *Die Entwicklung der Zürcher-Oberländischen Baumwollindustrie*, Diss., Berne 1924.
Honegger, W., *Die wirtschaftliche Entwicklung der Landgemeinde Hinwil*, Diss., Berne 1948.
Keller, B., *Das Armenwesen des Kanton Zürich vom Beginn des 18. Jahrhunderts bis zum Armengesetz des Jahres 1836*, Diss., Zurich 1935.
Keller, J., *Die Hungersnot im Kanton Zürich in den Jahren 1816–17*, Zurich 1948.
Kläui, P., and Imhof, E., eds., *Atlas zur Geschichte des Kantons Zürich*, Zurich 1951.
Kramer, K.S., 'Haus und Flur im bäuerlichen Recht', *Bayrische Heimatforschung*, 2 (1950).
Krebser, H., *Wald im Zürcher Oberland*, Wald 1951.
Das erste Bevölkerungsverzeichnis der Gemeinde Wald aus dem Jahre 1634, Wald 1952.
Künzle, E., *Die Zürcherische Baumwollindustrie von ihren Anfängen bis zur Einführung des Fabrikbetriebes*, Diss., Zurich 1906.

Leumann, P., *Das Haus als Träger von markgenossenschaftlichen Rechten und Lasten*, Diss., Zurich 1939.

Lüssi, H., *Chronik der Gemeinde Fischenthal*, Wetzikon and Rüti 1932.

Meier, F., *Geschichte der Gemeinde Wetzikon*, Zurich 1881.

Messikommer, H., *Aus alter Zeit: Sitten und Gebräuche im Züricher Oberland*, 3 vols., Zurich 1909–11.

Meyer von Knonau, G., *Die Volkszählung des Kantons Zürich am 9.10., und 11. Mai 1836 – ein Nachtrag*, Zurich 1837.

Der Kanton Zürich, St Gall and Berne 1844.

Morf, H., *Neujahrsblatt der Hülfsgesellschaft von Winterthur*, vol. 12: *Aus der Geschichte des zürcherischen Armenwesens*, Winterthur 1873.

Niederer, A., *Gemeinwerk im Wallis*, Basle 1956.

Peuckert, W.E., *Volkskunde des Proletariats*, Frankfurt a. M. 1931.

Schmidt, C.G., *Der Schweizer Bauer im Zeitalter des Frühkapitalismus*, Berne 1932.

Silberschmidt, M., 'Zur Geistesgeschichte der industriellen Revolution', *Schweizerische Hochschulzeitung*, 29, no. 6 (1956).

Sombart, W., 'Die Arbeiterverhältnisse im Zeitalter des Frühkapitalismus', *Archiv für Sozialwissenschaft und Sozialpolitik*, 44 (1917).

Spoerry-Jaeggi, H., *Zeit des Überganges von der Heimindustrie des Zürcher Oberlandes zum industriellen Betrieb*, Wald 1927.

Die Baumwollindustrie von Wald, Wald 1935.

Strehler, H., *Beiträge zur Kulturgeschichte der Zürcher Landschaft*, Part I: *Kirche und Schule im 17. und 18. Jahrhundert*, Lachen 1934; Part II: 'Aberglaube, Armut und Bettel', in *Zürcher Taschenbuch auf das Jahr 1935* (1935).

Strübin, E., *Baselbieter Volksleben*, Basle 1952.

Tawney, R.H., *Religion and the rise of Capitalism*, Harmondsworth 1938.

Weber, M., *Gesammelte Aufsätze zur Religionssoziologie*, 3 vols., Tübingen 1920–1 (the relevant parts of this study are translated in *The Protestant Ethic and the Spirit of Capitalism*, London 1930).

Weiss, R., *Volkskunde der Schweiz*, Erlenbach and Zurich 1946.

Häuser und Landschaften der Schweiz, Erlenbach and Zurich 1958.

Wyss, F., 'Die Schweizerischen Landsgemeinden', *Zeitschrift für schweizerisches Recht*, 1 (1852).

Index

adultery, 46, 47
agriculture, 5; and attitudes to work, 137;
and cottage industry, 127–30; field
systems, 31, 128–9, 130, 137, 190;
importance of the working year, 81–2;
outworkers' attitudes to, 149–50; and
proto-industrialisation, 190; redeployment
of outworkers in, 158
almsgiving, 154–5, 157, 162; and loss of
parish rights, 20, 155, 175; recipients of
alms, 10–11, 13, 16
Appenzell, 146, 175, 179; cottage industry
house, 119–20; Hirzel's description of, 135
Ascetic and Economic Societies, 97
associations, *see* societies

bailiffs, 193
Bäretswil: entry charter, 24; poverty in, 166,
172
Bauma parish, number of residents, 115–16
Baumberger, Hans, 13
beggars' weddings, 42–3, 45, 60; and
poverty, 158, 165
begging, 16, 155–6, 157, 158, 172–5
Bernhard, Hans, 30, 113, 114
Bertschinger, Hans, 18
Beyel (district captain), 146
Billeter, Kaspar, 102
Birch, Inspector von, 137
Bodmer, Anna, 16
Boller, Johannes, 120
books: in country schools in Zurich, 95–6; at
the Wädenswil Reading Society, 103
Bösch, Michael, 78
Bosshart, Elsbethli, 16
Brägger, Ulrich, 68, 72, 109, 152
bread consumption, 63, 65
bread dole, 155, 175
bread prices, 162–3
Breitinger, Jakob, 101
Brennwald, Pastor, 105–6
Brunner, Hans, 19

Bubikon: entry charter, 24; poverty in, 166
building restrictions, 33; and the decline of
agriculture, 130; in villages, 31, 51, 112,
122–4
Bülach, population, 53
Burg, Magdalena, 15
Bürkli, David, 157

calico industry, 179–80
carriers, 139; and attitudes to work, 142,
143–4; and payment of outworkers, 143–4,
145; and poverty, 160
Caspar, Josef, 12
charcoal-burners, 13, 137
cheating, among outworkers, 142–3, 144
childbirth, attitudes to, 51, 55
children: attitudes to, 51, 54–5; migration of,
14–15; of the poor, 17, 158; and *Rast*-
giving, 54, 55–9; as spinners, 12, 13, 16,
17, 18, 132–3, 139, 152; at spinning
places, 92–3; and the work ethic, 132–3
chimneys, and village rights, 121, 123
churches: inauguration of Wädenswil, 99,
100; and the outworkers, 93–5; parishes,
193, 194; and Poor Relief, 155; sittings in
(*kirchenörter*), 61–2; *see also* clergy;
Protestant work ethic; religion
class consciousness, 151
clergy: attitude to poverty, 163–4, 165, 168,
169; *see also* churches; religion
clothes, 69–74; clothiers, 80; outworkers,
69–74; women in Maschwanden,
105–6; young unmarried girls, 86–7
clothiers, 4, 80–1; and attitudes to work,
143–4; clothes, 80; education and culture,
98, 101; houses, 126; and payment of
outworkers, 143–4, 145; and poverty, 160;
and revolutionary philosophy, 108
clubs, 106; *see also* societies
coffee, consumption of, 64–5
community: need for, 2–3; sense of, among
outworkers, 149–53

conversation circles, 101–2
cotton spinning, 144
cotton weaving, 145, 148 179–81
courtship, 42–6, 83, 85–6, 192
Custer, Annemarie, 108

daughters: attitudes to work, 140, 141; lack
    of housework skills, 66; obligations of, 54
day-labourers, 14, 19, 20–1, 137, 193;
    attitudes to work, 138; poverty of, 11–12
diet, *see* food
divorces, 45, 46, 47
dress, *see* clothes

earnings, *see* payment system; wages
Ebel, J., 126
economic rationalism, and attitudes to work,
    141, 146
education: country schools in Zurich, 93,
    95–6; and cultural change, 97–105
Egli, Hans, 19
Ehrsam, Hans, 12
embezzlement, *see* cheating
entry charters to villages, 22–5, 122, 124,
    193–4
Erisman, Margaret, 15
Escher, Heinrich, 95, 96
Escher, Johann Kaspar, 70, 88

Factory Ordinance (1717), 142, 144, 145
famine, 162–3
farmers, *see* peasants
farming, *see* agriculture
farmsteads: and churches, 93; and the
    collapse of the spinning industry, 179;
    cottage industry smallholdings, 118–19;
    house design, 118–19; living conditions,
    125; neglect of, 57, 165; numbers of
    inhabitants, 116; selling of (Stutz family),
    149; and spinning work, 124
fertility, 53–4, 191
Fischenthal: landless outworkers in, 172;
    numbers of marriages, 39; population, 53,
    166; poverty in, 166
Flarz houses, 48, 117–18, 120, 121, 123, 127,
    186
flax, growing and spinning, 8, 9
folklore analysis, 1–3
food, 62–8; of clothiers, 80; and
    entertainment of visitors, 82; price rises,
    159, 160, 181–2; in times of poverty, 151
French Revolution, influence of philosophy,
    108
Fretz, Diethelm, 97, 99, 100–1, 103
Frey, Jakob, 12
Furrer, Jagli, 18

geographical distribution, of the cotton
    putting-out industry, 33–4, 35
Goethe, J. W. von, 140
going to the light (*zu Licht gehen*), 44, 46
Graaf, Salomon, 160
Grob, Adam, 160
Grüningen district: agriculture, 128, 129;
    earnings and attitudes to work in, 148;
    and revolutionary ideas, 108
Grüningery, Elsbeth, 11

Halbherr, Hans, 18
hamlets: growth of, 48, 93, 115, 116; living
    conditions, 125; and spinning work, 124
hawking, 173
Heidegger, Johann Heinrich, 88, 89
Helvetic Revolution (1798), 61, 87, 89, 130,
    176, 179
hemp, growing and spinning, 8, 9
Hess, Elisabeth, 63
Hess, Heinrich, 16
Hess, Senator Heinrich, 63
Hinausbauen, see villages: building restrictions
Hinwil: entry charter, 25; population, 52, 53
Hirzel, J. C.: on agriculture and cottage
    industry, 127–8, 129, 130; on attitudes of
    outworkers, 69; on attitudes to work,
    134–5, 136, 138; on clothes, 71;
    description of the Oberland, 30–1, 32; on
    food consumption, 64–5, 66, 67–8; on
    landless outworkers, 171; on marriage
    patterns, 38, 39, 40, 42, 45; on population
    growth, 51–2, 53–4, 114–15; on the
    propertied outworkers, 171; on *Rast-
    giving*, 58; on religion, 95; on village
    living conditions, 51
Hochholzer, Samuel, 156
Hofmann, Anna, 18
Hottinger, Johann, 163
house ownership, 17–19; and sittings in
    church, 62; and village rights, 18, 19, 22,
    27–8, 120–1
housekeeping, and putting-out work, 126–7,
    140–1
houses, 111–27; building materials, 127;
    construction of new, 112, 113; *Flarz*, 48,
    117–18, 120, 121, 123, 127, 186; living
    conditions in villages, 51, 122–7
Hübscher, Anna, 18

industrial landscape, 184–5
inheritance patterns: changes in, due to
    industrialisation, 38–9; and cottage
    industry, 165
insurance, attitudes to, 169, 182–3
International Association of Workers,
    151

Karasek-Langer, A., 185
Keller, Bertha, 166
Keller, Wilpot, 18
kinship groups, and housing, 117–18
kitchens, communal, in shared houses, 121
Klaüi, Paul, 34
Köchli, Heinrich, 101
Köllin, Major (of Zug), 135
Krebser, Heinrich, 53, 67, 107
Kunz, Hermine, 141
Kyburg district: agriculture, 128;
    revolutionary ideas in, 108

Lähner, Hans, 19
land: dividing up of common land, 130;
    patterns of use, 31–2, 128–9
landless outworkers, 19–20; conspicuous
    consumption of, 73–4; families, 55; and
    potato growing, 68; and poverty, 165–70,
    171–3; and *Rast*-giving, 57–8
landowning outworkers, *see* propertied
    outworkers
Lichstubeten (lighted rooms), 83, 84–6, 192
linen weaving, 8
Lise and Salome (Stutz), 56
Lochmann, Hans, 12
luxury: changing attitudes to, 72–80; and
    living conditions, 125–6; and the
    Protestant work ethic, 136

Maater, Jörg, 13
Männedorf, minister of, on silk weavers,
    141, 142–3
manufacturers, *see* clothiers
marriage patterns, 38, 39–40, 41–7, 59–60,
    122; beggars' weddings, 42–3, 45, 60, 158,
    165; and changes in life style, 126;
    community of the unmarried, 83–9; and
    fertility, 53–4; numbers of marriages, 39;
    and proto-industrialisation, 191, 192
Maschwanden, 105–6; living conditions in,
    123
meat consumption, 63, 64, 65
Medick, Hans, 192
Meier, Johann Ludwig, 67
Meiners, C.: on diet of factory workers, 65,
    66; on houses of factory workers, 125; on
    improvements after industrialisation, 129;
    on life style of factory workers, 68, 71; on
    marriage patterns, 39, 54; on new
    settlement patterns, 48; on poverty and
    crises, 159
Meister, Leonhard, on luxury and
    ostentation, 75–6, 78, 79
Mendels, Franklin, 188–9, 190, 191
Meyer, Gerald, 52–3

migration, from the Oberland, 14–16, 34, 173
military bands (*Feldmusikanten*), 98–9
money, attitude to, of factory workers, 68–9
Moos, Lienhart, 11
Morf, Hans, 166
Müller, Barbel, 14
Müller, Felix, 15
Müller, Heinrich, 160
Müller, Jörg, 13, 14
music societies, 99–100, 101, 102, 106

Nägeli, Johann Jakob, 99
Niederer, Arnold, 136
Nüscheler, J. C.: on churches, 93; on
    courtship practices, 44–5; on living
    conditions in villages, 122–3, 127; on
    population growth, 61; on *Rast*-giving, 57;
    on village living conditions, 51

Oberholzer, Jakob, 63
Oeri, Jakob, 141
Oetelin, Jakob, 15
Orelli, Salomon von, 71–2; on life style of
    clothiers, 80–1; on ostentation among
    outworkers, 82; on the Stäfa Music
    Society, 99–100; on Wadenswil societies,
    98, 99–100
ostentation: changing attitudes to, 72–80;
    clothiers, 80–1; and living conditions,
    125–6; and the Protestant work ethic, 136
ovens, and village rights, 121, 122, 123

parish rights, *see* village rights
payment system, in the putting-out industry,
    143–5, 146
peasants: attitudes to work, 136–7, 147; and
    day-labourers 20; outworkers' attitude to,
    149–51, 168; security arrangements,
    169–70; and putting-out work, 17, 32; in
    Zurich, 3–5
Pestalozzi, Johann Heinrich: on Appenzell
    and Zurich, 146; on attitudes to work,
    141; on the clothiers and culture, 98, 101;
    on culture and education, 97; on luxury
    and ostentation, 75, 76–7, 78, 79; on
    unemployment among outworkers, 159
Peterhans-Bianzano, G., 107
Pfaffhuser, Felix, 12
Pfister, Barbara, 11
Picture from the Life of the Common People
    (Stutz), 149–50
Plato, 156
poor people: attitudes to work, 137–8; in the
    Oberland, 10–17, 23–4; *see also* poverty
Poor Relief, 154–8, 164, 193; and landless
    outworkers, 172; and propertied
    outworkers, 171

population: concept of over-population, 21; growth, 24, 34, 51–4, 60, 61, 114–16, 129, 191; numbers in poverty, 166
potatoes, consumption of, 65, 66–8
poverty: attitudes to, 151, 153, 154–83; in the Oberland, 10–17, 20, 23, 28–9, 166
pregnancies, pre-marital, 44, 45, 122
price rises: and the collapse of the spinning industry, 178; food, 159, 160, 162–3, 181–2; and poverty, 159, 160; and propertied outworkers, 170
proletarianisation, 148–9
propertied outworkers: attitudes to poverty, 170–1; and clothing, 69–70; diet, 62–4; families, 54, 55, 56–7; and *Rast*-giving, 56–7, 59
property, attitudes to, 20
prostitution, 46, 47
Protestant work ethic, 74, 131–6, 138, 153; and poverty, 155, 157, 161
proto-industrialisation, 188–92

Rast, the, 139
Rast-giving, 54, 55–9, 66
reading societies, 98, 101, 102–5
Regensberg, population, 52, 53
regional bifurcation, 190
religion: and begging, 155–6; and the outworkers, 93–6; and Poor Relief, 155–7; and poverty, 161–2; *see also* churches; clergy; Protestant work ethic
rights, *see* village rights
Ruegger, Heinrich, 11
Rügger, Elsbeth, 16
Russeger, Maria, 16

Sänn, Hans, 16
Schänkel, Barbara, 15
Scheller, Martha, 16
Schinz, Salamon, 166; on the clothiers, 81; on marriage patterns, 40, 41–2; on population growth, 51; on spendthrift habits of factory workers, 68; on the starvation year (1817), 72–3
Schmidli, Anna, 18
Schmidt, C. G., 80, 155
Schneller, the, 139, 140
Schönenberg, silk weaving in, 128
schools, *see* education
Schulthess, Johann: on attitudes to children, 55; on beggars, 173; on corruption among outworkers, 142; on diet of factory workers, 65; on marriage patterns, 42, 44, 45–6; on population growth, 51; on spinning places, 90
Schweizer, L. J., 172
Seidel, Robert, 134

Shrove Tuesday nights, 85, 86
Sigg, Anna, 18
silk weaving, 128, 141, 142–3, 148
Singing Schools, 98–9; *see also* songs
smallholdings, cottage industry, design of, 118–19
social class: in the countryside, 193, 194; and the putting-out industry, 181; in Zurich, 3–4
societies, 97–108; conversation circles, 101–2; importance of statutes, 104, 105; music, 99–100, 101, 102, 106; reading, 98, 101, 102–5
songs: of spinners, 139–40, 149–50; sung at spinning places, 90–1, 92
spinners: attitudes to work, 138–41; children as, 12, 13, 16, 17, 18, 132–3, 139, 152; clothes, 69; eating habits, 66; living accommodation, 124, 125; songs, 139–40, 149–50; wages, 164
spinning: collapse of hand spinning, 37, 177–81; hemp and flax, 8, 9; and poverty, 10–14; and the work ethic, 133
spinning parlours (*Spinnstuben*) 85, 86, 90–3
spinning places, 90–3
Spörri, Jorg, 16
Stäfa Music Society, 99–100
statutory regulation, of the putting-out industry, 144–5
stealing, among outworkers, 142–3, 144
Steinmann, Jakob, 15
Sternenberg, poverty in, 166
story-telling, at spinning places, 90, 91, 92
stoves, and village rights, 121–2
Straub, Anna, 16
Strehler, Hedwig, 84
Stucki, Barbel, 16
Stutz, Jakob: on attitudes to work, 142; on beggars, 173; on clothing of outworkers, 74; on food consumption, 66; on poverty, 162; on *Rast*-giving, 56; sale of parental farm, 149; on Shrove Tuesday practices, 85; songs of spinners, 139–40; on spinning places, 90, 91, 92; on the starvation year (1817), 168; stories of childhood, 132–3; on tradition, 147; as weaver, 152
Sulzer, J. C., on food consumption, 63
Sundays: observance of, 132; social life of the unmarried on, 86–7
Swiss Farmer in the Age of Early Capitalism (Schmidt), 80

Tawney, R. H., 157
Temperli, Jageli, 13
tithes, payment of, and potato growing, 66–7
Toggenburg, 175; cottage industry house, 119–20

town burghers: clothes, 70; houses, 127; and
   the transmission of culture, 97–8, 99, 100;
   in Zurich, 3–5
town councils, 193
tradition: and attitudes to work, 136–7,
   146–8; belief in, 2–3
Trüb, Elsbeth, 14–15
Trüb, Jagli, 14

unemployment, 14, 158, 159
unmarried, community of the, 83–9

vagrants, *see* beggars
vandalism, 83–4
village rights: and agriculture, 130; and
   entry charters, 22–5, 122, 124, 193–4; and
   forms of housing, 120, 121–4; and house
   ownership, 18, 19, 22, 27–8, 120–1; loss of,
   by alms recipients, 20
villages: administrative structures, 193–4;
   building restrictions, 31, 51, 112, 122–4;
   living conditions, 51, 122–7; and
   population growth, 114–16
villeins, 19, 194; and village communities,
   25–6, 27
Vogel, Heini, 12
Vogler, Magdale, 12

Wädenswil: agriculture in, 129; inauguration
   of church, 99, 100; population, 52;
   societies, 98, 102–5, 107–8
wages (earnings): and attitudes to poverty,
   157; in the calico industry, 180; hand
   spinners, 17, 177; and marriage patterns,
   40; of outworkers, 88, 148, 150–1; and
   poverty of outworkers, 158, 159, 160, 164
Wald parish: care of poor children, 158;
   development of, 48–9; potato growing in,

66–7; sittings in church, 61–2; societies,
   106, 107
weavers: attitudes of different types, 152;
   attitudes to work, 138, 140, 141; life style
   of women, 72; living conditions, 124–5,
   126–7; male, 91; wages, 164
weaving: silk, 128, 141, 142–3, 148; linen, 8;
   transition to domestic weaving, 179–81
Weber, Hans, 16
Weber, Hans Jageli, 12
Weber, Max, 130, 134, 157
Weiss, Richard, 109
Werndly, Jageli, 14
Wettstein, Jakob, 16
Wildberg, poverty in, 166
Winkler, Jageli, 15
Wirth, Jageli, 11–12
Wohlegemut, Jakob, 18
women: abandoned wives and widows, 15,
   16–17; attitudes to work, 140–1; in
   Maschwanden, 105–6; weavers, 72, 126–7
work, attitudes to, 131–53; and the
   outworkers' sense of community, 149–53
work places, 89–93
worker movement, Swiss, 151
Wyla, poverty in 166
Wyss, Klein-Jagli, 18

yarn production, 8
yarn spinners, 152
young people (community of the
   unmarried), 83–9

Zappert, Conradt, 14
Zschokke, Heinrich, 103
zu Licht gehen, see going to the light
Zuppinger, Heinrich, 12
Zurich, textile industry, 3–6, 8–10
Zwingli, H., 131, 132

DATE DUE

NOV 1 5 2006			